Withdrawn

Praise for *The Business of Race*

The issue of race is now a business imperative we can no longer neglect in this century. This book goes beyond making a case on why businesses must understand the economics of race. It equips us with ways organizations can evolve the diversity, equity, and inclusion programs we are used to. This is a book every business leader needs to read slowly and take time to reflect on every chapter.

JANE EGERTON-IDEHEN
Head of Sales, Middle East and Africa at Facebook, and author of *Fearless*

A practical workbook to help you have hard conversations about race—and drive real systemic change in your workplace.

ADAM GRANT
#1 *New York Times* bestselling author of *Think Again*,
Wharton professor, and host of the TED podcast *WorkLife*

This timely book brilliantly unpacks complex concepts such as structural racism and color blindness. Rich with stories and historical perspectives, the authors show how understanding key constructs will transform "do nothing policies" into courageous DEI conversations and practices that promote health and wealth for individuals, corporations, and society at large.

HELEN RIESS, MD
Associate Professor of Psychiatry, Harvard Medical School,
CEO at Empathetics, Inc., and author of *The Empathy Effect*

The authors' approach of weaving together history, real-life examples, and tangible frameworks make the sometimes-difficult concepts of DEI accessible and engaging. As a DEI practitioner with over 12 years in the field, I knew the events of 2020 would necessitate change in the work—the stories and tools in *The Business of Race* can be practically applied in the workplace and to personal continuous learning journeys.

MARVIN MENDOZA
Global Head of DEI at PPG Industries Inc.

Margaret Greenberg and Gina Greenlee are right: Now is the time to talk honestly about race in the workplace. This book is just what is needed to help address the hard issues of systemic racism in real and practical ways. Study this book well, make it required reading for everyone in your organization. Your business—and you—will be better for it.

THE MOST REV. MICHAEL B. CURRY
Presiding Bishop of The Episcopal Church
and author of *Love Is the Way*

The keen analysis and practical solutions Greenberg and Greenlee offer in this remarkable book move the conversation about race in the workplace beyond platitudes and promises and toward genuine understanding and action. *The Business of Race* is timely, urgent, and essential.

DANIEL H. PINK
#1 *New York Times* bestselling author of
When, *Drive*, and *To Sell Is Human*

Greenberg and Greenlee provide a clean, reader-friendly, theory-based, nonjudgmental, and results-oriented approach to the prickly topic of race in the workplace. With great case examples, anecdotes, frameworks, tools, and reflection questions, *The Business of Race* is designed to be in the hands of every business leader, manager, DEI professional, and anyone interested in creating an antiracist work environment. It addresses how to align racial identity with work identity. Chapters can be used for leadership briefings, lunch and learns, business resource groups, race dialogue sessions, and workplace antiracist skill training. A must-read book during this time of racial reckoning that supports organizations to be less vulnerable in their brand reputations, strengthen their talent acquisition and retention practices, and increase their capacity for innovation and growth.

DEBORAH L. PLUMMER, PhD
Diversity and Inclusion Thought Leader and author,
Handbook of Diversity Management and *Advancing Inclusion*

We're all struggling with not only how to constructively talk about race in the workplace but what to do about it. *The Business of Race* guides you through creating a racially equitable workplace. It should be required reading for all business leaders, no matter their level in an organization.

DAN SCHAWBEL
New York Times bestselling author of *Back to Human*

Rarely does a book emerge that is so timely, germane and vital to the current conversation around race in the United States. Authors Greenberg and Greenlee, with keen insight and provocation (and humble authenticity about their personal journeys on race), take us through step by step the application of "race work." Underpinned by powerful and practical examples and tips, the authors push us to confront and rethink race at work. *The Business of Race* is a manual for learning and action. It is for current and future DEI practitioners and champions, as well as those who seek to better understand our race challenges, and who truly want to drive change.

TINA KAO MYLON
Chief Talent and Diversity Officer, Schneider Electric
and 2021's Top 100 HR Tech Influencers

I am a white guy; a big corporation successful white guy. Like many people, I don't get it. I don't fully understand this thing called racism. I underestimate it. I under-sympathize. I despise that it exists without even knowing the depth of it. . . . So what is different here? . . . What is different here is this is not about help; it's about fundamental change. It's about creating change. It's about driving change. It's about owning the outcome. It's about recognizing and then not tolerating racism. In any form, however subtle or disguised. This book is about the compelling case for antiracism as a positive business "strategy" on many levels from diversifying experiences to broader marketing, to better and deeper talent. . . . This book clearly makes the case for businesses taking a stance against racism because it is logical and good business. Read the book, broaden your perspective. My eyes are definitely more open. And my engine is running.

KEVIN MCCARTHY
Retired CEO at Unum US

I am in awe when I think about the approach to global change the authors are proposing and how it must be executed in a sustainable and consistent way. Key to making impactful progress is identifying a place to adopt an approach that is process-driven with a measured methodology and an understanding of how to use it. Picking the workplace is like "duh," what a natural setting to add an inflection point in the race journey.

ROBERT L. ANDRIS
VP/GM Value Chain SaaS Solutions

As a minority leader at a higher education institution, I'm absolutely thrilled about the timely publication of *The Business of Race* and would like to applaud the two authors' boldness in discussing the intricacy and sensitivity around race and racism. The book cites useful data and examples that provide an excellent basis for teaching and research. I plan to use the book to guide myself in my decision-making and to follow the roadmaps and methods described in the book. I will also encourage my faculty to consider adopting the book to help enrich their classroom discussions and to use it as a reference for their research projects.

DR. AMY Z. ZENG
Dean and Professor, Sawyer Business School, Suffolk University Boston

This is not just a book about race in the workplace. This is the essential, indispensable guide to improving the workplace through diversity, equity, and inclusion. It makes a compelling case that diversity is in a business's own best self-interest, and not just about selfless altruism. It treats the issue holistically, from historical, legal, business, and personal perspectives. And it lays out actions, for us as individuals and as workplace actors, that are necessary to create an antiracist workplace. It's not an easy journey: four hundred years of history cannot be brushed aside overnight. But it's a journey we all must undertake. Greenberg and Greenlee show us how.

PAUL C. CLEMENTS, PhD
Vice President of Customer Success at BigLever Software

Greenberg and Greenlee have given us insightful work presented in *The Business of Race*. The book provides a scope for what is necessary before one embarks upon the work in diversity, equity, and inclusion with an opportunity to reflect on the nuggets gained in each chapter. It gives us ways to approach race and racism in the workplace and how to champion there for a more diverse, equitable and inclusive environment.

BRENDA (NEAL) PINKNEY, EdD
Director of Diversity and Inclusion at State College of Florida

Diversity, equity, and inclusion are important, intertwined, and complex issues. Addressing them effectively requires forethought, planning, and commitment. *The Business of Race* draws on research and corporate experiences to help leaders become confident agents of positive change. The journey will not be easy, but the effects on organizational culture will be well worth the investment.

MARTIN S. ROTH
President, University of Charleston

The Business of Race is essential reading for all employees in all US workplaces. It educates and inspires us to see workplaces as critical sites for the changes essential to achieving the vision of an antiracist society. This book compels us toward a deeper understanding of race work as necessary and doable by equipping readers with resources, guides, stories and examples. And calls on us to expand our imagination toward what is possible for—as individuals and collectives—to create and sustain an antiracist workplace.

JANE E. DUTTON
University of Michigan Distinguished Professor Emerita
and coauthor of *Awakening Compassion at Work*

The Business of Race is a comprehensive road map that seamlessly connects the dots of profitable business and antiracist culture, walking the reader through how to accomplish it. It speaks to the internal work that must be done as a leader and the critical decisions that need to be made from a business perspective. After reading the first few pages, I set myself up with a notebook and highlighter to accompany my daily reading and will undoubtedly come back to several saved reference points again and again. Particularly the policy portion and the historical foundations make this a critical read for today's organizational leaders. As DEI professionals we must be continuous learners with an inherently open mind. I recommend this book for the rejuvenation of your mind frame and perspective around DEI.

CARMELLA GLOVER
President at Diversity Action Alliance

Symbols are important. The curated statements and actions employed by businesses around the world in response to the mass movements demanding social change have indeed been powerful. And yet, symbols are most effective when they reflect sincere policy and cultural changes in institutions. *The Business of Race* will help companies and their leaders do just that. If you are serious about doing more than just posting the right phrases on social media or making a few new hires, and if you truly want your workplace to be not just diverse, but a space of equity, inclusion, and justice—then this is the book for you.

THE REV. CHARLES LATTIMORE HOWARD, PhD
Vice President for Social Equity & Community and University Chaplain,
University of Pennsylvania

THE BUSINESS OF

RACE

How to Create and Sustain

an Antiracist Workplace—And

WHY IT'S ACTUALLY

GOOD FOR BUSINESS

MARGARET H. GREENBERG

GINA GREENLEE

New York   Chicago   San Francisco   Athens   London   Madrid

Mexico City   Milan   New Delhi   Singapore   Sydney   Toronto

1 2 3 4 5 6 7 8 9   LCR   26 25 24 23 22 21

ISBN   978-1-264-26884-9
MHID   1-264-26884-X

e-ISBN   978-1-264-26885-6
e-MHID   1-264-26885-8

McGraw Hill products are available at special quantity discounts to use as premiums and sales promotions or for use in corporate training programs. To contact a representative, please visit the Contact Us pages at www.mhprofessional.com.

CONTENTS

PART III

YOUR INNER JOURNEY

PART IV

CULTURE AND LEADERSHIP

PART V

NEW POLICIES, NEW PRACTICES

CONTENTS

PART VI

PUTTING IT ALL TOGETHER

FOREWORD

A benefit of being in my line of work is that hundreds of authors, new and established, send me prepublication copies of their books to review. Those who know me well send drafts early on in the process, as they know I am a tough and candid critic. The more I read, the more repetition I see. So when I see something novel, it commands my attention.

When I read an early draft of *The Business of Race*, it grabbed my attention as one of those rare books that is both new and practical. The book is also timely and important. The ideas and activities in these pages are what the business world needs—now.

Race is an emotionally charged and polarizing topic. For decades we've been told not to talk about race, especially at work. Every year I meet with leaders, managers, and employees who want to have these conversations, but they don't know how. *The Business of Race* is truly a remarkable and practical guide for employees, managers, and senior leaders alike.

Coauthored by two women, one White, one Black, Margaret Greenberg and Gina Greenlee model what they describe in the book through their own collaboration. Through interviews with dozens of leaders, they describe the often messy but necessary work businesses must undertake if they are going to remain competitive. The authors are not traditional diversity experts, and that is precisely why their ideas are fresh. With deep backgrounds in business, coaching, and OD (organizational development), they get us to explore what's needed at the individual, team, and organizational levels to reimagine a workplace that mirrors the customers we serve.

I first read a draft of *The Business of Race* while on a family vacation. I found myself rereading several passages because Greenberg and Greenlee kept making me stop and think. Really think.

In the Introduction the authors suggest this book be read one chapter or part at a time and then put down to reflect on what you learned. I couldn't do it, as I was drawn into the stories and driven to share what I was learning. And I can't wait to share this book with business leaders I know.

This is a topic we all need to address, now. It is a conversation we all need to have, today. In the pages that follow, you will begin your own inner journey. Through that discovery you'll learn how to engage with colleagues, customers, team members, and your organization to make substantive changes in your workplace. Your friends and family will benefit from your discovery, too.

Tom Rath
Speaker, researcher, and #1 *New York Times* bestselling author
of *StrengthsFinder 2.0*, *How Full Is Your Bucket?*, *Eat Move Sleep*,
and most recently, *Life's Great Question*

INTRODUCTION

CLAIMING A LANE

Setting Expectations

The workplace. Race. Applying a strategic business lens on the latter to reimagine the former. That's the lane we're in.

Why focus on the workplace? Simply, that's what we know. We are organizational development professionals, coaches, and educators with a combined business experience of 50-plus years with Fortune 5, 50, 100, and 500 companies in roles as both external consultants and internal employees. Beyond the workplace, numerous complex, intersecting facets of structural racism are rampant across our institutions: health, education, law, childcare, housing, banking and finance, law enforcement, and the penal system. We respect and support the work being undertaken to dismantle racism in these domains; however, that is not the focus of *The Business of Race*. Our lane is the workplace.

The Business of Race uses a business lens, not a social justice lens, to address the emotionally charged, polarizing, and deeply complex dynamic of race. Further narrowing the width of our lane is particular attention to the interactions between and among Blacks, African

Americans, and Whites. Why? Gina self-identifies as both Black and African American. Margaret self-identifies as White. Neither of us is in a position to examine the dynamics of dominant and nondominant groups in, say, Hong Kong, Honduras, Trinidad, Brazil, Ghana, or Croatia, which include wide-ranging cultures and ethnicities within racial identities. That would be committing an injustice to people in those communities and around the globe. We can, however, speak to our own experience. And share additional insight through the interviews we conducted with business professionals in Western nations.

WHO IS *THE BUSINESS OF RACE* WRITTEN FOR?

"Is this a book for White people?" A frequent question we received from friends, colleagues, and complete strangers, upon hearing the title, *The Business of Race*. Our reply? An emphatic "No." We wrote this book for the human race and specifically for people working in the business world. If you are a business leader, individual contributor, Human Resources or DEI professional, educator, coach, or consultant then we wrote this book for you.

WHAT ARE RACE WORK AND RACE TALK?

Throughout this book we write with caution the word "diversity." That broad term is often wielded to avoid specific discussion of race and racism in the workplace. We are staunch supporters of all aspects of diversity including gender, religion, sexual orientation, veterans, and individuals with (dis)abilities, in every sector of society including the workplace. However, those affected groups are beyond the scope of these pages. Instead, we use the terms "race work" and "race talk."

Race work includes the *inner work* of raising our awareness and building new ways of thinking and being in the world. The term also includes the *outer* work that organizations perform to develop, implement, and measure policies and practices to create and sustain an antiracist workplace. There's a difference between a *nonracist* and an *antiracist* workplace. A nonracist workplace is one in which a company does not consciously discriminate against people of color. But neither does it acknowledge racism's metastatic toxicity. So no actions are taken to address racial inequities in how the company operates. An antiracist workplace, first, acknowledges that racism exists. And then forges a connection between that history and the toll it exacts on individuals, the organization, and society at large. In response to that understanding, leaders in antiracist companies actively engage the entire organization in a strategic imperative to create and sustain business practices and policies that advance racial diversity, equity, and inclusion (DEI).

Race talk is a subset of *race work*. Conversations that encompass topics of race, racism, racial identity, and racial equity are what we mean by *race talk*. It is filled with intense emotions that reveal major differences in worldviews, which can at times feel threatening. Unless prompted, many employees in the workplace would prefer to avoid such discussions, minimize their importance, or dilute their meaning by talking about diversity in general terms.

As a society we tend to react and mobilize only in response to a *perceived* isolated incident captured on cell phone video that goes viral. For example, a violent attack or murder of an Asian American Pacific Islander (AAPI) or an unarmed Black man. These incidents, however, are but symptoms of intentionally-enacted, centuries-long inequities. Systemic change will only come when we connect individual acts of racial violence and economic oppression to their daily expression in every societal institution including the workplace.

OUR PROCESS

We are not diversity, equity, and inclusion experts, so we had to educate ourselves first. We read. Researched. We took a course. Read some more. Took another course. We conducted a survey of more than 50 racially diverse professionals to learn their burning questions and struggles about race and racism in the workplace.

We also conducted interviews with more than two dozen business professionals to explore their stories. They represent myriad industries including financial services, construction, advertising, healthcare, high tech, real estate, and manufacturing and distribution. Their fields include education, diversity, human resources, law, marketing, organizational development, psychology, and research.

The professionals we interviewed work for, lead, or own micro, small, medium-size, and large multinational businesses. Also, they represent different organizational levels. Their roles range from individual contributors, supervisors, and middle managers to C-suite executives and board members. Their business experience spans careers of seven years to longstanding tenures of up to four decades. Britain, Cuba, India, Korea, Mexico, and the United States are their countries of origin. These business professionals also have wide-ranging racial identities. We include their race when we share their stories so you can get a feel for how their lived experiences shape their perspectives. You will also notice that we capitalize both Black and White when referencing racial identities. Capitalizing these words in this context is a recent phenomenon in the writing world. And whether or not to do it continues to be hotly debated. Not here. Simply stated, we've engaged our own race work and this writing through an asset lens. To lowercase one racial identity and not the other runs counter to that view. A few professionals we surveyed and interviewed preferred that we only include their racial identity, not their name or company name. We wanted their voices heard. So we included their perspectives while still honoring their request for anonymity.

Not every company or business professional we approached granted us an interview. People have much on their plates. Perhaps, too, it is symptomatic of the avoidance in discussing the undiscussables—race and racism. As much as we learned from our coursework, reading, and research, we learned even more from the people we interviewed. Also, the following 11 companies are featured prominently in *The Business of Race*: Amazon Web Services, CFRA Research, CVS Health, EVERFI, Living Cities, MassMutual, McCormick &

Company, Prudential, Shawmut Design and Construction, Truss, and Walton Isaacson. We've woven their stories throughout *The Business of Race* with no vested interest in any of these companies other than wanting to share their approaches to race work. Not as formulas but to inspire your own race work. Our hope is that you can learn from them like we did, and that their journeys will spark your own.

Finally, we share asset-based models, research, and tools to help you better appreciate how the individual journey buttresses race work in the business cases we cite. We'll also remind you of the business toolkits you use nearly every day to manage projects, people, and systems and show you how to apply them to your race work. Many of these tools will feel familiar and accessible to you. But don't confuse accessibility with ease. This is hard work. Don't expect to reimagine 400 years of racially imbalanced norms in one financial quarter.

OUR JOURNEY

The Business of Race would never have been written were it not for George Floyd—a man we would never know personally but whose public loss of life spawned a global movement. His murder by a White police officer, and captured on cell phone video, not only sparked protests around the world, but also a phone call.

Margaret called her friend Gina and said, "I've been thinking about you and wanted to hear your voice. What is going on in the world?!" And that's where Margaret left the space for Gina to share her feelings.

In our 20-plus-year friendship, we rarely talked about race, until now. Gina grew up in a White neighborhood and had mostly White friends during her childhood. Today she lives in a predominantly White town and works around mostly White people.

"You're one of only two White people of the many in my circle who reached out to me," said Gina.

She shared how isolated she felt. She shared her anger, frustration, and sadness. That fateful call between two friends prompted a series of LinkedIn articles. Not alone. Together. We felt compelled to act. We would use our friendship and love of writing to bring voice to what nobody wanted to talk about—race and racism.

OUR HOPES

Fifty years from now, social psychologists, cultural anthropologists, epidemiologists, and historians will still be studying the year 2020. As the pandemic ravaged the globe, many businesses were ahead of governments by mandating work-from-home policies to protect employees. Worldwide, kitchen tables, basements, and bedrooms became the new workplace and the new classroom. "Social distancing" became a new norm to help "flatten the curve" of the Covid-19 infection spread rate.

The year 2020 was also when the murders and attacks against Black and Asian people in the United States, and around the world, galvanized people of all races to protest against systemic racism. Our hope is that *The Business of Race* instills in you the courage to talk about race and racism. Moreover, to do something constructive about it—no matter your level in the organization, no matter your racial identity. We don't pretend to know what that "something" is for you. It may be reshaping your thinking, conversations, and decision-making. It also may be evolving your business strategy, policies, and practices. Our hope is that *The Business of Race* will inspire *you* to use your voice, to create and sustain an antiracist workplace. Now let's get down to *The Business of Race*.

GINA AND MARGARET
August 2021

USING *THE BUSINESS OF RACE* AS A WORKBOOK

We've taken the complex and emotionally charged topics of race and racism, and distilled them into digestible chunks for the busy professional. While you might be tempted to read *The Business of Race* in one sitting, we suggest you read one chapter or part at a time. This approach will allow opportunities for reflection. We help you do this by ending each chapter with a handful of questions. You might want to use *The Business of Race* as a personal journal or workbook; a place to jot down your thoughts so you can recall them later or discuss with others in the workplace, book club, or classroom.

Let's begin now.

Take a moment and reflect on *why* you have this book in your hands. Maybe it's because you ethically believe addressing systemic racism is the right thing to do, but you don't know where to begin. Maybe your company has made a public #BLM (Black Lives Matter) statement, but now what? Perhaps you're getting pressure from your board, boss, employees, or spouse to use your positional influence to create meaningful change. Or, you want to avoid another discrimination lawsuit. Possibly you're frustrated with all the talk and media attention on race and racism, with little to show in substantive difference.

Regardless of why you picked up this book, you are about to embark on a journey. A journey that will be both exciting and daunting. One that is fraught with missteps and filled with surprising giant steps. A journey that is both self-reflective and other-focused. In the space below, write down the reason why you picked up *The Business of Race*. It will serve as a convenient guidepost.

My "why": _____

PART I

THE
BUSINESS CASE

I t's time for a new approach.

Talking about race and racism at work historically has been taboo. However, we can't solve what we don't talk about. For nearly 60 years, workplaces have focused on diversity specific to gender and many historically underrepresented groups. Attention to *racial* diversity has been less tenacious. The events of 2020, emblematic of racial inequities rooted in a long history of systemic discrimination, forced that to change. While we believe that no single societal sector can disrupt the status quo on its own, we also believe that innovative businesses can lead the way. In Chapter 1 we outline six reasons why the workplace is the perfect place to discuss race and racism, and by extension, undertake race work.

Some organizations will actively persist in creating an antiracist workplace, firm in the belief that it is morally right. Others need evidence that their business survival depends on it. In Chapter 2 we lay out the business case for why embarking on or advancing your racial diversity strategy actually makes good business sense, no matter the size of your company or the industry you represent.

CHAPTER 1

YOU CAN'T SOLVE WHAT YOU DON'T DISCUSS

Why the Workplace Is the Perfect Place to Talk About Race and Racism

I ask people, "How are you defining diversity?" When I tell them we are specifically talking about race and Black people in particular, I get pushback. They say, "We don't just talk about one group." My reply is that we have to, because we haven't been talking about it all these years and look what's happened. People are still so afraid to talk about race.

ERNESHIA PINDER
Black American, Director of Strategic Diversity Management
at CVS Health[1]

t's hard enough to talk about race and racism at the family dinner table or neighborhood barbeque. What makes us think we can talk about it at work and make any progress? For decades we've been told not to talk about race at work.

Thirty years ago, the late Harvard Business School professor emeritus Chris Argyris wrote about discussing the undiscussables in his book *Overcoming Organizational Defenses.*[2] Of the many undiscussables, "race" and "racism" are chief among them. The term "diversity" often takes center stage in company press releases, interview sound bites, annual reports, and training programs. It's all-encompassing, and includes race, religion, gender, LGBTQ+, disabled persons, other historically underrepresented groups, and thinking preferences. In business, though, you cannot advance a strategy you do not name. To create and sustain an antiracist workplace we must normalize conversation on "race" and "racism." Here are six compelling reasons why.

#1 WHERE WE INTERACT

Work—often the first and perhaps only place in our daily lives where we regularly engage with someone from a different race, culture, religion, or neighborhood. We, the authors of this book, never would have crossed paths had we not connected through work.[3] Margaret and her husband chose to raise their two daughters in a rural Connecticut town, different from the Connecticut cities where they both grew up. Gina, whose chosen lifestyle is partner-free and child-free, relished a five-minute work commute. So she chose to live in Hartford, the capital city, where Margaret, a business owner of a consulting firm, saw many of her clients. A workplace in Connecticut's capital city first brought Gina and Margaret together. Personal choice on where we live may be one reason the workplace is often the only place where we interact directly with someone of a race, ethnicity, or culture different from our own.

Here is another reason:

In 2002 Nealie Pitts of Richmond, Virginia, was house hunting for her son when she spotted a For Sale sign in front of a modest brick bungalow.[4] She stopped to ask the owner about it. He said, "This house is going to be sold to Whites only; it's not for colored." Three years later in 2005, Rufus Matthews, the homeowner, testified before the Virginia Fair Housing Board that he believed a clause in his deed prohibited him from selling to a Black buyer. Specifically, a 1944 deed on his property restricted owners from selling to "any person not of the Caucasian race."

Restrictive covenants are binding agreements that hold homeowners to behaviors and practices in renting or selling their house.[5] "Racial restrictive covenants" prohibit the homeowner from selling or renting to anyone of a specific race or ethnic background. The wording may differ, but the crux of the issue is the same: racial restrictive covenants were designed to create and maintain neighborhood segregation.

Figure 1.1 shows a page from the 1921 deed of the Los Angeles home that Rochelle Newman-Carrasco and her husband purchased in 1990.[6] The racially restrictive language of the deed reads:

> No portion of said premises shall ever be leased, rented, sold or conveyed to any negro, or any person of African descent, or of the Mongolian race, or of any race other than the White or Caucasian race. That, as to the grantor of said premises, its successors and assigns, a breach of any of the foregoing conditions or restrictions shall cause said premises to revert to the said grantor, its successors and assigns, each of whom, respectively, shall have the right, in the event of any such breach, to immediately, or at any time during the continuation of any such breach, re-enter or take possession of said premises and to remove all persons therefrom.

inclusive in said Tract No. Three Thousand Four
Hundred Seventy (3470), said premises shall be
used for residence purposes only; that, no
apartment house, flat, lodging house, hotel or
any building or structure other than a first-
class private residence or one-story double
bungalow, with the customary outbuildings, shall
be erected, placed or permitted on said
premises, or any part thereof; that any such
residence shall cost and be reasonably worth not
less than Three Thousand Dollars ($3,000.00),
and any such residence shall be so located on
said property that no part thereof except the
front steps, shall be within Twenty-five (25)
feet of the said front line of said premises;
that no garage or temporary building of any
kind, or any part thereof, shall be erected, or
placed on said premises more that forty (40)
feet from the rear line of said premises, and
that the above conditions and restrictions shall
be in full force until January 1, 1935.
        That, no part of said premises shall ever
be leased, rented, sold or conveyed to any
negro, or any person of African descent, or of
the Mongolian race, or of any race other than
the white or Caucasian race.   That, as
to the grantor of said premises, its successors
and assigns, a breach of any of the foregoing
conditions or restrictions shall cause said
premises to revert to the said grantor, its
successors and assigns, each of whom,
respectively, shall have the right , in the
event of any such breach, to immediately, or at
any time during the continuation of any such
breach, re-enter or take possession of said
premises, and to remove all persons therefrom;
provided, however, that any re-entry made by
reason of any such breach shall not defeat or
render invalid the lien of any mortgage or trust
deed, placed on said premises in good faith and
for value, but said conditions and restrictions,
and each of them, shall be binding upon any and
all persons acquiring title of possession of

FIGURE 1.1 1921 deed of the Los Angeles home purchased in 1990 by Rochelle Newman-Carrasco and her husband. (*Permission by Rochelle-Newman Carrasco.*)

Racial restrictive covenants were deemed illegal many decades ago. The Supreme Court ruled against them in 1948. Twenty years later, the federal Fair Housing Act of 1968 outlawed them. However, historians who track such data say that thousands of racist deed restrictions, as well as restrictive covenants governing homeowner associations, survive in communities across the United States. "Every city, large or small, that I'm aware of, where anybody has looked for racial covenants, they have found them," said historian Kirsten Delegard.[7] She is the founder of the Minneapolis-based Mapping Prejudice project, which researches the covenants that barred non-Whites from buying property in the city's most desirable neighborhoods. Consequently, many rural, suburban, and urban neighborhoods across the United States remain segregated. This minimizes our opportunities to meet people of different ethnicities or races, until we enter the workplace.

#2 A READYMADE COALITION

At workday's end we go home to our respective neighborhoods, some of which may be de facto segregated. By contrast, the workplace is an organic form of coalition, the center of shared meaning. This place is where unique individuals from wide-ranging lived experiences come together to advance common goals. They produce products and services for the marketplace or implement new systems and processes. This organic community exists whether we work remotely, in an office, on a factory floor, or in a retail establishment. That sense of "we" among employees is essential to creating and sustaining an antiracist workplace.

In 1995, the game of rugby became the "we" that united Black and White South Africans. Nelson Mandela's election to the presidency in 1994 divided the nation. Not everyone was happy with the new majority rule government, or that native Africans would hold the same civil rights as minority Whites. What could bring South African Blacks and Whites together?

Rugby had long been viewed as a symbol of White supremacy in South Africa. During apartheid, the Whites-only National Team, the Springboks, proudly wore the antelope emblem on their green and gold jerseys. Black South Africans identified the national team as synonymous with minority rule. When South Africa found itself in the unusual position of welcoming the world after years of apartheid-enforced sporting isolation from international rugby, there were widespread fears of a racial bloodbath. Some Black groups were keen to avenge years of racial oppression. Some Whites were plotting violent protests against the new Black majority rule.

Mandela embraced the South African National Team during its 1995 Rugby World Cup run. And he asked reluctant Black citizens to join him. When the Springboks won the international championship, *all* South Africans cheered the victory for the team and for their nation.

The Nelson Mandela rugby story is well known, given South Africa's visibility on the world stage as a once openly apartheid nation. And also because Mandela was incarcerated for 27 years on a deserted island. Four years after his release, he became president. Not so well known is how Israelis united around cottage cheese.

Serbian political activist Srdja Popovic tells the story of Itzik Alrov, an Orthodox Jewish insurance salesman in Israel who makes ends meet by moonlighting as a singer in local synagogues.[8] A thoughtful and passionate man, Alrov didn't like "piggish capitalism," but he understood that for anything to change, he needed to make the fight relevant to everyone, including individuals who were relatively well-off. He knew that most people wouldn't join an effort to do something that sounded really daunting, like forcing the prime minister to resign or outlining an alternative economic program. He knew instinctively that when advancing what Popovic calls "a vision of tomorrow," you cannot pick the cataclysmic fight as your first confrontation. Alrov knew he couldn't take on Israel's entire economy right out of the gate. What he could do was something about cottage cheese.

Alrov sparked a nationwide boycott of the region's major dietary staple. The cost of living in Israel in general was high, as was food in particular. Issues too big to wrestle with as a start. Instead, Alrov knew everyone would rally behind cottage cheese when, within three years' time, the price rose by 45 percent of its original price. In June 2011, Alrov used Facebook to call on the public to stop buying cottage cheese. Within a short time, 100,000 users joined the Facebook protest page. And as the boycott gained momentum, it sparked a public debate on the high cost of living in Israel.

Rugby and cottage cheese served as successful coalition builders to unify South Africans and Israelis, respectively. The workplace is a readymade coalition. At least 40 hours weekly it brings together large groups of uniquely disparate people for a shared purpose.

#3 WHERE ACQUIRING NEW SKILLS IS THE NORM

The third reason why the workplace is the perfect place for race work is because, routinely, like it or not, we must venture outside our comfort zones to acquire new skills. Companies must do this to remain competitive, and workers must do this to remain employable. For example, an increasing number of retail cashiers are not only collecting cash and swiping credit cards. They've also had to learn new hardware and software skills to serve as technical support for self-checkout machines.

Similarly, the jobs high school and college students will hold in five years or a decade after graduation likely don't yet exist. When Margaret graduated from college, the profession she is in today—positive psychology coaching—didn't exist. Both coaching and positive psychology are younger than the internet. The year 1995 marked the coaching industry's official start. Positive psychology as a discipline debuted in 1998. None of us knows what our jobs will look like next year, next month, or next week.

Employees worldwide learned that in 2020. Companies adapted and pivoted their business models, job offerings, and footprint in response to the Covid-19 pandemic. Today's business environment requires us to be continual learners, always on the lookout for opportunities and trends. Learning more about race and racism is no different. Diversity programs have been a mainstay in many companies for almost six decades. Yet many employers did not encourage discussion on race or racism except in specific training contexts. Some prohibited it. When George Floyd was murdered on May 25, 2020, that changed. Constructive discourse on these dynamics is a twenty-first-century workplace competency.

#4 CIVILITY STILL EXISTS

The workplace is one of society's few settings in which a modicum of civility still exists. Workplaces are governed by a set of norms, written and unwritten, that guide professional behavior. Try to talk about race or racism in line at the supermarket or coffee shop. It's likely to turn into name-calling, a brawl, or worse. Behave like this at work, and you'll incur economic sanction: potentially fired or slapped with a lawsuit.

#5 CATALYST FOR
TRANSFORMATIONAL CHANGE

Every society has influential institutions: education, religion, health-care, and government. The workplace is another center of influence. From the industrial revolution to the digital revolution, the work-place has been where we experience exponential change in the making: from personal computers on every desktop and the ability to work from anywhere in the world, to on-site daycare and flexible work hours. For businesses to compete, grow, and remain relevant for consumers, they must solve problems that drive innovation: boosting productivity, retaining talent, and, in the case that follows, managing a crisis.

Johnson & Johnson (J&J)'s decision to remove Tylenol from store shelves in 1982 has been cited for decades as a platinum case study in business ethics and crisis management. We cite it here as a catalyst for global societal change. On September 29, 1982, three people died in the Chicago area after taking cyanide-laced Tylenol at the outset of a poisoning spree that would claim seven lives by October 1.[9] No suspect was ever identified. Public outrage could have fallen on Tylenol—the nation's leading painkiller, with a market share greater than that of the next four top painkillers combined—and its parent corporation, J&J. Instead, the company took a proactive role with the media and announced a massive recall of Tylenol from store shelves. This move cost J&J millions of dollars. In addition, J&J issued national warnings urging the public not to take Tylenol and established a hotline for customers to call with their questions and concerns. The company emerged as a leader in putting consumer safety above profit.

Tylenol reestablished its brand, recovering the entire market share lost during the cyanide scare. Within a year, and after an investment of more than $100 million, Tylenol's sales rebounded to their healthy past. And Tylenol became, once again, the nation's top over-the-counter pain reliever.[10] J&J's handling of the crisis also changed the way we consume medication globally.

The company developed new product protection methods, which included foil seals and other features that would make foul play obvious to a consumer. J&J also worked with Federal Drug Administration (FDA) officials to introduce new tamper-proof packaging that soon became the industry standard for all over-the-counter medications.

In 1983, the US Congress passed the "Tylenol bill," making it a federal offense to tamper with consumer products.[11] In 1989, the FDA established federal guidelines for manufacturers to make all such products tamper-proof. Industry has frequently been the source of innovation that influences government policy.

Another example of the workplace as a catalyst for societal change is compensation. The first federally mandated minimum wage in the United States was established in 1938 as part of the Fair Standards Labor Act. This was also in response to labor disputes and the desire to alleviate suffering from the Great Depression. However, the federal minimum wage does not automatically adjust to the rising cost of living. It hasn't increased since 2009.

The current federal minimum wage is $7.25 an hour. US workers in the retail, fast-food, and home-healthcare industries have seen their compensation rise at a much slower pace than their output per hour.[12] Minimum wage increases have long been subject to debate among economists and politicians. Many argue they hinder job creation by making it costlier for employers to hire people. That view has been questioned lately as several US states and cities raised their hourly minimum wage to $15 without appearing to damage labor markets.

> Businesses are capable of leading another transformational change: advancing an antiracist society. It starts with setting as a strategic priority, an antiracist workplace.

Many companies are not waiting for the federal government to recognize that $7.25 an hour wage is below the poverty line. They have taken matters into their own hands. Shake Shack, Trader Joe's, Ben & Jerry's, Whole Foods, Costco, IKEA, Amazon, Target, Bank of America, and the Gap are starting entry-level workers at wages ranging from $12 to $17 an hour.[13]

More recently, the Covid-19 pandemic caused worldwide lockdown mandates for all but essential workers. With millions working from home, videoconferencing became the office communication standard between clients and colleagues. Now this technology routinely connects family and friends and is a learning platform for K–12 and college students. Apps like Zoom, Microsoft Teams, Google Meet, and GoToMeeting, once used exclusively for business, have become popular in households around the world. From bridal showers and happy hours, to holiday shindigs and funeral services, gathering over a once business-only platform has become the new norm. Businesses are capable of leading another transformational change: advancing an antiracist society. It starts with setting as a strategic priority, an antiracist workplace. Then applying resources (enormous in the case of large corporations) to educating their workforce, facilitating constructive conversations, and evolving their policies and practices.

#6 BUSINESSES DON'T OPERATE IN A VACUUM

All stakeholders—employees, executives, customers, suppliers, shareholders, and boards—are members of the larger society. Current events at the local, national, and global levels impact both our personal and our professional lives.

Most adults living in the United States and beyond remember where they were when they learned the World Trade Center in New York City tumbled to the ground on September 11, 2001, after terrorists flew two planes into the Twin Towers. This event directly and indirectly affected businesses worldwide. No one was concentrating on work that day and the days following. Especially not employees in New York City.

Similarly, most Californians remember exactly where they were when four LAPD officers were acquitted for beating the late Rodney King in April 1992. In addition to the outcry from African Americans around the country, reaction to the verdict sparked riots in Los Angeles that affected local businesses from April 29 to May 4, 1992. These events were the subject of the theatrical piece *Twilight: Los Angeles, 1992*, written and performed by actor and playwright Anna Deavere Smith and published in 1994.[14] For the one-woman shows she has written, Smith conducts hundreds of interviews about high-profile civic events. Through a miracle of compression, she presents verbatim the answers of her subjects, one after the other, retelling recent history as an audiovisual collage.

> Bradley said that the Rodney King beating was nothing new. What he questions, though, was why the law firm partner took no action in response to police treatment of the company's intern.

Of the many personas she embodies in the Tony-nominated *Twilight* is that of former Democratic senator Bill Bradley from New Jersey, who served in the Senate from 1979 to 1997. In his monologue, performed by Smith, Bradley acknowledges that the law treats different people in different ways. One of the incidents that stood out for him was the story of an African American man who was interning at a large LA law firm. The police pulled him over while he and his White female friend were driving to a function at a law partner's home. The police threw the man to the ground and handcuffed him at gunpoint. After the intern finally made the police understand who he was and why he was in that neighborhood, they let him go. Then drove away like nothing had happened.

Bradley said that the Rodney King beating was nothing new. What he questions, though, was why the law firm partner took no action in response to police treatment of the company's intern.

Harassment such as this happens daily to Black employees all over the country. And they bring this to work. And in many cases, keep it to themselves. Unless they work for an employer who has the awareness to help them do otherwise.

In more recent events, shortly after George Floyd's murder, an Edelman poll found that "Americans expect brands to play a key part in addressing systemic racism."[15] The global spice manufacturer and distributor McCormick & Company, headquartered in Baltimore, Maryland, was among the many US corporations that issued public statements. In it, they expressed their continued commitment to dismantle systemic racism following the deaths of Floyd and countless other Black men and women.[16] McCormick also demonstrated public support during the pandemic for its Asian employees, both in the United States and abroad. This included the company signing a national agreement to denounce scapegoating China and other Asian countries for the Covid-19 pandemic.

> Race needs to be a conversation that people can have with anyone: a direct supervisor, company president, a peer or direct report. We have to normalize the conversation around race.

In our interview with Nereida Perez, global head of diversity and inclusion at McCormick & Company, she recounted what happened shortly before McCormick's annual Global Town Hall meeting in June 2020. Organizers had arranged to broadcast the meeting around the world to McCormick's 14,000 employees. The external speakers had been confirmed. The agenda was set: How could McCormick emerge from the Covid-19 pandemic stronger as an organization? Then, just one week before the event, the news of George Floyd's murder in Minneapolis spread around the globe. "There was so much impacting our employees from a crisis management perspective," said Perez.

> I immediately started getting emails from employees, and from our employee groups, saying, "Are we going to talk about what just happened in Minneapolis [referring to the peaceful Black Lives Matter protest that turned into a riot when police started arresting people and used tear gas]? Are we prepared to have a deeper discussion globally?"
>
> At the same time, I was talking to our CEO and our head of HR. "We really need to respond to this," I urged.
>
> Our CEO said, "Yes, let's talk about it, but let's make sure we're prepared from an HR perspective."
>
> I reached out to the speakers and we pivoted. We talked a bit about Covid-19 because it was still very much a relevant issue. It was in the middle of June. We didn't know where things were going, and so we wanted to have some dialogue.
>
> And then we talked about this other very important issue—Black Lives Matter. That event led to a series of other dialogues and requests for more information, support, guidance, training, and coaching that we have never seen before in the organization.

McCormick began rolling out virtual awareness sessions for employees in response to the requests at the Global Town Hall meeting. The purpose: take a deeper look at race in both their communities and work environment. McCormick's pivot in its town hall agenda demonstrated the company's understanding of how societal events affect its workforce. Employees are already talking about what's going on in the world anyway, whether online or with colleagues whom they trust. McCormick's response also shows how companies can create environments that advance meaningful discussions and productive actions for society at large to model.

Erneshia Pinder from CVS Health says: "Race needs to be a conversation that people can have with anyone: a direct supervisor, president of a company, a peer, a subordinate. What we don't talk about, or can't acknowledge, we can't solve for. Race is a persistent problem in America and around the world. It's kind of like mental health. We know it's there, but we don't want to talk about it. We have to normalize the conversation around race."[17]

> For too long we've outsourced the uncomfortable conversations of systemic racism to the police, politicians, talk show hosts, celebrities, red carpet sound bites, and "reality" TV. It's time for businesses to use their outsized influence to take a stand.

And where better than work, the places and spaces that occupy much of our adult lives? The workplace is the perfect place to address racial diversity, equity, and inclusion. Though, this organic coalition in no way guarantees ease. In some environments it may be especially difficult. One of our survey respondents who works for the federal government shared with us that "there are quite a few rules regarding what to do or not to do when it comes to topics you should or shouldn't discuss. This can make things tricky when trying to promote openness and new thinking."[18] We get it. Remember, though, you can't solve what you don't talk about. For too long we've outsourced the uncomfortable conversations of systemic racism to the police, politicians, talk show hosts, celebrities, red carpet sound bites, and "reality" TV. It's time for businesses to use their outsized influence to take a stand.

THE FINE POINTS

The workplace is the perfect place for six reasons:

- Often the first or only place where we interact with others from a background, ethnicity, race, or religion different from our own.

- A readymade coalition where hundreds to tens of thousands of people come together daily in a shared purpose.

- Where we routinely move beyond our comfort zone to learn new skills. The ability to talk about race and create a more equitable culture are twenty-first-century competencies we all must learn to remain professionally relevant.

- One of the few places where a modicum of societal civility still exists.

- An influential institution that can catalyze societal change.

- Does not operate in a vacuum: society influences the workplace, and the workplace influences society.

REFLECTION

- How have current events impacted your life? Work? Where in the world you live?

- How racially diverse are the people you connect with professionally? How racially diverse are your relationships outside of work? How comfortable are you talking about race and racism at work? With friends? With family members? If you are uncomfortable, what dynamics need to be present for you to feel safe?

- Outside of work, when have you come together with people different from you for a shared purpose? What was the experience like? What learning can you bring from the experience to race work at your company?

- How do you define the term "diversity"? How does your company define "diversity"?

- When was the last time you acquired a new skill at work? In other areas of your life? What was the learning experience like for you at the time? How do you feel about it now?

- How relevant do you find the six reasons we cited for why the workplace is the perfect place to discuss race and advance race work?

CHAPTER 2

WHY RACIAL DIVERSITY, AND WHY NOW?

A Competitive Advantage

Many of us know intuitively that diversity is good for business. The case for establishing a truly diverse workforce, at all organizational levels, grows more compelling each year. The moral argument is weighty enough, but the financial impact—as proven by multiple studies—makes this a no-brainer.

VIJAY ESWARAN
Malaysian-Indian, Executive Chairman of the QI Group,
a multinational e-commerce company,
and an economist by training[1]

Creating and sustaining an antiracist workplace is this decade's business imperative. Business leaders must first recognize that racial diversity can be a competitive advantage. Next, they must make it a strategic priority. But sometimes they need convincing, and what better way than to review data. There are four main reasons why racial diversity is actually good for business: profitability, innovation, productivity, and talent.

RACIAL DIVERSITY INCREASES PROFITABILITY

Greater racial diversity results in greater profitability. Consulting giant McKinsey & Company compared results from its multiyear studies between 2015 and 2019.[2] McKinsey found that companies with more ethnically and culturally diverse executive teams were likely to be more profitable than their less diverse competitors. These findings are correlations. However, the relationship found between greater levels of diversity at the executive level and financial performance is statistically significant.

Stand in your customer's shoes. Would you buy products from a company whose values do not align with your own? Give your hard-earned money to companies that seem oblivious to societal issues? According to a study reported by the World Economic Forum, 60 percent of respondents said they would either buy from or boycott a brand based on how the company reacted to the protests following the murder of George Floyd. This figure rose to 70 percent among 18- to 34-year-olds. Ignoring systemic racial inequities will cost a company its customers, and by extension, profits.

RACIAL DIVERSITY LEADS TO GREATER INNOVATION

Innovation isn't limited to tech companies and startups. In today's ever-changing and competitive business world, innovation is essential for any company, large or small. Yet, if the same people repeatedly return to the idea-generation table, results will be incremental at best. A key factor in innovation is different perspectives.

Research bears this out. In 2018 global consulting firm Deloitte conducted a survey of Millennials that showed 74 percent of respondents believe their organization is more innovative when it promotes a culture of inclusion.[3] Another consulting giant, BCG (Boston Consulting Group) conducted a 2018 study of employees at more than 1,700 companies across eight countries. They found that companies with more racially diverse management teams have 19 percent higher revenues resulting from innovation.[4]

RACIAL DIVERSITY LEADS TO GREATER PRODUCTIVITY

Dr. Stephanie Creary, who self-identifies as Black, and her team of researchers at the University of Pennsylvania's Wharton People Analytics found that employees who feel a greater sense of belonging to their organization take 75 percent fewer sick days than employees who feel excluded.[5] The studies have also found that employees demonstrate a 56 percent increase in job performance when they feel like they belong. And, have a 50 percent lower rate of turnover than employees who feel excluded. You already know from experience that your team's productivity is linked to the goals you set and the training you provide. You also know that the tools, resources, and processes employees use are crucial to their productivity. Now you have another lever to boost productivity—creating an environment where all your employees feel like they belong and can contribute.

RACIAL DIVERSITY EXPANDS YOUR TALENT POOL

Millennials (people born between 1981 and 1996) and Generation Z (people born in 1997 onward) are our future leaders and hold different perspectives on race than the Baby Boomers who grew up during the civil rights era.

As Baby Boomers retire, Millennials and Gen Zs will move into leadership positions, and businesses must be able to attract and retain them. In another recent study by marketing firm The Manifest, researchers found that 70 percent of job seekers now want to work for a company that promotes diversity and inclusion.[6]

Racial diversity and inclusion is the "what." Racial equity is how we measure it. If your company tracks broad diversity numbers, you might think you have racial equity. If you have representation across the BIPOC (Black, Indigenous, people of color) spectrum of employees, yes, you have a racially diverse culture. However, if you track the ratio of White to non-White employees at differing levels within your organization, the numbers may tell quite another story, one about inclusion.

A Black business leader who responded to a survey we administered in the late summer/early fall of 2020 asks, "Why is it the norm for there to only be two Black leaders in a room of 400 White leaders?" Another asks, "Why do companies and senior leaders claim to be devoted to diversity but the top still looks the same and no one meaningfully calls them out?"[7]

We have before us a great opportunity to bring more racial diversity to all organizational levels. Doing so will attract talent who value working for a diverse and inclusive company. In Part V you'll learn where and how to expand your talent pool and hire more racially diverse employees. Profitability, innovation, productivity, and talent—that is your business case; it's what you need to move your board to action, lead your organization, or influence those in positional power no matter your role or title.

THE "DO-NOTHING" STRATEGY IS NO LONGER AN OPTION

If you went to business school or you work in strategy and planning, mergers and acquisitions, or product development, you already know that there are three common business strategies: cost differentiation, product differentiation, and growth. There is one more, however, that we often overlook: the do-nothing strategy. The do-nothing strategy comes into play when, say, a business that has performed its due diligence decides *not* to acquire another company as part of its growth strategy. The do-nothing strategy is an option and sometimes effective, but *not* when advancing racial diversity and inclusion in the workplace. "There is a penalty for opting out," says McKinsey and Company in its 2019 "Delivering Through Diversity" report.[8] "The penalty for bottom-quartile performance on diversity persists. Overall, companies in the bottom quartile for both gender and ethnic/cultural diversity were 29 percent less likely to achieve above-average profitability than were all other companies in our data set. In short, not only were they not leading, they were lagging."

With the rise of social media, businesses are now more accountable than ever for taking a public stance against systemic racism.

There's been an awakening in the United States and around the world. The high-profile murders of Black Americans Ahmaud Arbery, Breonna Taylor, and George Floyd in the winter/spring of 2020, along with the murders of Asian American Pak Ho in March 2021, and many others, have sparked a reckoning. Law professor Kathy Taylor, who self-identifies as Black, sums it up best when she says, "There's an acknowledgment that our past is still with us. There's an acknowledgment of systemic racism. There's an acknowledgment that if we do nothing to address it, then we are complicit. There is no neutral ground."[9]

The do-nothing strategy intentionally ignores the elephant in the room in the hope that it "will go away," a repeated lament from several of the business leaders we interviewed. The elephant will never leave the room if we don't open the door. We liken ignoring racism in the workplace to ignoring dysfunctional team dynamics. Have you ever tried to develop a business strategy or implement a project with a dysfunctional team? Don't address that norm and you will collide with it every step of the way, slowing down decision-making and impeding overall progress. At this moment in history, the do-nothing strategy is no longer an option.

Closing racial inequities in wages, education, housing, and investment today could boost US GDP by $5 trillion over the next five years, a September 2020 Citigroup report said.[10] But it won't be easy. Citigroup economists laid out a blueprint for how US corporations can address inequality in meaningful ways. A sampling of the policy suggestions include:

- Hiking the minimum wage—currently 38 percent of Black employees work for minimum wage, and yet Black employees represent only 11 percent of the workforce.

- Banning employers from asking job candidates to reveal their salary history to prevent wage discrimination.

"To emerge from a history of entrenched segregation and active discriminatory policy into an era of genuine equity will require conscientious reform at individualistic, corporate, and governmental levels," the Citi economists said.

DON'T THROW MONEY AT IT

Have you heard the expression "Put your money where your mouth is"? Companies must do precisely that to create and sustain an antiracist workplace. That doesn't mean tossing money haphazardly into DEI initiatives or donating to a big-name nonprofit organization. If you are tired of all the media attention on race and racism with little to show in positive change, then it is time to put your money where your mouth is. Invest in educating yourself and others in your organization. Ben Hecht, who self-identifies as White, is president and CEO of Living Cities, a New York City–based organization that collaborates with the world's largest foundations and financial institutions. He sums

> "We needed to invest in understanding our country's history, or the globe's for that matter, and come to terms with it. We needed to invest in being able to take the blinders off ourselves and commit to making racial equity a daily practice. It's not a program. It's structural, and it's institutional. You have to do this work from the inside out."

up his company's commitment this way: "We needed to invest in understanding our country's history, or the globe's for that matter, and come to terms with it. We needed to invest in being able to take the blinders off ourselves and commit to making racial equity a daily practice. It's not a program. It's structural, and it's institutional. You have to do this work from the inside out."[11]

Working from the inside out means weaving the measure of racial equity into the fabric of your company's operating model. For example, tying a percentage of executive compensation to achieving racial equity goals, as Starbucks, Prudential, and other innovative companies have done. "Historically, leaders have not been rewarded for doing this work," says Hecht. "Until they are rewarded—however you want to define reward, be it money, recognition, or social leadership—it's not going to change to any great degree."

Working from the inside out can also be investing and volunteering in the communities where your company does business. Prudential does this in its headquarter city of Newark, New Jersey. In the summer of 1967, racial protests erupted across cities in the United States and turned violent. Newark was one of them. In five days, twenty-six people died and hundreds were injured. Property was looted and destroyed in response to the beating of a Black cab driver, John Smith, by two White police officers after a minor traffic violation.[12] The riots sped up the "White flight," but Prudential stayed. It invested in Newark then and continues to do so. In the last decade that investment totaled over a billion dollars to help the city rebuild and enrich the lives of its citizens. Prudential's chief marketing officer Susan Somersille Johnson, who self-identifies as Black, referred to this community investment this way: "We feel it is both a moral and a business imperative."[13]

Another company investing in creating and sustaining an antiracist workplace is EVERFI. Founded in 2008, the international tech company is driving social change through education. It partners with the private sector to funnel into classrooms around the globe, essential life skills such as financial literacy, social-emotional intelligence, and now diversity and inclusion. In the fall of 2020, the company committed $100 million to teach social justice and racial equity skills to children in grades K–12. "We can't just talk about racial equity internally anymore. We have to go and do the work," says cofounder and president Ray Martinez, who is a first-generation college graduate and self-identifies as Latino.[14] "These conversations around allyship and managing unconscious bias need to happen much earlier. While the shift to talking about racial equity in the workplace is great, we have to start having these conversations up stream. All of the research demonstrates that by seventh and eighth grade, students are developing their norms and values, so it is a great intervention point," Martinez explained. Imagine more and more employees entering the workplace of the future already grounded in the history of systemic racism and who see racial differences as an asset not a deficit.

> Creating and sustaining an antiracist workplace cannot fall on one person. It requires that the entire organization actively engage in creating a culture where all people can thrive and bring their best selves to work.

EVERFI began its race journey in August 2019 when it hired an SVP of diversity, equity, and inclusion. She reports directly to Martinez and oversees EVERFI's DEI initiatives both internally and externally. However, the company recognizes that creating and sustaining an antiracist workplace cannot fall on one person. It requires that the entire organization actively engage in creating a culture where all people can thrive and bring their best selves to work.

Says Martinez, "Organizations that do this well are going to get the best talent, have the best results, and be here in the long-term." That's what we mean by competitive advantage. Companies that attract and retain a racially diverse workforce are more profitable, more innovative, and more productive than those companies that "play it safe" or do nothing.

THE FINE POINTS

Creating and sustaining an antiracist workplace may be a moral imperative for some, but it is also a sound business strategy for four main reasons. A racially diverse workplace has been found to:

- Increase profitability

- Improve innovation

- Boost productivity

- Attract the next generation of workers and expand your talent pool

The do-nothing strategy may be effective in some business circumstances. It is not, however, an effective strategy for addressing racism in the workplace. Countless studies show that diversity and inclusion make economic business sense and must be built into overall strategy and executable plans.

REFLECTION

- What is your company's business case for creating a racially diverse, equitable, and inclusive workplace?

- What are you and/or your company doing today to create and sustain an antiracist workplace?

- If your answer to the last question was "nothing," then what is one small step you will take today to begin your own journey?

- What does "Don't throw money at it" mean to you and your company?

- Whether you lead a small team or a large organization, or are an individual contributor, what are two actionable steps you will take to create a greater sense of inclusion and multicultural cohesion?

PART II

THE WORK BEFORE THE WORK

How often have we stumbled our way through a new project with cross-functional team members who use their own siloed jargon or have no context for what has come before? Gina, one of the coauthors, always began initiatives with foundational work during her 20-plus-year career in strategic planning and project management at companies such as J&J, Aetna, the Johns Hopkins Health System, the Hartford Courant, and Phoenix Life (now Nassau Life). This included establishing a common vocabulary before launching into the heart of a project. Margaret, the other coauthor, learned the benefits of a common vocabulary the hard way. Many years ago a large corporation brought her in to consult on developing a change management plan for a massive technology initiative. She was 45 minutes into facilitating the project team's meeting when it hit her. They all spoke English, but for the project, didn't share common language. "Change management" connotes one dynamic to an organizational development consultant and quite another to technology professionals. Margaret called a time-out. Then spent the next half hour clarifying the terms they were using.

When developing a new product, implementing new systems, or creating alignment around a marketing or investment strategy, you will get nowhere without a common language and shared context (history of what's come before). Race work is no different.

In the next two chapters we begin our journey of creating and sustaining an antiracist workplace by sharing how society has shaped over time, the lexicon of race and racism. The do-nothing strategy is not benign. Yet neither is speaking in euphemisms. Both authors know how failing to name what needs naming derails any business endeavor.

That's a certain outcome if euphemisms are applied to race talk and race work. We encourage you to use direct, constructive language to name what must be named, without shaming or blaming.

In many of our interviews with business professionals who generously shared their stories, we had to unpack opaque phrases such as "What happened last May" and "The events of last summer 2020." Even companies that agreed to speak with us on the record do not have a lexicon for describing those events. Yet for the business professionals who spoke with us, the events have triggered personal reflections and even stronger organizational commitments to building an antiracist workplace. We will make little headway in our conversations today if among us we don't share a lexicon and basic knowledge about what led us here, about the history of race and racism in the United States, the Americas, and globally. No, this isn't a history book. We will, however, distill relevant context about race and racism in our society, a requisite foundation, *before* jumping into action at your workplace. Our hope is that the next two chapters will pique your interest to explore the Additional Resources at the end of this book for more information.

Change is a constant. The evolution of diversity, equity, and inclusion (DEI) in the workplace is like the evolution of anything else. What was once considered pioneering thinking in behavioral and cognitive psychology during Sigmund Freud's era can be challenged now because we know more. We've grown more. We have new technologies that measure human behavior. Today MRIs easily link psychology with biology. Freud's work has a place in the evolution of the discipline of psychology. Without it we would not have new branches such as positive psychology and organizational psychology.

In January 2021, the American Psychiatric Association (APA), the nation's oldest physician association, issued an apology to its members, patients, their families, and the public for "enabling discriminatory and prejudicial actions within the APA and racist practices in psychiatric treatment for Black, Indigenous and People of Color (BIPOC)."[1] These actions include "abusive treatment, experimentation, victimization in the name of 'scientific evidence,' along with racialized theories that attempted to confirm their deficit status. Similar race-based discrepancies in care also exist in medical practice today as evidenced by the variations in schizophrenia diagnosis between White and BIPOC patients, for instance." Deeming these past actions "appalling," the APA, which has historically remained silent on these issues, committed to put an end to institutional racism in the psychiatric profession, a profession whose mission it is to "benefit society and improve lives."

The field of DEI is not exempt from evolution. In Part II we explain how the focus has changed since the passage of Title VII of the Civil Rights Act of 1964. We began by educating ourselves. What follows is a summary of what we learned from our research and from the DEI professionals we interviewed. We give voice to the practitioners who have undertaken this work for nearly six decades.

CHAPTER 3

WHO SNUCK THE "E" BETWEEN THE "D" AND THE "I"?

The Evolution of DEI

A journey is called that because you cannot know what you will discover on the journey, what you will do, what you will find, nor what you find will do to you.

JAMES BALDWIN

Black American novelist, playwright, essayist, poet, and activist[1]

LET'S START WITH THE "D"

On the eastern edge of California's San Francisco Bay Area lies a premier research and development laboratory dedicated to national security—that's code for keeping the United States's nuclear weapons safe, secure, and reliable. It was here, in February 1980, that a young, multicultural woman joined the organization, not as a scientist, but as an administrative assistant. Her name was Lorie Valle. The organization was Lawrence Livermore National Laboratory (LLNL), a sprawling city within a city. For Valle and many other women at that time, including Margaret, one of the coauthors of this book, getting your foot in the door of a large organization often meant you began your career as an administrative assistant.

When Valle started, she supported several executives who were scientists in the director's office.[2] "There was this new initiative, which was not called diversity at the time, but that's what it was," she told us in an interview. "It was proactive efforts, above and beyond any compliance efforts the company was already doing around affirmative action and EEO [Equal Employment Opportunity], because the lab is a federal contractor. I eventually lobbied to change my job. I was doing a lot of diversity work off the side of my desk, so to speak, so I went to my boss and said, 'I want to be your diversity awareness program manager.'"

Asking for what she wanted, rather than waiting to be asked, started Valle's (now Valle-Yañez) 30-plus-year career in diversity, equity, and inclusion. LLNL created paid internship and apprenticeship programs for students of color. After a year, if the students worked out, the lab would hire them full-time. "We were essentially letting our scientists try before they buy," says Valle-Yañez. "It definitely wasn't philanthropy. In fact, that would not be a good thing at the lab, as we were using taxpayer money. You couldn't just give away money without any return on investment."

In the Beginning

Let's back up a bit. Initial diversity efforts began 20 years before Valle-Yañez began her career. Diversity in the 1960s centered on legislation and compliance.[3] The civil rights era focused on formally addressing the historic discrimination that had legally denied Blacks and people of color full rights to citizenship. Title VII of the Civil Rights Act of 1964 made it illegal for employers with more than 15 employees to discriminate in hiring, termination, promotion, compensation, job training, or any other term, condition, or privilege of employment based on race, color, religion, sex, or national origin.

This landmark legislation spawned an era of training in the late 1960s and 1970s, largely in response to the barrage of discrimination suits that were filed with the Equal Employment Opportunity Commission (EEOC). The multibillion-dollar Coca-Cola Company didn't know it in 1973, but that was the year it would begin its journey toward being the defendant in a class-action racial discrimination lawsuit more than 20 years later.

In 1973 Maynard Jackson became the first African American mayor of Atlanta, a home to numerous HBCUs (historically Black colleges and universities) including Morehouse College and Spelman College. At the time, Coca-Cola, headquartered in Atlanta, contributed to several high-profile Black causes; yet its workforce clustered Blacks at the bottom of the organization, and most of the managers were White and male. "In 1988, Linda Ingram joined Coca-Cola as an information analyst," writes journalist Pamela Newkirk in her 2019 book, *Diversity, Inc.: The Fight for Racial Equality in the Workplace*.[4] "Ingram, who is African-American, took pride in her association with the company. But her life significantly deteriorated in 1996 after she said her White supervisor berated her and allegedly told her, 'This is why you people don't get anywhere.' Ingram, the only African American in her unit, was stunned and humiliated and reported the incident to human resources." Coca-Cola fired the supervisor, and yet Ingram's colleagues blamed her for the popular supervisor's dismissal, and her situation worsened.

One day Ingram saw an article about Bari-Ellen Roberts, the lead plaintiff in *Roberts v. Texaco*, a discrimination lawsuit against Texaco that had in 1996 resulted in a $176 million settlement. At the time, it was the largest settlement for a workplace discrimination lawsuit in legal history. Roberts recounted her experience in the book *Roberts v. Texaco: A True Story of Race and Corporate America.* In 1989 Roberts accepted a position as a senior financial analyst, becoming the first Black woman to hold a professional position in Texaco's Finance Department.[5] Denied an expected promotion despite high marks on her performance review, Roberts suspected a pattern. She began to talk to other Black employees at Texaco. And those conversations revealed patterns of discrimination throughout the company. And that became the basis for Roberts and other Texaco employees to initiate a class-action lawsuit in March 1994. In November 1996, audiotapes surfaced containing dialogue among Texaco executives. These conversations were filled with racial remarks and plans to destroy or alter documents sought in evidence.[6] With the release of these tapes, Texaco agreed to pay $176 million to approximately 1,400 Black employees across the country. After reading an article about Roberts's account of her experiences at Texaco, Linda Ingram, whose problems had worsened at Coca-Cola, reached out to Roberts at a book signing. By then Ingram had identified potential plaintiffs. So when Roberts shared her attorney's name and number, Ingram called the attorney to say she had a case. On April 22, 1999, attorney Cyrus Mehri, Iranian American, filed the lawsuit in the US District Court in Atlanta, accusing Coca-Cola of systematic racial discrimination.

In the "E" section of this chapter, we will resume the specifics of the Coca-Cola lawsuit and where the company is today, because its journey parallels the course of the diversity industry over the decades. As it relates to the "D" portion of our tracing the evolution of DEI, it's important to know that during this early period in diversity history, not all companies took a "check-the-box" approach—legitimizing legislation compliance with bare minimum programming. Notable exceptions were IBM and Xerox. They adopted beyond-compliance, social responsibility positions in the 1960s, write Rohini Anand

and Mary-Frances Winters in their article, "A Retrospective View of Corporate Diversity Training from 1964 to the Present."[7] Most companies, though, wanted to avoid costly lawsuits such as those at Texaco and Coca-Cola. So before the EEOC or state agencies found "probable cause" for discrimination, companies voluntarily implemented diversity "training" that focused on imparting legal requirements to managers and employees.

The rate of organizational change through affirmative action stalled during the 1980s except for increased numbers of women entering the workplace. The decreased focus on compliance was partly due to federal government deregulation, the belief that employers should be more responsible for policing their own workplaces. With less government scrutiny, many companies turned their attention to other pressing concerns such as offshore competition and quality improvement. Companies still included affirmative action and equal employment sessions in training catalogs, though scaled back as a cost-cutting effort.

HOW THE "D" EVOLVED
TO INCLUDE THE "I"

An organization can work hard to be diverse; however, that doesn't necessarily mean it is inclusive. Hiring more people with varied backgrounds and lived experiences does not automatically guarantee that these employees and those from the dominant group will work together effectively. After LLNL formed strategic partnerships with diverse colleges and universities to recruit more racially diverse talent to the company, Valle-Yañez found that the Black and Brown people she hired from these schools were not having a good experience at work.

Valle-Yañez explained:

> There was this feeling by their managers that they were less than; that they weren't of the same quality as the people we were hiring through the "front door." We had

created a "back or side door," but these people were not being embraced or seen as good enough. I've always had a strong belief that you reach people through education, so I started to think, "How can I teach people to have an open mind? How can I teach people to treat everyone with respect and dignity? How can I teach people to understand what it's like not to feel included in an organization?"

Those questions that Valle-Yañez asked herself—essentially, how to create more *inclusion*—were the same questions other diversity practitioners were asking of themselves during this period, prompted by their own experiences and, notably, following the publication of the study *Workforce 2000: Work and Workers for the 21st Century*.[8] Published in 1987 by the Hudson Institute, a leadership think tank founded in Croton-on-Hudson, New York, in 1961, the study showed that the demographic makeup of additions into the workforce would be composed of more women and people of color. The publication created a major shift in thinking about the future composition of the workforce and is credited with putting the term "workplace diversity" into the business lexicon.

Workforce 2000 also prompted a shift in the diversity discussion from how to satisfy legal recruitment mandates to how to assimilate more women and people of color into existing, homogeneous corporate cultures. "In the past, most companies believed that assimilating new hires into the organization required that employees be socialized to conform to the company's existing culture. Over the last 30 years, however, companies have realized that the corporate culture itself must adapt if it hopes to attract and retain a competitive workforce."[9] And so practitioners appended the "I" for "inclusion" to the "D" in "diversity." Recruitment, in other words, was no longer believed to be the core issue. What needed specific attention was what happens *after* someone is hired.

Yes, there were increases in the number of racially diverse employees during this period; yet employer statistics showed them clustered at the bottom of the organization, with few entering higher-level positions. And so another set of questions needed answers: How do organizations create and sustain work environments that welcome and nurture the *professional development* of all employees? How do we enable people to perform at their highest potential? If, as Valle-Yañez experienced, new recruits are made to feel solely like "diversity hires," the organization is not creating an environment that encourages employees to tap their strengths—a missed opportunity that businesses cannot afford. As Nereida Perez, global head of diversity and inclusion at McCormick & Company, points out, 'I've worked at a number of different companies, and I've had employees tell me, 'Yeah, I knew exactly what they [management] could do to fix the issue, but rather than ask me how would I go about fixing it or providing an opportunity to fix it, they decided to spend $50,000 on a consultant, when I could have solved it for free.'"[10]

Three years after the publication of *Workforce 2000*, the discussion shifted again, this time to *business survival.* This shift paved the way for the next iteration of managing diversity: stronger focus on measurement. This brings us to the "E."

AND NOW ... THE "E"

"E" for "equity" is a relative newcomer to diversity and inclusion professional practice. Many "D&I" (diversity and inclusion) professionals and business leaders are still wrestling with what it means and how to implement it. Some are suspicious of the "E." They consider it undefined and ambiguous and point to it as a lexical trend, a fashionable meme to lead blogpost headlines. Still others think of "E" as evolutionary, the forward progression of the currently established "D&I," even if few share a definition. Some view it as a goal. A process. A system. Others as a power dynamic. And still others say racial equity is the complete absence of systemic racism in the workplace. McCormick's Nereida Perez, who describes herself as "old school" (having worked for UPS in the 1990s and five other large corporations over the last 30 years), had this to say about equity: "Many organizations are using the term 'equity' now which seems kind of sexy to people, like the term 'belonging' is being introduced. While their intentions and aspirations are on the mark, let's get grounded first through robust discussions and setting meaningful goals. Maybe a year or two from now, we can introduce equity, or belonging, or whatever the new term is, but I don't feel like we are deep enough in our journey to start throwing in new terms."[11]

"F" for failure. We keep reading about and hearing about the "failure" of diversity as an entire industry. We deemed it too broad and overstated. Yes, there were probably aspects of workplace diversity programs that over the decades were ineffective. However, through our own workplace experiences as employees and OD (organizational development) consultants, we knew of companies that had made great strides in this area. And our research for this book affirms this. So to make sense of this often-repeated "failure" mantra, we dug deeper to better understand what, in particular, might be driving such a broad-brush declaration. In doing so we found *five* dynamics that might account for such a claim: mixed messaging, overstated training outcomes, expertise limitations, no formal follow-up, and no connection to the core business.[12]

Mixed Messaging

During the 1990s, many companies continued to combine compliance and diversity content in their training, even though the new thinking was that affirmative action and legal compliance were different from diversity. It was common for training content to start with legal compliance topics and then move to discussing identities and valuing differences. This mixed-topic curricula confused learners, who left these types of training believing that "diversity" was nothing more than a new euphemism for the legal mandate called "affirmative action."

Overstated Training Outcomes

There were great expectations for the outcomes of early diversity training. These trainings varied widely in content and length, from one hour to a full day, with a typical length of four hours. For most companies the training was a one-time event, but some also required brief, periodic refreshers of company policies. This included signatures from all employees to acknowledge that they had read and understood the policies and the consequences of noncompliance. In other words, CYA, cover your assumptions. Although it is unrealistic to expect sustained change as an outcome for a one-day training, company management expressed much disappointment when observing no real difference in the work environment.

Expertise Limitations

Many diversity training programs were well designed. When faced with cost constraints, though, the content was sometimes squeezed into short time frames or facilitated by internal trainers who lacked subject-matter expertise. This resulted in little time for discussion or reflection. And led to managers and employees alike not fully grasping the complex and controversial concepts presented. Some of the unintended outcomes were that many left confused or with more animosity toward differences.

With little internal expertise during this era, many Fortune 500 companies hired diversity firms to train all employees. An unavoidable trade-off surfaced: on the one hand, the need to design a robust learning experience to meet the goals of shifting behaviors and mindsets. And on the other hand, the

> By the end of the 1990s, practitioners were more likely to understand that diversity could not be reduced to a training program. The greatest effectiveness in managing diversity came from viewing it as an ongoing business process integrated into the organization's core marketplace strategy.

business requirement to develop cost-effective approaches to train vast numbers of employees without impacting customer service, production, or productivity.

No Formal Follow-Up

After these training sessions, employees were left on their own to interpret and internalize what they had learned rather than experience a facilitated group process. The result? Some employees walked away from training sessions believing that they had to cherry-pick words around women and people of color so as not to offend. Others concluded that women and people of color were too sensitive. And some decided that White men were villains, while others believed they would lose their jobs to people of color and women.

No Connection to Business Results

During the period of the 1980s and 1990s, workplace diversity training sessions made little connection to how recommended behavior changes would improve business results. Few business professionals made the connection either. Many of those who hired D&I professionals didn't directly fund this work from their department budgets or invest in data collection beyond what was required legally, let alone analyze the data to drive business decisions.

By the end of the 1990s, practitioners were more likely to understand that diversity could not be reduced to a training program. The greatest effectiveness in managing diversity came from viewing it as an ongoing business process integrated into the organization's core marketplace strategy. With this evolution, positioning diversity education as a business driver gained solid footing by 1999.

The twenty-first-century variety of diversity is focused on building skills and competencies throughout the organization, to enable learners to value differences and also effectively use them to drive better business decisions. Positioning diversity as a competency has created another major paradigm shift. The assumption is no longer that only certain groups need training but that all employees need to be more cross-culturally competent in an increasingly global world. More to come on this in Chapter 6.

It is important to note that what were considered "failures" were nearly *six decades* of iterative learning and application to workplace norms we now take for granted thanks to an industry that arose out of the government mandate known as "civil rights legislation." *There was no blueprint for this.* Educators, scholars, social justice workers, human resources professionals, learning program developers, and corporate attorneys were literally making this up as they went along. That is how change happens. That is the nature of evolution. Design, experiment, and learn from what works and what doesn't one step at a time. This is not accomplished in a vacuum or in the privacy of your home. Rather, this growth dynamic of "fall down seven times, get up eight" is on public display in response to individuals, teams, organizational culture, societal norms, the media, the court of public opinion, and government policies.

> Neither finite nor absolute, "E" measures how and to what extent "D" and "I" are embedded into an organization's business strategy and every business policy and practice. The organization's "E" perpetually monitors and, as necessary, recalibrates "D" and "I" to stay ahead of potential relapse and continually advance toward an antiracist workplace.

The professionals who pioneered the diversity industry over the last 60 years are to be commended not pilloried: for the challenges they faced, the risks assumed, and the lawsuits that changed their lives and ours. They endured bruises borne from hard thinking and heavy lifting that positioned them deeply outside of their comfort zones. On these girded shoulders we stand in the twenty-first year of this twenty-first century to move their work forward.

Nereida Perez, of McCormick & Company, believes that understanding workplace racial equity surfaces from cross-functional conversations about how your company will measure progress, like you do for any other strategic business priority. You first explore what your company is trying to achieve. Then you use that information to set aspirational goals. From there you establish a baseline from which to begin your measurement. Perez told us, "What I've seen in the industry is the term 'equity' being introduced, but these deeper conversations are not happening."

We agree with Perez. Your organization's expression of equity surfaces from deep and ongoing conversations with a cross section of stakeholders throughout your organization, notably your employees. Throughout this book you will note an emphasis on leadership, which we define as the ability to influence, inspire, and advance racial diversity and inclusion by *any employee at any level in the organization*, not only hierarchically. Voices engaged throughout the levels and across the functions of your organization will shape the conversations that surface your "E" with far more credibility and relevance than confining them to C-suite meetings. We share, in detail, in Parts IV and V, how other organizations have approached this work, along with relevant tools, models, and assessments we've discovered along our own journey. For now, through our own exploration, we define "E" as a measure of "D" and "I." Neither finite nor absolute, "E" measures how and to what extent "D" and "I" are embedded into an organization's business strategy and every business policy and practice. The organization's "E" perpetually monitors and, as necessary, recalibrates "D" and "I" to stay ahead of potential relapse and continually advance toward an antiracist workplace.

BRIDGING "D "AND "I" WITH "E"

So how exactly does "E" act as a checkpoint between "D" and "I"? To answer this question, we'll need to return to the Coca-Cola story and find out how the company found its "E." In June 2000 the Coca-Cola Company settled a discrimination lawsuit for $192.5 million, with relief paid to roughly 20,000 Black employees.[13] Though Coca-Cola had once been the poster child for institutional bias, as a result of the lawsuit, the company would now begin a decade-long journey toward becoming a gold standard for corporate racial diversity and inclusion.

The settlement required the company to create an action plan to address the systemic and cultural issues in the lawsuit. The settlement's bedrock was the formation of a seven-member task force, to serve as a watchdog to ensure the company's compliance with the agreement.

The action plan included designing a system that would result in fair compensation, promotion, and evaluation, and to set measurable business goals toward that aim. Coca-Cola's board of directors were required to monitor progress by reviewing, and amending as needed, policies on salary, promotions, merit pay, bonuses, stock options, and performance evaluations.

The first report in July 2002 acknowledged Coca-Cola's efforts toward evolving its system for determining salaries, promotions, and raises to ensure fairness. It had created a central pay scale for roles aligned with the market and routed prospective candidates' offers to the corporate legal department for review. The company had also designed an external recruitment program to build a racially diverse candidate pipeline.

Over the course of the next four years, Coca-Cola continued to favorably change. It adopted transparency and created accountability by putting in place a detailed, systemwide assessment involving data collection and review. This measured the actual numbers of people hired, promoted, and recruited along racial and gender lines.

Next, from within its human resources department, the company internally recruited a global marketing professional to become global chief diversity officer, who served in that role for more than a decade. From the close working relationship among the global chief diversity officer, the settlement task force, and the plaintiffs' attorney, Coca-Cola began to quantitatively measure every process that touched an employee to ensure that it was just and fair. The goal was "triage, not forensics," meaning the team, now led by the chief diversity officer, was looking at the data *before* performance ratings, stock option grants, and promotions. This allowed the company to address issues in real time, before inequities became systemic.[14]

Coca-Cola's "E" measured progress toward diversity and inclusion in nine key areas: performance management, staffing, compensation, diversity education, equal employment opportunity, problem resolution, career development, succession planning, and mentoring.[15]

> How might we operate if we didn't require others to make invisible their unique, layered, and complex identities inside the world of the dominant group?

In 2005 the task force reported substantial improvement in the racial diversity of new hires and at the senior job levels at Coca-Cola. "More than 51 percent of new hires at the positional job grade of 14 and above were people of color, with African Americans accounting for 35.9 percent of the new hires." During this time, the company also had appointed new senior officers. In 2000, 16 percent of those officers were female and 8 percent were people of color. In 2005, the numbers were 27 percent and 21 percent, respectively. "That is a 68 percent increase in women and a 161 percent increase in people of color within the officer ranks in a five-year time period," the task force report said.[16]

By 2005, more than 30 years after the city of Atlanta elected its first Black mayor, the corporation, headquartered in the predominantly Black city, had finally found its "E."[17] "A senior leader at Coca-Cola who, at the time, played an active monitoring role alongside the settlement task force, shared this with us: "While the lawsuit was painful, it forced a discussion that might have never occurred. I believe everyone involved learned from the experience and made the organization better."[18]

Learning from challenging experiences is a theme we heard from the business leaders we interviewed for *The Business of Race*. Using tested models, in Chapter 5 we deconstruct how we go about learning just about anything. And in Chapter 6 we spotlight how to learn from our mistakes.

MORE EVOLUTION TO COME

Jordana Cole, learning and development manager at Custom Ink, says, "Organizations have a tendency to ascribe social categories through demographics which are disempowering and can create feelings of tokenism. Maybe diversity and inclusion should evolve into identity and belonging."[19] As we described in the introduction to this section, the DEI discipline will continue to evolve. In fact, in the time it took to write this book, the industry's lexicon has already morphed. Before we finished writing this chapter, someone appended a "J" (for "justice") and a "B" (for "belonging") at the end of DEI, to form "DEIJB."

Future researchers looking back on our current decade will tease out the workplace shifts that occurred as a result of societal shifts. This longer, historical lens will show how the lexicon we use today evolved to reflect new norms. For example, Rochelle Newman-Carrasco, cultural marketing strategist at Walton Isaacson, writes, "The more I hear the phrase 'diversity and inclusion,' the more I believe that the pairing of these words is doing our [ad] industry more harm than good. The words have become rather meaningless, even dangerous. They lull us into a false sense of security, providing a feel-good mantra that checks all the right boxes but does none of the heavy lifting."[20] Now is the time for companies to consider these terms not as a semantic exercise but in deep exploration. One that asks, how might we operate if we didn't require others to make invisible their unique, layered, and complex identities inside the world of the dominant group? And from that exploration, the authentic lexicon for each organization's work will surface.

THE FINE POINTS

- Diversity, equity, and inclusion can best be described as an evolution.

- Motivation for the earliest diversity initiatives was in response to legal compliance after passage of Title VII of the Civil Rights Act of 1964. By the late 1980s and much of the 1990s, the focus became fostering sensitivity and respect for differences to enhance working relationships.

- Practitioners broadened the definition of diversity beyond race to include gender, age, sexual orientation, people with disabilities (mental, physical, emotional, or cognitive), religion, veterans, and thinking preference.

- Many workplaces today have begun integrating diversity and inclusion into the company's values and core business strategy. This is a key distinction from earlier efforts. However, most companies have yet to fully implement processes and measurement tools to create and sustain an antiracist workplace.

REFLECTION

- During your career at the companies you have worked with or for, what exposure have you had to DEI training? What was your experience like?

- At your workplace, what deeper conversations need to occur to uncover the company's "E"?

- What do you believe is the next stage of evolution for DEI?

- If you live or work outside the United States, how has DEI shown up or evolved in your workplace?

CHAPTER 4

SHARED CONTEXT

The Evolution of Race

If we want to talk about how we got here, it's important to remember that we got here on purpose. It's about a structure built on systemic racism that the United States created intentionally and now needs to dismantle intentionally and replace with one that takes into account the needs of the people that it actually serves.

JOHN OLIVER

White British-American comedian, writer, producer, political
commentator, actor, and television show host[1]

A White consultant shared with us how the Black Lives Matter movement isn't well understood by some White people: "I was working with an organization last year right after the murder of George Floyd. We were all wearing masks because of Covid, and a White person came up to me and said, 'I don't understand Black Lives Matter. All lives matter.' And I said, 'You need to be careful who you say that around or in front of. Let me tell you why we have this movement called Black Lives Matter.' When you give people the history, they start to get it."[2]

Unfortunately, most people in the United States didn't learn the country's history of race and racism in our schoolroom classes. Liz Rowan is a biracial millennial who is a marketing professional at Amazon Web Services. She shared with us an exchange she had with one of her White friends: "She couldn't believe what she was seeing [referring to the murder of George Floyd and other unarmed Black people]. She said to me, 'I was so naïve. I never totally understood just how big this problem is.' People think because slavery ended and the Jim Crow era is over that wide-sweeping racial equity already exists. They don't realize that there are Black men who are afraid to go outside, afraid to get pulled over by police because they will be racially profiled."[3]

Or worse, murdered by police officers with little or no accountability. Most recently, some people have described the trial verdict of former police officer Derek Chauvin as a "victory." The jury found him guilty on all three counts, for the murder of George Floyd. The verdict in the Chauvin murder trial is right, but it's not justice. Also, it is extremely unusual.[4]

The Staten Island police officer who put 43-year-old Eric Garner in a chokehold that killed him on July 17, 2014—the incident was filmed by a bystander—was later fired but never prosecuted.[5]

The officer who fatally shot 18-year-old Michael Brown in Ferguson, Missouri, on August 9, 2014, was cleared of wrongdoing, based on dozens of eyewitness reports. However, the DOJ report was scathing about institutional problems in the Ferguson police force and racial disparities in the justice system.[6]

In December 2020, the BBC reported that "the US Justice Department says it will not bring charges against two White police officers involved in the 2014 fatal shooting of Tamir Rice, a 12-year-old Black boy in Cleveland, Ohio, who was holding a toy gun." The Justice Department said that prosecutors had "found insufficient evidence to support federal criminal charges."[7]

One of the two police officers who fatally shot 37-year-old Alton Sterling in Baton Rouge, Louisiana, on July 5, 2016, was suspended; the other was dismissed. Neither faced criminal charges.[8]

The police officer who fatally shot 32-year-old Philando Castile on July 6, 2016, while he was out driving with his girlfriend in St. Paul, Minnesota, was cleared of murder charges.[9]

In March 2019, authorities announced that the two officers who fatally shot 22-year-old Stephon Clark on March 18, 2018, in Sacramento, California, would not face criminal prosecution, as the officers had feared for their lives. Only a mobile phone was found at the scene, and Clark was unarmed.[10]

On March 13, 2020, Breonna Taylor, a 26-year-old emergency medical technician, was shot eight times when officers raided her apartment in Louisville, Kentucky. A grand jury charged one police officer not with Ms. Taylor's death, but with "wanton endangerment" for firing into a neighboring apartment. Three officers involved in the raid have now been dismissed from the police force.[11]

On September 12, 2017, the US Justice Department announced in a press release that "the independent federal investigation into the death of 25-year-old Freddie Gray, Jr., on April 19, 2015, in Baltimore, Maryland, found insufficient evidence to support federal criminal charges against six Baltimore Police Department (BPD) officers."[12]

Four police officers were tried on charges of excessive use of force in the March 3, 1991, beating of 25-year-old Rodney King in Los Angeles, California. On April 29, 1992, the jury acquitted three of the officers and failed to reach a verdict on one charge for the fourth.[13]

Like the Chauvin verdict, another rare exception to the pattern of no charges brought—or if so, acquittal—is the White police officer who on April 4, 2015, fatally shot 50-year-old Walter Scott in the back five times in North Charleston, South Carolina. The officer was later fired and eventually sentenced to 20 years in prison.

At the time of this writing, there was yet another fatal shooting of a biracial Black man by a White police officer in Minnesota, just 10 miles from where Chauvin's trial was in progress. On April 14, the police officer was charged with second-degree manslaughter in the death of 20-year-old Daunte Wright.

Clearly, this is a pattern. So how did we get here? There are two narratives of how the system of US policing developed. Both are true.

"The more commonly known history—the one most college students will hear about in an Introduction to Criminal Justice course—is that US policing can trace its roots back to English policing," writes criminal justice researcher Connie Hassett-Walker.[14] She is an assistant professor of justice studies and sociology at Norwich University in Vermont. Centralized municipal police departments in the United States began to form in the early nineteenth century, beginning in Boston and soon cropping up in New York City, Albany, Chicago, Philadelphia and elsewhere. "This is the history that doesn't make us feel bad," says Hassett-Walker.

> "At the current rate, it will take Black Americans 95 years to reach workforce parity in all levels of US private industry— having 12% representation at every level of a company, according to a February report from McKinsey & Co."

In the South, however, the economics that drove the creation of police forces were centered on the preservation of the slavery system. That's the second historical narrative about the origins of law enforcement. "Policing in southern slave-holding states had roots in slave patrols, squadrons made up of White volunteers empowered to use vigilante tactics to enforce laws related to slavery. They located and returned enslaved people who had escaped, crushed uprisings led by enslaved people and punished enslaved workers found or believed to have violated plantation rules."[15]

The first slave patrols arose in South Carolina in the early 1700s. University of Georgia social work professor Michael A. Robinson has written about members of slave patrols forcefully entering anyone's home, regardless of their race or ethnicity, based on suspicions that they were sheltering people who had escaped bondage.[16]

As Eastern Kentucky University criminologist Gary Potter explains, officers were expected to control a "dangerous underclass" that included African Americans, immigrants, and the poor. Through the early twentieth century, there were few standards for hiring or training officers.[17]

Beginning in the 1870s until 1965, Jim Crow laws mandated separate public spaces for Blacks and Whites, such as schools, libraries, water fountains, and restaurants. Enforcing them was part of the police's job. Blacks who broke laws or violated social norms often endured police brutality. "The authorities didn't punish the perpetrators when African Americans were lynched," writes Hassett-Walker. "Nor did the judicial system hold the police accountable for failing to intervene when Black people were being murdered by mobs."[18]

Since the time that Floyd died under the knee of former police officer Chauvin on May 25, 2020, "more than 80 companies in the S&P 100 have promised to improve hiring for Black, Brown and other historically underrepresented workers," writes Jeff Green, managing diversity reporter for *Bloomberg News*. "Almost half have goals for improving representation in management, according to data collected by Bloomberg. Twenty-two S&P 100 companies have joined the OneTen Coalition, a pledge to add 1 million middle-income jobs for Black workers in a decade."[19] Corporations such as Microsoft Corp., Target Corp., and Starbucks Corp. have made specific promises for hiring more Black workers. That's the good news.

However, a majority of large companies still haven't set quantifiable racial diversity goals. Many companies remain reluctant to disclose details about the racial composition of their workforce, says Green. "At the current rate, it will take Black Americans 95 years to reach workforce parity in all levels of US private industry—having 12% representation at every level of a company, according to a February report from McKinsey & Co."[20]

In isolation, without the context of history, the Chauvin verdict lets us off the hook for the real work: institutional reckoning; and across society's institutions, structural change. Green says, "The jury is still out on whether US companies will make a measurable, lasting change to their system of governance, and thus whether the status quo will shift."

It is our hope that this book, *The Business of Race*, will influence that shift.

THE FUNDAMENTALS

The language of race is always changing in tandem with the culture that shapes it. That is why we must be in sync with how it has evolved over time, from its origins to modern day, to reflect the racial dynamics of the twenty-first century. We all need context and a common language when creating cultural change, aligning around a business strategy, or advancing goals. The same is true in our conversations and race work. If we don't share basic education in the history and evolution of race and racism, we will make little headway. And another reason to have at least a working knowledge of race, racism, and diversity? Some employers are now asking these questions in job interviews for values alignment, as you will see in Chapter 10.

You have a business to run or a job to perform, which means your time for amassing large volumes of historical knowledge is limited. However, assimilating the *basics* of racial history will help you be more proficient. The two fundamental concepts to know before embarking on race work are (1) race is not biological and (2) race is a social construct.

We've recommended four resources on the history of race and racism to provide you with a shared lexicon and context for your organization's journey. All are available online. Three are free and one is nominally priced. And we provide their links in the back of this book under Additional Resources. Two are documentaries—one from *Frontline*: "A Class Divided"[21] and the other from California Newsreel: *Race: The Power of an Illusion*.[22] The remaining two resources are free online courses. One is produced by the University of Illinois at Urbana–Champaign: Race and Cultural Diversity in American Life and History.[23] The other is produced by Microsoft: Global Diversity and Inclusion: Beyond Microsoft.[24]

RACE IS NOT BIOLOGICAL

The idea of race as biology assumes that simple external differences such as skin color, eye color, and hair form are linked to other, more complex internal differences. Like athletic ability. Musical aptitude. Intelligence.

Legal scholar and microbiologist Pilar Ossorio says, "We have a notion of race as being clear-cut, distinct categories of people that are deep and unchanging. All of our genetics now is telling us that that's not the case.[25] We can't find any genetic markers that are in everybody of a particular race and in nobody of some other race."[26]

We (this book's coauthors) both studied anthropology and biology during our undergraduate days, so this information—that there are no distinct genetic or biological markers for race—is not new to us. However, this information may surprise you and others. Evolutionary biologist Joseph L. Graves explains that understanding race means understanding how different people perceive and define it.[27] And most people assume that there are biological races and that "these racial categories align with physical features." In other words, we can see differences among populations, but can populations be bundled into what we call races?

Graves further explains that "the measured amount of genetic variation in the human population is extremely small. Genetically, we aren't very different." Humans are among the most similar of all species. Only one out of every thousand nucleotides (the building blocks of the nucleic acids RNA and DNA) that make up our genetic code is different among individuals. Though penguins look very much alike, they have twice the amount of genetic difference, one from the other, than humans do with each other. In fruit flies it's ten times the amount. So how do you explain the differences in skin color, eye shape, and hair form? Geography.

People who trace their ancestry back to Europe, sub-Saharan Africa, Asia, or the early Americas lived isolated from each other for long enough periods to evolve different physical traits in response to their environment. People who trace ancestry to the Southern Hemisphere adapted to their geography with darker skin to protect them from the sun's ultraviolet rays. People who trace their ancestry to the Northern Hemisphere tend to have lighter skin to better absorb the sun's vitamin D. Humans have migrated around this planet over the last 200,000 years, resulting today in multitudes of skin color variations.

There hasn't been time for the development of much genetic variation, other than what regulates superficial features like skin color and hair form. Most importantly these superficial features do not represent differences in overall genetic variation.[28] Meaning by the time these variations arose, more complicated traits such as speech, abstract thinking, and physical aptitude had already evolved.

> "Race is a fluid concept used to group people according to various factors including, ancestral background and social identity. Race is also used to group people that share a set of visible characteristics, such as skin color and facial features. Though these visible traits are influenced by genes, the vast majority of genetic variation exists within racial groups and not between them. Race is an ideology and for this reason, many scientists believe that race should be more accurately described as a social construct and not a biological one."
>
> —*National Human Genome Research Institute*[29]

RACE IS A SOCIAL CONSTRUCT

Human beings are tribal at their core.[30] Since the nineteenth century, social psychologists and cultural anthropologists, and now more recently neuroscientists, have studied this phenomenon. Our brains are like digital folders or analog filing cabinets. We love to make sense of the world we see by performing a function that US journalist

Bill Bishop calls "the big sort." In his book, *The Big Sort: Why the Clustering of Like-Minded America Is Tearing Us Apart*,[31] Bishop is referring to modern-day humans, noting that this sorting goes back to our early survival. Forming bonds with others who looked like us helped us feed our families (think hunter-gatherers) and protect ourselves from danger.

Tribalism goes back millennia. Both slavery and indentured servitude have existed for thousands of years and span many cultures, nationalities, and religions from ancient times to the present day. The social, economic, and legal positions of slaves have differed vastly in different systems of slavery in different times and places. The concept of race, though, is a relatively recent human invention, only hundreds of years old, and it's deeply tied to the development of the United States.

"The term 'race,' used infrequently before the 1500s, was used to identify groups of people with a kinship or group connection," write the authors of the Smithsonian's website for the National Museum of African American History and Culture. "The modern-day use of the term 'race' is a human invention, a shorthand to describe and categorize people into various social groups based on characteristics like skin color, eye shape and hair form." In Western countries, *this social construct of race gives or denies benefits and privileges.* It is embedded in Western institutions, invented to disproportionately channel resources, power, status, and wealth to the dominant group, White people.

US society developed the social construct of race early in its formation to justify its new economic system of capitalism, which depended on the institution of forced labor, especially the enslavement of African peoples. As explained on the homepage of the "Talking About Race" section of the website for the National Museum of African American History and Culture at the Smithsonian, "To more accurately understand how race and its counterpart, racism, are woven into the very fabric of US society," including the workplace, "we must explore the history of how race, White privilege, and how anti-blackness came to be."[32]

The social construct of race, as we understand it today, evolved alongside the formation of the United States and was deeply connected with the evolution of two other terms, "White" and "slave," writes the Smithsonian. The words "race," "White," and "slave" were words Europeans used in the 1500s. And they brought these words with them to North America. However, the words did not have the meanings that they have today. Instead, the needs of the developing United States, would transform those words' meanings into new ideas. Four hundred years ago in the US colonies that would come to be known as the United States, land was plentiful. Labor was not. A new human resources model had to be created. It would provide workers to plough the fields, pick the cotton, dry the tobacco, and eventually construct the railroads. It was called slavery and indentured servitude.

> "The world got along without race for the overwhelming majority of its history. The US has never been without it."
>
> *David R. Roediger, White, American Studies and History*
> *at the University of Kansas, coauthor of* The Construction of Whiteness[33]

The Seeds of Racism

For those of us who grew up in the United States, what we did learn in history class was that Thomas Jefferson was one of the country's Founding Fathers.[34] Specifically, he was the primary author of the Declaration of Independence, the document that demanded independence for the United States from the rule of Great Britain. Also, he was the third president of the United States; Jefferson penned the revolutionary words "All men are created equal," proclaiming human equality in the Declaration. However, the contradiction between the claim that all men are created equal and the existence of US slavery (Jefferson himself owned 225 slaves) garnered criticism when the Declaration was first published.

Jefferson also wrote a lesser known yet influential document, *Notes on the State of Virginia.* Written in response to questions from France about the American colonies, the book reads like a sales pitch for the newly forming country. *Notes on the State of Virginia* was not about race.[35] But among Jefferson's descriptions of rivers, seaports, mountains, and climate, he expressed his views on the people of the new land, from America, Europe, and Africa: "I advance it as a suspicion only that the Blacks whether originally a distinct race, or made distinct by time and circumstances, are inferior to the Whites in the endowments both of body and mind."[36] Jefferson's words appear to justify slavery at a time when many were admonishing the Declaration's authors for espousing freedom while continuing to support a system of human bondage.

Historian Robin D. G. Kelley writes that "the problem that they had to figure out was, 'how can we promote liberty, freedom, democracy on one hand and a system of slavery and exploitation of peoples who are non-White, on the other?'"[37] The only way to justify owning slaves, while at the same time espousing "All men are created equal," was to create a plan—a business plan. In that plan it was necessary to define one of the key stakeholders—the laborers who were Black Africans—as inferior to the White stakeholders.

We're not suggesting that Jefferson was alone in justifying and perpetuating this social construct called race and its counterpart, racism. Slavery, upheld by the necessary rationalization of the construct to support a way of life, was an institution—intentionally systematized. Alongside Jefferson, many of the Founding Fathers owned numerous slaves—among them George Washington, the first president of the United States; James Madison, Jefferson's secretary of state and the fourth president of the United States;[38] Benjamin Franklin in Pennsylvania, one of the drafters of the Constitution and founder of the University of Pennsylvania; and John Hancock, first Massachusetts governor from 1780 to 1785. Hancock was also the first member of Congress to sign the Declaration of Independence. Other Founding Father slave owners included John Jay of New York, Samuel Chase of Maryland, and several more. Some of those who didn't own slaves themselves, such as Alexander Hamilton of New York,[39] married into large slave-owning families.[40] Former commanding general of the Union Army Ulysses S. Grant was the last president to personally own slaves. He served two terms as president between 1869 and 1877.

Similar logic rationalized the taking of Indigenous lands—people who were non-White were inferior to those who were. In 1830, a year after Andrew Jackson became president, he signed a law he had proposed during his first State of the Union address in 1829—the Indian Removal Act. Shortly after Congress approved the Indian Removal Act, Jackson and his War Department began enforcing it, targeting tribes in the southeastern United States. By Jackson's second term in office, his administration was already relocating the Choctaw, Chickasaw, and Creek tribes to lands west of the Mississippi that had been designated "Indian Territory." The Muscogee and Seminole, established, autonomous nations like the other tribes in the southeastern United States, would soon join them.

The Indian Removal Act forcibly relocated tens of thousands of Indigenous people from their homelands east of the Mississippi.[41] Their removal gave 25 million acres of land to White settlement and to slave plantations. Jackson defended Indian removal by saying that it was not the greed of White settlers that drove the policy, but the inevitable fate of an inferior people established "in the midst of a superior race."[42]

The operational force behind Jackson's Indian Removal Act of 1830 was Martin Van Buren, the eighth US president from 1837 to 1841. Van Buren, who served as secretary of state during Andrew Jackson's first term in office and vice president during Jackson's second term, pledged to continue enforcing policies established by his predecessor.

Just as the scarcity or abundance of resources—people, products, or services—drives your business today, the need for land and labor was the rationalization for and driver of the creation of racism in America. But seeds must not only be planted in people's minds; they must be nourished to turn them into deeply held beliefs.

The United States has a long history of systemic oppression justified by the social construct of race. "Since the 1840s, anti-Latino prejudice has led to illegal deportations, school segregation and even lynching—often-forgotten events that echo the civil-rights violations of African-Americans in the Jim Crow-era South," writes Erin Blakemore.[43]

Blakemore continues, "Though Latinos were critical to the US economy and often were American citizens, everything from their language to the color of their skin to their countries of origin could be used as a pretext for discrimination." This was a pattern of welcome until you are no longer useful as a source of cheap labor. Or if you were perceived as a threat to the economic opportunities of Whites such as access to the wealth yielded by Californian mines during the Gold Rush of 1848 to 1855. Also, forced deportations were common during the Great Depression. When the stock market tanked and unemployment grew, fears about jobs and the economy spread. In response, the United States forcibly removed people of Mexican descent from the country—about 60 percent of whom were US citizens. Euphemistically referred to as "repatriations," the removals were not voluntary. Sometimes, private employers drove their employees to the border and kicked them out. In other cases, local governments cut off relief, raided gathering places, or offered free train fare to Mexico. Blakemore writes:

> Colorado even ordered all of its "Mexicans"—in reality, anyone who spoke Spanish or seemed to be of Latino descent, including Mexican immigrants who had already become US citizens, and US-born children—to leave the state and blockaded its southern border to keep people from returning. People with disabilities and active illnesses were removed from hospitals and also deported. . . . When deportations finally ended around 1936, up to 2 million Mexican-Americans had been "repatriated," including nearly a third of both Los Angeles' and Texas' Mexican-born population. . . . Unlike the South, which had explicit

laws barring African American children from White schools, segregation was not enshrined in the laws of the southwestern United States. Nevertheless, Latino people were excluded from restaurants, movie theaters and schools.

Latino students were expected to attend separate "Mexican schools" throughout the Southwest beginning in the 1870s. At first, the schools were set up to serve the children of Spanish-speaking laborers at rural ranches. Soon, they spread into cities, too. By the 1940s, as many as 80 percent of Latino children in places like Orange County, California, attended segregated schools.

THE 1904 WORLD'S FAIR: THE ULTIMATE RACISM MARKETING CONVENTION

By the mid-nineteenth century, race and racism had become the accepted, "commonsense" wisdom of Whites in the United States, explaining everything from individual behavior to the fate of human societies. Academic journals legitimized race "science," which was also popularized in the new monthly magazines of the day such as *Harper's*. Its advancement took a giant leap forward in the "remarkable Indigenous people" displays at the 1904 World's Fair in St. Louis, Missouri.[44] Here, US popular culture reinforced and fueled racial explanations for the country's progress and power. These ideas of racial difference and White superiority were deeply imprinted into the US consciousness and that of Western culture overseas.

The 1904 World's Fair was positioned as a triumph of civilization, imperialism, and a new century. The organizers wanted to show the United States's unbridled progress. Attendees go to have fun, to be sure, but world's fairs are not about entertainment; they're billed as the world's universities. In what was hailed as "palaces of progress," fairgoers wandered through technological and cultural exhibits. But on the other side of the fairgrounds, visitors were captivated by human exhibits—people on display in their so-called natural habitats.

Human beings were organized (there's that "big sort" again) on a continuum from *savagery* to *civilized*. Savages were portrayed by Brown and Black people, civilized by White people. Some White fairgoers had their photo taken next to so-called savages to show their friends back home how "civilized" they were—an example is shown in Figure 4.1. The seeds of racism that were planted then, flourish today.

FIGURE 4.1 From the Philippine Exhibit, 1904 World's Fair, St. Louis. (*Harvard Art Museums/Fogg Museum, Transfer from the Carpenter Center for the Visual Arts, Photo President and Fellows of Harvard College, 2.2002.3160.*)

On display for all to see at the fair were the subjugated people of the United States's recent past. An exhibit titled "Old Plantation" served up a bucolic view of slave life. At another exhibit titled "American Indians," and described as vanquished people, sat a man dressed as Geronimo, the legendary and recently defeated Apache warrior, signing autographs for a fee. Fairgoers saw an enormous number of people who perhaps they had only read about, maybe never even heard about. The fair was an opportunity to showcase Manifest

Destiny—the nineteenth-century cultural belief that the expansion of the United States throughout the continent was both justified and destined by God—and the country's burgeoning drive to expand overseas. One of the largest and most popular exhibits was the Philippine Exposition. Created to demonstrate the benefits of the United States's civilizing presence, the exhibit gave fairgoers a chance to see the people they had recently conquered: The United States had taken possession of Guam, Puerto Rico, Cuba, and the Philippines after defeating Spain in war.

The St. Louis World's Fair closed on December 1, 1904. Its grand exhibit halls were demolished soon after. But race, a story first told to rationalize and justify deep divisions in a society that proclaimed its belief in equality, would be carried forward into the twentieth century and beyond.

In the seven months the fair was open, nearly 20 million people attended. Visitors received an object lesson that connected this social construct abstraction called race to a concrete, literally hands-on vision of the United States's future. Newspapers around the world also promoted this enduring narrative for all the world to see: Whites are the superior race, Whites are the shapers of history, Whites are the symbol of progress.

The St. Louis World's Fair closed on December 1, 1904. Its grand exhibit halls were demolished soon after. But race, a story first told to rationalize and justify deep divisions in a society that proclaimed its belief in equality, would be carried forward into the twentieth century and beyond. Most US citizens believed that race was one of the most important parts of national life; that race mattered because it guaranteed the United States's future in the history of the world. The United States would rise toward glory, toward history, toward its destiny.

DO NOT PASS GO OR COLLECT
ANY MONEY . . . FOR 400 YEARS

In the weeks following the police killing of George Floyd, protests brought to the forefront of US consciousness the perspectives of numerous Black leaders, artists, intellectuals, and authors. Among them is young adult author Kimberly Jones, whose nearly seven-minute video, *How Can We Win*, gained national media attention with more than 2 million views.[45] The content of her video will be expanded and published in book form by Henry Holt and Co. in November 2021 (*How We Can Win: Race, History and Changing the Money Game That's Rigged*). In her video, Jones passionately describes one among countless historical episodes when Black people were able to break free of the grips of oppression and advance both economically and educationally, only to have that freedom taken away again.

"Economics was the reason that Black people were brought to this country," Jones says midway into the video. "We came to do the agricultural work in the south and the textile work in the north."

She continues the metaphor of the 400-year wealth-building advantage of Whites in the United States that began by enslaving Black Africans: "[Let's say] right now I decided that I wanted to play Monopoly with you, and for 400 rounds of playing Monopoly I didn't allow you to have money, I didn't allow you to have anything on the board. And then we played another 50 rounds of Monopoly and everything that you earned while playing those 50 rounds was taken from you: that was Tulsa."

Black Wall Street: Tulsa, Oklahoma

In 1906, O. W. Gurley, a wealthy African American from Arkansas, moved to Tulsa and purchased over 40 acres of land that he made sure was only sold to other African Americans. By 1921, Tulsa's Greenwood District, which would come to be known as Black Wall Street, was one of the most prosperous African American communities in the United States. In this district, the average hourly wage of

Black families in the area exceeded what the federal minimum wage is today. This community prospered with banks, hotels, cafés, clothiers, movie theaters, its own school system, and contemporary homes with indoor plumbing.

Gurley created this community as a refuge and economic opportunity for those migrating from the harsh oppression of segregation laws in Mississippi. This movement was part of the Great Migration, the exodus of 6 million African Americans from the Jim Crow South to the cities of the North and West, from the time of World War I in 1916 until the 1970s.

This Great Migration was not simply relocating from one part of the country to another like we might today, say, for a new job. Isabel Wilkerson in her book *The Warmth of Other Suns* weaves a beautifully-crafted yet brutal story, based on more than 250 personal interviews, of what the Great Migration was like; the courage it took for African Americans to leave the familiar for the unfamiliar; the escape from violent attacks, lynchings, and economic oppression; and the desire for a better education for their children and future generations.[46] Those that fled the South, often under false pretenses for fear of retribution, sought economic and social asylum, much like immigrants do today. The big difference? The Great Migration was within the borders of their own country. African Americans were escaping a caste system known as Jim Crow—an artificial hierarchy in which everything that you could and could not do was based on the color of your skin.

The Jim Crow Museum of Racist Memorabilia explains, "After the Civil War (1861–1865), most southern states and, later, border states passed laws that denied Blacks basic human rights. The minstrel character's name 'Jim Crow' became a shorthand for this racial caste system—the laws, customs and etiquette that segregated and demeaned African Americans primarily from the 1870s to the 1960s."[47]

The name "Jim Crow" was popularized by a White entertainer, Thomas Dartmouth Rice, well before the Civil War. Throughout the 1830s and 1840s, Rice performed a popular song-and-dance act supposedly modeled after a slave. He named the character Jim Crow. Rice darkened his face, acted like a buffoon, and spoke with an exaggerated and distorted imitation of African American Vernacular English. In his Jim Crow persona, he also sang "Negro ditties" such as "Jump Jim Crow." By 1838, the term "Jim Crow" was being used as a collective racial epithet for Black people. Rice was not the first White comic to perform in blackface, but he was the most popular of his time, touring both the United States and England. As a result of Rice's success, "Jim Crow" became a common stage persona for White comedians' blackface portrayals of African Americans. The popularity of minstrel shows aided the spread of Jim Crow as a racial slur. It represented the legitimization of anti-Black racism and a system of laws and customs that oppressed Black people as a way of life. This system was fortified by the rationalizations that Whites were superior to Blacks in all important ways, including but not limited to intelligence, morality, and civilized behavior.[48]

And it was regularly enforced by violence, actual and threatened, as a method of social control. As author Ijeoma Oluo says, "The way in which systemic racism works, and has always worked, has not necessarily always been this reign of terror."[49] That's an enforcement of the system itself. The most extreme forms of Jim Crow violence were lynchings. Blacks who violated Jim Crow norms, for example, drinking from the Whites-only water fountain or trying to vote, risked their homes, jobs, and lives. Any White person could physically beat any Black person with impunity. Blacks had little legal recourse against these assaults because the Jim Crow criminal justice system was all White: police, prosecutors, judges, juries, and prison officials.

The Black Code laws known as Jim Crow, began their foothold during the period known as Reconstruction. This is a period in US history, from 1865 to 1877, that followed the Civil War. During this time, the nation attempted to redress the inequities of slavery and its political, social and economic legacy.

The Equal Justice Initiative's website cogently connects the dots between Reconstruction, the post-Reconstruction period, Jim Crow and where we are today:

After the Confederacy's 1865 defeat in the Civil War, Reconstruction amendments to the United States Constitution abolished slavery, established the citizenship of formerly enslaved Black people, and granted Black people civil rights—including granting Black men the right to vote. For the Reconstruction period, federal officials and troops remained in Southern states helping to enforce these new rights and administer educational and other programs for the formerly enslaved. As a result, Black people in the South, for the first time, constituted a community of voters and public officials, landowners, wage-earners, and free American citizens.

The federal presence also addressed deadly violence Black people faced on a daily basis. Continued support for White supremacy and racial hierarchy meant that slavery in America did not end—it evolved. The identities of many White Americans, especially in the South, were grounded in the belief that they were inherently superior to African Americans. Many White people reacted violently to the requirement to treat their former "human property" as equals and pay for their labor. Plantation owners attacked Black people simply for claiming their freedom. In the first two years after the war, thousands of Black people were murdered for asserting freedom or basic rights.

Congressional efforts to provide federal protection to formerly enslaved Black people were undermined by the U.S. Supreme Court, which overturned laws that provided remedies to Black people facing violent intimidation. In the 1870s, Northern politicians began retreating from a commitment to protect Black rights and lives, culminating in the withdrawal of troops in 1877. In response, racial terror and violence directed at Black people intensified and legal systems quickly emerged to restore racial hierarchy: White Southerners barred Black people from voting; created an exploitative economic system of sharecropping and tenant farming that would keep African Americans indentured and poor for generations; and made racial segregation the law of the land.[50]

During the post-Reconstruction era of the South, the biggest fear for Black people was economic terrorism: the very real threat felt by people whose jobs could be taken at a moment's notice, whose homes could be taken out from under them, who couldn't get any medical help, who had no security for themselves and their family, who couldn't get their kids to school. "Yes, terror helped push Black people out," says Oluo "But it was economic opportunity that propelled them north and west during the Great Migration." And that includes the parents of coauthor Gina Greenlee. Her mother and father migrated from Virginia and South Carolina, respectively, in the 1950s. They met and married in New York City, where Gina was later born.

The Game Is Fixed

Tulsa was a place "where we built Black economic wealth," continues Kimberly Jones in her video *How Can We Win*, "where we were self-sufficient, where we owned our stores, where we owned our property, and they burned them to the ground. So that's 450 years. . . . So if I played 400 rounds of Monopoly with you and I had to give you every dime that I made, and then for 50 years, every time that I played, if you didn't like what I did, you got to burn it, like they did in Tulsa . . . how can you win? How can you win? You can't win. The game is fixed."

A century ago, on May 31, 1921, the *Tulsa Tribune* reported that a 19-year old Black man, Dick Rowland, attempted to rape a White woman, Sarah Page, 17 years old. Whites in the area did not wait for the investigative process to play out, sparking two days of unprecedented racial violence. Thirty-five city blocks went up in flames, 300 people died, and 800 were injured.

Accounts vary on what happened between Page and Rowland in the elevator of the commercial Drexel Building in downtown Tulsa. Yet as a result of the *Tulsa Tribune's* racially inflammatory report,

Black and White armed mobs arrived at the courthouse. Scuffles broke out. Shots were fired. The outnumbered Blacks headed back to Greenwood. But the enraged Whites were not far behind, looting and burning businesses and homes along the way. As a result of mass migrations to the area, driven in part by increased job opportunities, Tulsa became the city with the most African Americans in the state. Tulsa's rapid change in racial demographics made the city ripe for a riot motivated by White animosity against Black economic progress.

THE BOOTSTRAP MYTH

A common dominant-group narrative about underrepresented groups sounds like this: "I'm sick and tired of people who act like victims and complain about not being able to get ahead. Nothing was ever handed to me. I've worked hard my whole life. Why can't they?" This narrative perpetuates what's called the "bootstrap myth," rationalized by people who have, yes, made it—but only in part—by hard work; they also made it in part by another dynamic. "For centuries, White households enjoyed wealth-building opportunities that were systematically denied to people of color," said Amy Traub, one of four coauthors of the 2017 racial wealth study, "The Asset Value of Whiteness: Understanding the Racial Wealth Gap—How Past Racial Injustices Are Carried Forward as Wealth Handed Down Across Generations and Reinforced by 'Color-Blind' Practices and Policies."[51]

The researchers' analyses show that individual behavior is not the driving force behind racial wealth disparities. Typical Black and Latino households in which the children attend college and live in two-parent households still have much less wealth than similarly sit-uated White households. Black and Latino households that include a full-time worker have much less wealth than White households with a full-time worker. Differences in spending habits also fail to explain wealth disparities between Black and White households.

Additional research traces the causes of the racial wealth gap to its origins in historical injustices, from slavery to segregation to redlining—this third injustice being the practice of denying creditworthy applicants a house loan because they lived in certain neighborhoods even though these applicants may otherwise be eligible. Further, the great expansion of wealth in the years after World War II was fueled by public policies such as the GI Bill, which mostly helped White veterans attend college and purchase homes with guaranteed low mortgages, building the foundations of an American middle class that largely excluded people of color. The outcomes of past injustices are carried forward as wealth is handed down across generations and are reinforced by ostensibly color-blind practices and policies in effect today. Yet many popular explanations for racial economic inequality overlook these deep, systemic roots, asserting that wealth disparities must be solely the result of individual life choices and personal achievements. The misconception that personal responsibility accounts for the racial wealth gap is an obstacle to the policies that could effectively address racial disparities.

Those policies continue to impede efforts by African American and Latino households to obtain equal access to economic security. "Research shows that racial privilege now outweighs a fundamental key to economic mobility, like higher education," says Traub. US policy makers have been slow, at best, to acknowledge this one, of many, structural inequities and to create policies that address it.

Even more recently, a 2020 study by the financial giant Citigroup found that the failure of the United States to address wide gaps between Black and White communities has cost the economy up to $16 trillion over the past 20 years. The study focused on existing gaps in wages, education, housing, and investment. The 104-page report by Citigroup's economists highlighted the residual effects of slavery in the United States that are still with us today despite legislation: "The dual health and economic crises resulting from the coronavirus lays bare long simmering racial tensions and inequities that have plagued the United States for centuries."[52] The economists connected the dots between the economic impact of the pandemic, repeated incidences of police brutality against unarmed Black men and women, and the ensuing protests, claiming this trifecta proved "too great to ignore" and calling for a general reassessment of the "very soul of the nation."

The findings in the Citigroup report make clear that the United States has made some strides in addressing inequality. Still, huge gaps exist today. These gaps are restraining the economy at large. "Societal inequities have manifested themselves into economic costs, which have harmed individuals, families, communities, and ultimately the growth and well-being of the US economy," the Citi report said.

GAPS BETWEEN BLACK AND WHITE COMMUNITIES IN THE UNITED STATES

- White families have eight times more wealth than Black households.

- The US homeownership rate among Whites is nearly 80 percent, compared with 47 percent for Blacks.

- Blacks are five times as likely to be incarcerated as Whites and make up 33 percent of the US prison population even though they only represent 12 percent of the total US population.

- Income levels peak for Black men sooner and lower (ages 45–49 and $43,849) than for White men (ages 50–54, $66,250).

- The total wealth held by US billionaires ($3.5 trillion) is equal to three-quarters of all Black wealth ($4.6 trillion).

Source: Citigroup, September 2020.

This is not only an issue in the United States but also in other parts of the world, such as the United Kingdom.

GAPS BETWEEN BLACK AND WHITE COMMUNITIES IN THE UNITED KINGDOM

- Black male university graduates are paid 17 percent less than White male university graduates—the equivalent of £3.90 an hour, or £7,000 over a year.

- Black female university graduates are paid 9 percent less than White female university graduates, or £3,000 less over a year.

- For every £1 a White British family has, Black Caribbean households have about 20p.

- For every £1 a White British family has, Black African and Bangladeshi households have approximately 10p.

- There is a lack of diversity at the top of the UK's largest companies. Among FTSE 100 companies, 62 percent of board members are White males, and they occupy 84 percent of executive directorships. Fewer than one in ten directors is Black or Asian or is from another underrepresented group.

Source: The Guardian, June 2020.[53]

A HISTORY OF VIOLENCE AGAINST AAPIs: MURDERS, ATTACKS, IMMIGRATION RESTRICTIONS, AND MICROAGGRESSIONS

When we began writing this book, our focus was on the Black and White experience given what was happening in the world and our own racial identities. In the time it has taken us to finish the book for publication, we are compelled to write about the increased violence, hatred, and microaggressions targeted toward Asian Americans and Pacific Islanders (AAPIs) living in the United States and Asians living in Western nations. An increasing number of Asians have faced a rise in verbal and physical attacks as a result of racist scapegoating over Covid-19. In the period between March 19, 2020, through

February 28, 2021, there were 3,795 hate incidents reported against AAPIs. Stop Hate AAPI is a nonprofit organization that tracks and reports incidents of discrimination, hate, and xenophobia against AAPIs in the United States.[54] The 3,795 incidents reported likely represents a fraction of the actual number. Incidents include verbal harassment (68.1 percent); shunning—the deliberate avoidance of Asian Americans (20.5 percent); physical assault (11.1 percent); civil rights violations—workforce discrimination, refusal of service, and the barring from transportation; and online harassment. The primary location of these hate incidents may surprise you: 35.4 percent occurred in businesses, not in public places or online.

On March 16, 2021, eight people, six of them Asian American women, were shot and killed by Robert Aaron Long at Asian-owned businesses in the Atlanta area. The names of the eight people murdered are Soon Chung Park, Hyun Jung Grant, Suncha Kim, Yong Yue, Delaina Ashley Yaun, Paul Andre Michels, Xiaojie Tan, and Daoyou Feng. Elcias Hernandez-Ortiz was also shot, but survived.[55]

"After his capture, the police noted that the shooter said he was seeking to address a 'sexual addiction' and 'was not racially motivated.' But for Asian women, racism and misogyny are deeply intertwined," wrote Cady Lang in *Time* magazine.[56] Lang continued, "A 2018 report from the American Psychological Association outlined the ways in which Asian-American women are exoticized and objectified in media and popular culture, depicted as 'faceless, quiet and invisible, or as sexual objects.' The survey said these stereotypes 'contribute to experiences of marginalization, invisibility and oppression' for Asian-American women."

"Anti-Asian racism also surged during the pandemic in Britain and Australia, with incidents of discrimination and xenophobia reported last summer by Human Rights Watch in Italy, Russia and Brazil," says Mai-Anh Peterson, cofounder of besea.n (Britain's East and South East Asian Network).[57] She goes on to say, "We know that this isn't just a problem for North America."

This recent violence against Asians, Asian Americans, and Pacific Islanders who live in Western countries is not new and not isolated.

It is yet another part of a long, historical timeline of oppression by the dominant group against people of color. In 1864 the United States brought in thousands of Chinese workers as a source of cheap labor to build the transcontinental railroad. When their usefulness was over, US politicians, journalists, and business leaders demonized them racially to appease White workers who felt threatened by Chinese competition. "The result was White mobs lynching Chinese immigrants, driving them en masse out of towns, and burning down Chinatowns. Racism against Chinese immigrants climaxed when the 1882 Chinese Exclusion Act was passed." It was the first racially discriminatory immigration law in US history. Political scientist and director of Asian American Studies at the University of Maryland, College Park, Janelle Wong says, while "European immigrants were confronted with widespread hostility, they never faced the kind of legal racial restrictions on immigration and naturalization that Asian Americans experienced."[58]

Cady Lang notes: "This brutality runs through more than two centuries of US history, from the incarceration camps of World War II, when over 100,000 Japanese Americans were rounded up and imprisoned because of xenophobic fears, to the 1982 murder of Vincent Chin, who died after being beaten by White men in a racially motivated attack in Detroit."[59]

This most recent wave of racial violence against Blacks, Asians, and people of color has been repeatedly referred to by US elected officials as "un-American." At best, this statement represents denial, as racial violence is deeply rooted in the country's history. Ending anti-Asian racism in the United States means confronting centuries of discrimination, violence, and oppression and recognizing how it manifests in the present day. In her comments about the March 16, 2021, Atlanta shootings, Dr. Michelle Au (Chinese American), the first Asian American to be elected to the Georgia state senate, told *Time* magazine, "This is a new chapter in a very old story."[60]

JUST WHO WE'VE BECOME

The United States is long overdue for a new story—a business model founded on a different set of principles: not oppression but expression; not deficits but assets; not treating humans as resources but treating them with humanity; not fears but hopes. We believe innovative businesses can lead the way.

If race is a social construct and not biological, you might be wondering why we are continuing to focus on it. The answer is this: because our systems, from employment and education, to housing, healthcare, business, law, and government, were constructed with intention on a flawed narrative. "In order to write a new story," writes Cady Lang, "we have to acknowledge the ugly past that brought us here."[61] The belief that non-Whites were less smart, less able, less civilized, less overall than Whites. To this day, that narrative shapes and reinforces *every* societal institution, including the workplace.

We asked EVERFI's cofounder and president Ray Martinez what his hope was for the future. He offered this perspective: "My hope is that many years from now, we're not having this conversation; that racial equity and diversity are ingrained in the institutionalization of every organization across the globe. This is the moment where we can make sustainable change so that in the next generation or two it is just who we've become."[62]

WHERE TO BEGIN

Having a shared understanding of the origins of race and racism in the United States, or your own country, is essential to productive discourse on these topics. However, if you Google the phrase "race resources," you'll receive over a billion results (yes, that's a "b"). No wonder it's difficult to know where to begin, but you already have. You're reading this book. Yet we have only scratched the surface. Now what?

We believe race is core *to* your business, but it is not your core business, unless you are in the DEI consulting industry. You don't have time to sift through volumes of information. We've done the job for you. As part of our own race journey, we've curated the scholarship to four educational resources, mentioned briefly at the beginning of the chapter and presented in more detail below, to help deepen your knowledge of race and racism:

- *Race: The Power of an Illusion.* Produced by California Newsreel and originally screened on PBS, this three-hour documentary investigates race in society, science, and history. Of the four educational resources we suggest, this is the only one that has a cost. However the online, four-day streaming rental is under $5.00. Also, you may also purchase the video in disc format for repeated viewing. The documentary challenges the biological idea of race by examining contemporary science, including genetics. It also explores the roots of the race narrative in North America, the nineteenth-century science that legitimized it, and how it came to be so fiercely held in the Western imagination. And it uncovers how race resides not in nature but in politics, economics, and culture. Few of us in the United States learned this in school, unless your family was actively steeped in social justice or civil rights. We certainly didn't. Likely, during race talk at work, some people may disagree with these facts and even pointedly attempt to dispute them. Though a skilled facilitator will navigate these dynamics, what's inevitable is that without participant awareness gained from exposure to the same history, race conversation and race work will grind to a standstill.

- *Frontline*'s "A Class Divided." In 1968, the day after Martin Luther King Jr. was assassinated, Jane Elliott, a teacher in the small, all-White Iowa town of Riceville, divided her third-grade class into blue-eyed and brown-eyed groups and gave them a daring lesson in discrimination. This episode of *Frontline* (first aired in 1985) is the story of that lesson, its lasting impact on the children, and its enduring power 50 years later. Initially Elliott tried discussing issues of discrimination, racism, and prejudice with her third-grade class. Her efforts were not getting through. These students did not normally interact with any people of color in their all-White rural town. So Elliott got bolder. She devised a two-day "blue eyes/brown eyes" experiment. The first day, she gave students with blue eyes profuse preferential treatment and positive reinforcement. She consciously made them feel superior to the students with brown eyes. Day two: Elliott reversed the treatment she had given each group the day before—preference to brown-eyed students so they could now claim superiority over the blue-eyed students. The result: whichever group Elliott favored in class, those students engaged with enthusiasm. They answered questions quickly and accurately, and performed better on tests. Those who were discriminated against appeared downcast, were uncertain in their answers, and performed poorly on tests. In the documentary about her experiment, Elliott says, "I watched what had been marvelous, cooperative, wonderful, thoughtful children turn into nasty, vicious, discriminating, little third-graders in a space of fifteen minutes."

- University of Illinois at Urbana-Champaign's online course Race and Cultural Diversity in American Life and History. Coursera, the giant online curator, offers it for free. This self-paced, 12-hour course, led by African American Studies scholar Dr. James D. Anderson, picks up the baton from the PBS documentary *Race: The Power of an Illusion*. It guides learners through a deeper understanding of ways in which race, ethnicity, and cultural diversity have shaped US institutions, ideology, law, and social relationships from the colonial era to the present. The primary focus is on the historical and social relationships among European Americans, Native Americans, African Americans, Latinos, and Asian/Pacific Americans. Through a series of video lecturettes, Dr. Anderson prompts you to examine your own beliefs, relationships, and individual experiences.

- Microsoft's online modules, Global Diversity and Inclusion: Beyond Microsoft. This self-paced course includes four modules focused on building greater awareness of diversity and inclusion. Recognizing that systemic racism is bigger than any one individual or organization can address, Microsoft has made these modules and hundreds of videos available free of charge. The modules were developed in collaboration with a Japanese American and openly gay man, Kenji Yoshino, who is the Chief Justice Earl Warren Professor of Constitutional Law at NYU School of Law and the Director of the Center for Diversity, Inclusion and Belonging. Beginning with inclusion and bias, the modules also cover three other constructs related to inclusion: covering, allyship, and privilege.

Together these four resources create a shared context (history) and lexicon necessary for productive race talk and race work in the workplace. Our hope is that you will devote time to learn from these free resources (three of the four are free) and perhaps share them with others in your professional life and maybe even your personal life.

THE FINE POINTS

Having a shared understanding of the origins of race and racism in the United States, or your own country, is essential for productive race talk and race work:

- Race is not biological.

- Race is a social construct invented to favor and maintain power of the people in the dominant group.

- The business model that the United States was founded on is one of oppression; and in many societal institutions, the workplace included, remains intact to this day.

- Racism is hard to see when you are part of the dominant group in society.

- The four educational resources outlined in this chapter help organizational leaders and staff members explore shared history and individual biases.

REFLECTION

- How have you or your family been oppressed by or benefited from the United States's economic system?

- Think of a time when *understanding context* was critical to making a business decision, launching an initiative, or solving a problem. How did understanding the context help you?

- What's one small step you can take to educate yourself and others on the United States's history of race and racism?

- If you live or work outside the United States, how would you describe the evolution of race in your country?

PART III

YOUR INNER JOURNEY

C hange irritates. Saxophonist Billy Cox said, "Life will only change when you become more committed to your dreams than you are to your comfort zone." Most everyone over the age of 10 has experienced this. Doesn't mean they like it.

Measurable, sustainable race work will only happen when organizations become more committed to embracing yet unimagined possibilities rather than snuggling up to what's always been. Change requires a stretch. New muscles and new ways of being in the world. It's the recognition of an end to one lived experience, a transition period of not knowing, limbo, and experimentation. Then trials weathered, errors reconciled, skins shed, and discoveries revealed. In this re-created life, we bring with us parts we once knew and more of what we've unearthed that was previously unimaginable.

Some of the early diversity training of the 1970s through 1990s we introduced in the last section were deemed failures. Much of that is attributed to compliance box-checking and budget and time constraints. These dynamics only left room for short-term exposure to basic topics. And there was limited reinforcement of newly acquired skills. Organizations that persisted through this phase

> Measurable, sustainable race work will only happen when organizations become more committed to embracing yet unimagined possibilities rather than snuggling up to what's always been.

of isolated training evolved their race work over time. They did this through a willingness to sit in the discomfort of what they knew they didn't know. And while in that dissonant state, experimented their way to new learning and their unique expression of workplace racial diversity and inclusion.

Before we undertake team and organizational race work, we must first begin our journey from within. Part III is all about helping you understand, appreciate, and grow from the challenges (and discomfort) you will experience individually. We provide tools, models, and case studies to serve as your guide.

CHAPTER 5

CONSCIOUSLY COMPETENT

Insights for Your Own Race Journey

It starts with you. Look inside and connect with the issues of race through your own personal stories. If you don't have any, then talk to some Black men and women and hear their stories. Listen without judgment, without trying to fix anything or inadvertently bringing the conversation back to you. Leaders too quickly jump over this first step of cultural awareness and self-awareness of their own mindsets and want to move right to "what can I do?" And if you don't know any Black people then at the very least you can read about it.

JOANNA BARSH
White American, Director Emerita at
McKinsey & Company, Board Director at Genesco[1]

The "conscious competence learning model" has had staying power for more than 50 years. Developed at a time when learning and development was called "training," the model remains relevant today in coaching, education, and business. It is a simple yet profound deconstruction of the stages we enter and pass through when learning new skills or adopting new behaviors. Whatever we are learning, from navigating a new digital collaboration tool or speaking a new language, to developing more empathy, the conscious competence learning model helps us pinpoint where we are in the learning process. To the topic of race in the workplace, we apply the model depicted in Figure 5.1.

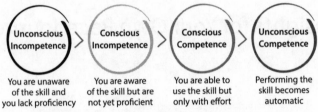

FIGURE 5.1 Conscious competence learning model. (*Illustration 85667805 © Vaeenma | Dreamstime.com.*)

In the first stage, *unconscious incompetence,* we don't know what we don't know. We are unaware of how systemic racism impacts ourselves, our coworkers, and society at large.

This was the stage coauthor Margaret Greenberg was in when she began learning more about systemic racism back in June 2020. Her first assignment, as part of the online course Race and Cultural Diversity in American Life and History you learned about in the last chapter, was to write a self-reflection essay answering this question: "How do you self-identify—ethnically, racially, social class, gender, sexual orientation?"

"When I first read this question I thought, I don't really self-identify with any of these categories," Margaret began her essay. She didn't know what she didn't know.

"I tend to identify myself as a parent, wife, author, business owner, and a lover of all things outdoors. However, upon further reflection the only one of these categories I really self-identify with is gender. Perhaps that is because that is the only category where I have experienced inequities in the workplace."

Not identifying White as a race, as Margaret initially did, is inherent in the concept known as "White privilege." As members of the nondominant group in the United States, people of color don't have the luxury of only seeing themselves as a parent, spouse, or professional or identifying themselves by their hobbies. They don't have the privilege of *not* seeing race.

If you are a member of a dominant group in your culture, such as male, White, and heterosexual, rarely do you have to come out of your cultural comfort zone. If, like Margaret, you've never thought much about yourself as having a race, learning about Whiteness as a racial identity is a great place to start your inner journey.

Stage two is *conscious incompetence*. In this stage we now know what we don't know. This is the most difficult, uncomfortable stage. We are now aware that we have a gap. Race plays a role in whom we hire and whom we promote? Really? As we begin to learn more, we stumble our way through conversations. We worry about putting our foot in our mouth or being perceived as a troublemaker. This is the stage where we often give up or are tempted to do so, but if we hang in there and embrace the uncomfortable, we grow our skills and ourselves.

Margaret reached the conscious incompetence stage in her own race journey when she realized that one gap in her knowledge was around the concept of White privilege. "When I first heard the term 'White privilege,' I was taken aback," she says, "because I didn't think I was privileged at all. I grew up in a middle-class family. My life was not easy, especially after my mother died by suicide when I was 12. My father, a foreman in a ball bearing factory, was thrust into the role of single parent to four kids under the age of 21. With no college education himself, he didn't believe girls 'needed' to further their education, as they were going to stay home and have babies. So I put myself through college by waitressing and doing other odd jobs. I have since learned that White privilege does not mean I haven't had struggles in my life. It means that the one struggle I haven't had to deal with is the color of my skin."

Conscious competence is the third stage. We now know what we need to know. We have context. We've learned about our history. Have a shared lexicon. We've sufficiently absorbed what we have learned to feel competent. And now we want to learn more. We may not exactly feel competent when engaging the emotionally charged topics of race and racism, but we can feel more open and curious, knowing that this is a journey, not a finite destination.

The last stage, *unconscious competence*, is when we no longer consciously think about our actions or behaviors. They have become what we call second nature. It is who we are.

WHY WE STRUGGLE

Being able to dialogue about race and racism is, of course, different from the ability to drive a car, generate Excel spreadsheets, or draft a marketing plan. One of the reasons we struggle with race talk is because we lack readiness. The US racial history narratives (books, school curricula, media, laws, policies) have been carefully constructed to obscure realities of dominant-group economic oppression. It's wishful thinking that, upon the global witnessing of George Floyd's murder, all of a sudden we will be ready to engage in new narratives. Or that a new lexicon should come easily to us.

Many White people in the United States watched that video and were *astonished* that the police officer didn't let up for more than nine minutes while Floyd pleaded that he couldn't breathe. The reality of the violence was nothing new for many Black Americans and Black people from the diaspora who live in the United States. Though Blacks have lived with violent, murderous attacks on their bodies for centuries despite laws in place to protect and serve, Floyd's modern-day lynching was rattling. Frightening. Devastating. The language to speak to such horrors, to connect them to the history that created them, is not one in which we are fluent. That fluency, like any other language, comes from the work we must first do as individuals. You don't grow up speaking English your entire life, and then boom, you're fluent in Mandarin. Rather, you set the foundation for fluency with the building blocks of grammar, vocabulary, and the cultural context that infuses language.

> In nearly every interview we conducted with more than two dozen business professionals, the need to do "your own, inner work" came up again and again, unprompted, as did the word "journey."

Readying yourself to begin or advance race work is a developmental process. It involves learning to assess your current capabilities, identifying your development needs, and recognizing your strengths. This will help foster meaningful, cross-cultural dialogue. Readiness is not a six-week crash course. It develops over time through knowledge acquisition and skills practice. Readiness asks for introspection and self-reflection. In nearly every interview we conducted with more than two dozen business professionals, the need to do "your own, inner work" came up again and again, unprompted, as did the word "journey." Let's look at three foundational pieces of inner work needed to become *consciously competent* in your own race journey.

DISCOVER YOUR ANTIRACIST STYLE

There are those who would cringe at the thought of being called a racist. Yet our silence perpetuates racism. Your workout buddy at the gym uses racial slurs that make you uncomfortable. Do you say something? A colleague confides in you that the only reason a new coworker was hired was because of her race. You disagree. Do you speak up? What is the racial identity of the influencers you follow on LinkedIn and other social media channels? Are you aware of facts and statistics that clearly disprove racial stereotypes, and yet when they are casually repeated in group settings, you remain silent?

Productive race work begins with self-awareness. Before you read on, take Dr. Deborah Plummer's Antiracist Style Indicator (ASI)—you can access it for free at https://asi.dlplummer.com/. This quick list of questions uncovers to what extent each of us acts to dismantle structural racism. The ASI measures *functionality*. Specifically, the tool identifies your antiracist style from *underfunctioning* to *functioning* to *overfunctioning*, without demonizing or shaming any one approach. This is a style assessment, not a test score. Not a judgment. And not for White people only. We all have something to learn, no matter our racial identity, as we will explore in detail later in this chapter

Race and racism are emotional and value-laden issues. Oftentimes we can get caught up in our feelings and overreact. As Dr. Plummer writes, "An antiracist overfunctioning style tends to rush in to fix a problem, give unsolicited advice and present themselves as expert on the lives of others as well as their own. A flame throwing antiracist can ignite more fires and keep them ablaze rather than put them out."[2] An underfunctioning antiracist style relies on others to solve problems. When overwhelmed, this style either avoids the problem altogether or shuts down when attempting to solve it. Unwittingly, race work can be stifled by well-meaning underfunctioning antiracists and interrupted by zealous overfunctioning antiracists. So, what is a *functioning* antiracist style?

A functioning antiracist style turns "us and them into we," says Dr. Plummer. This creates a stronger foundation for race work. She explains, "This style recognizes and understands the structures that shape and maintain racism. They understand racial dynamics and treat associated tensions as challenges to be mastered with education and learning." Our antiracist style is not fixed. It can evolve through awareness, self-evaluation, and the willingness to learn more about our history and the role systemic racism has played in shaping it.

We recommend all readers complete this free, online assessment. It takes less than 15 minutes to finish. And you will receive an automated report as soon as you click "send." We encourage you to take time to reflect upon your report.

If your results show that you have an *underfunctioning* antiracist style, take heart. Instead of feeling shame or guilt, this is your chance to recognize that you took a positive step in your learning—from *unconscious incompetence* to *conscious incompetence*. Attend a lecture, listen to a podcast, or watch a documentary about racism. Streaming channels now organize their movies and series not only by award winners, but also by genres including Black, LGBTQ+, and Latino, among others. Read articles to learn more about racial and ethnic groups other than your own. Read nonfiction books and novels written by authors of races or ethnicities other than your own. With more knowledge and skill building, when you retake the ASI a few months from now, you may find that you now have a functioning antiracist style.

If your survey results show that you have a *functioning* antiracist style, don't stop there. You might be tempted to say, "Whew, good news; I'm done." Deepen your learning. Engage the suggestions outlined in this chapter. Start a book club at work or in your personal life. Ask a close friend or trusted colleague to take the ASI. Then explore your results together.

If your ASI results show that you have an *overfunctioning* antiracist style, be self-compassionate. Your style isn't fixed. It morphs with your type and level of engagement in actively dismantling the status quo. If you find yourself in a perpetual state of anxiety or anger, look for ways to channel those emotions into positive actions. Protest marches are not the only way to demonstrate your commitment. For example, if you like to write, keep a journal or coauthor an article with a friend or colleague. Notice not only microaggressions but also positive interactions you experience firsthand or hear about in the media. We call these "micro-opportunities." If you are a daily consumer of podcasts on race, you might shift to once a week for the next four months. Today's 24-hour news cycle requires that we "appropriately disengage." This is a term positive psychologists use for giving ourselves a break. In doing so we protect our well-being.

DISCOVER YOUR RACIAL IDENTITY

Any learning and development program advises that the first step toward competence is self-awareness, not immediate action. Introspection involves slowing down, going inward, and being deliberate about how we think. Productive race work begins with self-awareness and how you navigate a multiracial workplace. That way of being is tied to many variables including family of origin, education, professional circles, and media exposure. Also, it is connected to how you racially self-identify and how society identifies you, as the two are often quite different. Our racial identity shapes our worldview and our lived experience. That includes the different opinions, ideologies, and assumptions that influence our every workplace interaction, conversation, and business decision whether or not we are aware of it.

_____

When we assume sameness, we excuse ourselves from being constructively curious about the life experiences of people from different races and ethnicities. And instead, treat them as a faceless homogeneous throng rather than as individuals.

_____

In the previous chapter, you learned that visible differences in our appearance are a function of geography, not genetics. Humans are 99.9 percent genetically the same. The superficial variations in our appearance—skin color, eye shape, and hair form—were used to create a narrative of inherent superiority of the dominant group (White people) and fundamental deficiency in abilities and humanity of non-White groups. This fabricated narrative deliberately conflates superficial physical traits with fundamental human abilities as justification for the social construct of race. That is, the _arbitrary classification_ of human beings. What's different is not our innate abilities (established genetically for all humans), which has been the perpetuated narrative for hundreds of years. What's different is the lived experiences created from this comparative superior-inferior narrative. Regardless of your skin color, these classifications shape many aspects of lived experiences, including how we self-identify.

If we are all basically the same, isn't our work done? No. When we assume sameness, we excuse ourselves from being constructively curious about the life experiences of people from different races and ethnicities. And instead, treat them as a faceless homogeneous throng rather than as individuals. The idea of sameness, of adopting a color-blind strategy for relating to individuals of different races, ethnicities, and skin tones, leaves people without the language to discuss race and racism and examine their own bias.

Color-Aware Instead of Color-Blind

"Color blindness" relies on the concept that race-based differences don't matter. It ignores the realities of systemic racism, that the United States was built on the arbitrary use of skin color as a sorting tool.[3] And yet the color-blind message—*I don't care if you're White, Black, purple, or blue, because I don't even see race*—remains esteemed in the United States and other Western nations. Many refrain from discussing race, even in situations where mentioning race would be useful, such as describing the only Black person in a group.[4]

The undercurrent in this refusal to see color is the conscious or unconscious desire to remain blind to racial disparities. For the first time in their lives, many non-Black people are having tough conversations about race and racial inequality in the United States, a realization brought on by the outcry over the ways Black Americans, Blacks from the diaspora who live in the United States and globally, have been mistreated, underserved, and underpaid.

The skin color sorting tool affected the ancestors of most current-day Americans. "Oppressed people from around the world, particularly from Europe, passed through Ellis Island, shed their old selves, and often their old names to gain admittance to the powerful dominant majority," writes bestselling author Isabel Wilkerson.[5] Europeans who were Czech or Hungarian or Polish or German or Irish now became "White." Serbs and Albanians, Swedes and Russians, Turks and Bulgarians who might have been at war with one another back in their mother countries became one and the same, now part of an artificially created dominant group. Not from shared ethnic culture, language, faith, or national origin. Solely on the basis of what they looked like. Wilkerson notes: "To gain acceptance, each fresh infusion of immigrants had to enter into a silent, unspoken pact of separating and distancing themselves from the established lowest group. They could establish their new status by observing how the lowest group was regarded and then imitate or one-up the disdain and contempt, learn the epithets, and join in on violence against them to prove themselves worthy of admittance to the dominant group."

Yes, White is a racial identity. It shows up in Whiteness being the "default," the center, and Black, Brown, and people of color as "other"—outliers and aberrations. Constructive race work requires us to be color-aware so that we may explore this collective history and unpack our own.

> "Where do South Asian and East Asian people fit in this conversation? They've been discriminated against based on their skin color, but it's not the conversation currently. I also get the sense that people think that I should feel guilty [for being White]. That feels rotten."
>
> *Anonymous, White female with more than 20 years of business experience*

We urge you to explore your own racial identity, no matter your skin color or which group you belong to (dominant or nondominant). This will help you to be more *color-aware* of others. One way to do this is to reflect upon the question: "How do you self-identify?"

Our first assignment in the online course Race and Cultural Diversity in American Life and History, mentioned earlier, was to write an essay answering that question. As one Black woman and one White woman, we each answered that question quite differently.

NATIONAL PUBLIC RADIO'S THE RACE CARD PROJECT

"Playing the race card" is an idiom that alleges someone has used race to gain unfair advantage.

Multiracial (White British father, Black Ghanian mother) *Guardian* columnist Afua Hirsch[6] wrote that whenever she offered either a structural or personal analysis of how racism has affected Black people's lives, she was told that she was "playing the race card." Accusing a Black person of playing the race card when he or she speaks about racism is intended to silence, threaten, or "shame someone into not mentioning the obvious racism they're being subjected to," writes Hirsch.

National Public Radio has turned this pejorative term on its head with The Race Card Project.

In 2010, US journalist and former *ABC News* television correspondent Michele Norris began inviting people to distill their thoughts on the word "race" to only six words. Calling her idea "The Race Card Project," Norris asked people around the world to share their experiences, questions, hopes and dreams, laments, and observations about identity—in six words—as the starting point for conversations about race.

Today the project has collected more than 500,000 personal narratives, from every US state and nearly a hundred countries beyond the United States. People often send backstories and photos to share more about what is behind their six-word statements. Many of these essays contain sentiments and hard truths rarely expressed out loud. In 2013, The Race Card Project was awarded the prestigious Peabody Award for excellence in electronic communications for turning a pejorative phrase into a productive dialogue on a difficult topic.

How would you distill your thoughts, experiences, or observations about race into one sentence containing only six words? Here are a half-dozen race cards from the site:

School Integration Enriched My White Life.

Mom, Why Do They Hate Us?

No, Where Are You Really From?

My Name is Jamaal. I'm White.

With Kids I'm "Dad," Alone, "Thug."

My Family Members Are Not Terrorists.

We invite you to share your identity story at The Race Card Project. Yes, you may do it anonymously. Visit the Race Card Wall at https://theracecardproject.com/. Read the cards and the stories behind them. Complete your own card, and encourage others to do the same. Take this exercise a step further and share your six-word statement with others both inside and outside the workplace.

DISCOVERY AND RESPECTING WHAT YOU DON'T KNOW

One of our colleagues, who is of Lebanese descent, wrote to us after she took the ASI you learned about earlier in this chapter. "The demographic info should have an 'Other' option in my opinion. I am not White but had to check that box." Our colleague's observation stopped us cold. Just as we were preparing to put this chapter to bed, we recognized we had more work to do.

The ASI lists seven race categories in its demographics section: (1) Native American, (2) Asian, (3) Black/African American, (4) Hispanic/LatinX, (5) Native Hawaiian/Pacific Islander, (6) White, and (7) Biracial/Multiracial. The six US Census race categories are (1) White, (2) Black or African American, (3) American Indian or Alaska Native, (4) Asian, (5) Native Hawaiian and Pacific Islander, and (6) "Some other race," which is a write-in answer, not a box check. In addition, the US Census provides write-in spaces for sub-categories within the Asian category such as Chinese, Filipino, Asian Indian, Vietnamese, Korean, Japanese, and Other Asian (for example, Pakistani, Cambodian, and Hmong). And it provides a write-in space for subcategories within Pacific Islander such as Tongan, Fijian, and Marshallese. The creators of the US Census write, "We recognize that the race categories include racial and national origins and sociocultural groups." So they've also made available subcategory write-in spaces for the Black/African and American Indian or Alaska Native categories. Write-in space for subcategories in the White category list these examples: German, Irish, English, Italian, Lebanese, and Egyptian. Which brings us to the feedback from our Lebanese colleague: she checked the "White" box in the ASI demographic section even though she does not self-identify that way. (The ASI does not offer subcategories of "White" as does the US census form.) This, in turn, prompted yet another discovery on our own race education journey.

In response to the ASI demographic questions, neither of us reacted the way our Lebanese colleague did, with the desire to check a box designated "Other." This is because Gina racially identifies as "Black" and Margaret as "White." On the race question of the ASI and on most government forms and job and education applications in the United States, the boxes "Black" and "White" exist. Those boxes, though, tend to fit fewer and fewer people. In our ever-increasing multicultural society, more and more people self-identify racially and ethnically in numerous, intersectional ways.

For example, US golfer Tiger Woods self-identifies as "mixed race." His father was of African American, Chinese, and Native American descent. His mother is of Thai, Chinese, and Dutch descent. During an interview in 1997, Oprah Winfrey asked Woods whether it bothered him being called "African American." He said it did. As a teenager, he had coined his own term to describe his racial identity: "Cablinasian"—a person who is Caucasian, Black, American Indian, and Asian. Another example is Robin Thede, comedian and the creator and producer of HBO's *A Black Lady Sketch Show*. Thede self-identifies as "Black" and "African American." Her mother is Black, and her father is White. And the not-so-famous San Franciscan who filmed a White couple confronting him about a Black Lives Matter message he stenciled in chalk outside his home is of Filipino descent and identifies as "a person of color." People who identify as Black, African American, mixed-race, or a person of color are no more homogeneous than White people.

On this newly discovered road of our race education journey, we wondered about the census questions for people who self-identify as Hispanic or Latino. Question 8 on the 2020 census reads: "Is Person 1 of Hispanic, Latino, or Spanish origin? For this census, Hispanic origins were not considered races. Hispanic origin can be viewed as the heritage, nationality, lineage, or country of birth of the person or the person's parents or ancestors before arriving in the United States. People who identify as Hispanic, Latino, or Spanish may be any race."

"Isn't Hispanic/Latino my race?" The National Association of Latino Elected and Appointed Officials (NALEO)[7] posed this rhetorical question in the Q&A section of its Hagase Contar# (Be Counted) campaign for the 2020 census.[8] Answering their own question, they write, "The short answer is *NO*. According to the Census Bureau, *Hispanic origin* and *race* are two different concepts, and everyone should answer both questions even though many Latinos consider their Hispanic background to be their 'race.' The Census Bureau says being Latino is an ethnicity, not a race." Respondents to the census question "Is Person 1 of Hispanic, Latino, or Spanish origin?," may answer by checking one of four boxes: (1) Mexican/Mexican-American/Chicano, (2) Puerto Rican, (3) Cuban, or (4) OTHER Hispanic. Which prompts the question "What if my origin is not listed?" A write-in section is available, and the examples given include Salvadoran, Guatemalan, Dominican, and Argentinian.

In this chapter, and in those following, you will hear from business professionals we interviewed who self-identify as Latino and Black. Latino and White. Or Latino. Or Hispanic. And others who self-identify solely with what the US census considers ethnicity and not with race.

Which leads us to . . .

Box-Checking Gone Wild

If you've immigrated to the United States from, say, Brazil and complete a job application, box-checking becomes even more complicated.

In Brazil, "pardo," also known popularly as "moreno," is an ethnic and skin color category used in the Brazilian census.[9] The term "pardo" most commonly refers to Brazilians of mixed ethnic ancestries, and represents a diverse range of skin colors. Pardo Brazilians are typically a mixture of Europeans, Sub-Saharan Africans, and/or Native Brazilians. Also, in Brazil there are up to 140 more categories, including branco ("White"), preto ("Black"), amarelo ("yellow," meaning East Asians), and indígena ("indigene," meaning Amerindians). The list continues to loira (blond hair and White skin), clara (literally clear—light), castanha (literally a chestnut—a cashew-like brown), jambo (after a deep red fruit), sarará (a mixture of White and Black with red hair), canela (cinnamon color), mulata (a mixture of White and Black), marrom (chocolate brown), and escura (dark). This complexity results from over 500 years of relationships among three groups in Latin America: Indigenous people, European colonizers, and the slaves the colonizers brought over from Sub-Saharan Africa.

The aforementioned examples clearly demonstrate the complexity of classifying people into racial categories based largely on skin color. Which brings us again to our colleague who identifies as "Lebanese" who, in the absence of the "Other" box on the ASI, reluctantly checked "White."

When in doubt, ask. We reached out to Dr. Plummer's research team, explaining:

> In our book we speak to the importance of spectrum and not dichotomous thinking. We suspect that our Lebanese colleague is not alone in wishing to check an "Other" box given the myriad ways to racially identify (note Brazil). Might Dr. Plummer be amenable to including an "Other" category as an option for the racial identity demographic question at the conclusion of the ASI?

This was the research team's prompt reply:

> We understand your request and appreciate what you are saying but the theoretical frameworks for the ASI do not align ethnicity and race in that way. Lebanese is an ethnicity and not a race in the US. Especially in the framework of racism, the visibility of color is an important aspect of

race. Also, Dr. Plummer uses the tool to align with other research that she and other teams do, and so uses the same categories for those metrics.

Dr. Plummer's research team encouraged us to read more about racial identity development and ethnicity. So we did. It's complex.

Dr. Jennifer DeVere Brody, director of Stanford University's Center for Comparative Studies in Race & Ethnicity, sums up race and ethnicity this way: "When looking at how society, scholars, and the government define the words, there is little agreement on core distinctions between race and ethnicity."[10] She explains that over the years, "law, medicine, and common sense" have blurred their true meanings.

Susan Somersille Johnson, Prudential's chief marketing officer, self-identifies as Black. "I was raised to be proud of my heritage," says Johnson,[11] whose mother is from Jamaica and father is from St. Thomas/St. Croix. Johnson is particularly attuned to the intersection between Black and Latino. Her husband, who is a journalist, self-identifies as both; his parents are from Costa Rica and Panama. Although Spanish is his first language, he had difficulty getting assigned to Latino stories on television in the United States because he "looks Black." His employer asked, "Why would we put you on that story in Puerto Rico?" His reply: "Because I speak Spanish, because I'm Latino."

Johnson says that since the emergence of Black Lives Matter and the public killing of George Floyd, she's had debates with several Latino people. She asks if they are "allies" or "actually in the fight"? Their response often depends on the color of their skin and how they self-identify. Some say, "I'm Black, so I am part of Black Lives Matter," and others say, "I'm an ally."

A Look at Ethnicity

Zakira Bhura is an IT executive director at CVS Health. She was born on the northwest coast of India in Gujarat but was raised and educated in the United States from the age of two. She could have easily been raised in Africa or the United Kingdom. Her father had visas to those countries, too, but he chose the job in the United States because a college buddy of his had moved there. He wouldn't be completely alone. That was 1969. A year later his wife, Zakira, and her sister joined him. Bhura is American (nationality), identifies as Asian (race), and is culturally Indian (ethnicity). In her own words, she says:

> People can usually tell by looking at me that I'm from the subcontinent of India. But as I was thinking about what happened over the summer [referring to the Black Lives Matter protests in 2020] and what happened on Capitol Hill [referring to the armed assault on the US Capitol in January 2021], I felt like an outsider. With everything that was happening with Black Lives Matter, the building of the wall against Mexico, those slurs against Latinos, and people confusing Indians and Spanish people, I felt like an outsider in my own country. It was really disturbing and made me think about my race, when I never thought about it before in my whole life. Even though I'm Indian and I'm American, I'm also Muslim, and unfortunately terrorism is associated with it. And even in India, I'm a minority because I'm a Muslim. I remember thinking, "OK, I'm not Black. I'm not really Indian. Sometimes people even joke and call me a "fake Indian" because I have no accent. For a moment in time, I was having a pity party and thinking, "I'm on an island by myself."[12]

Like Bhura, Manuel Meza, who is head of global markets for one of the biggest banks in Mexico City and who identifies as Latino, said he felt somewhat like a "spectator" when asked about his perspective on the racial protests in the United States and other demonstrations in Europe. Meza comments:

If you ask people in Mexico about what's going on in the United States, how police are treating Black people, they are very indignant. They say it's not fair how the United States is treating Mexicans that go there for work and are drivers, waiters, or whatever. We feel pity for them. But then when we look at what's happening in our own country, we don't talk about the people coming here from Central America—El Salvador or Guatemala. They get robbed. They get murdered. They are on the streets of Mexico City asking for food or a job. But we don't talk about it. It's like it's not happening here.[13]

Ethnicity most often refers to the way a person identifies *learned* aspects of themselves, such as nationality, language, and culture. When we contacted Dr. Plummer's team and said that we suspected our Lebanese colleague is not alone in her desire to check a box other than "White," one that she feels more accurately reflects the culture with which she identifies, our follow-up research confirmed that hunch (Figure 5.2).

Roughly 3 million people of Middle Eastern and North African (MENA) and Southwest Asian descent live in the US, reports a 2019 *Los Angeles Times* analysis of US Census Bureau data.[14] In Los Angeles County, more than 350,000 people can trace their roots to a region that stretches from Mauritania to the mountains of Afghanistan. In addition to Southern California, New York and Detroit have the largest groups of people from Southwest Asia, North Africa, and the Middle East. The analysis found that in past surveys more than 80 percent in this group have called themselves White. Arab and Iranian communities for years have lobbied the Census Bureau to create a separate category for MENA. However, in 2018 census officials said that a category would not be added to the 2020 census, citing that MENA was seen not as a race, but an ethnicity, which aligns with Dr. Plummer's response to our query.

The terms "race" and "ethnicity" also are often substituted for one another, based on how an individual chooses to identify and

What is this person's race?
Mark [X] one or more boxes **AND** print origins.

☐ White – *Print, for example, German, Irish, English, Italian, Lebanese, Egyptian, etc.* ↗

☐ Black or African Am. – *Print, for example, African American, Jamaican, Haitian, Nigerian, Ethiopian, Somali, etc.* ↗

☐ American Indian or Alaska Native – *Print name of enrolled or principal tribe(s), for example, Navajo Nation, Blackfeet Tribe, Mayan, Aztec, Native Village of Barrow Inupiat Traditional Government, Nome Eskimo Community, etc.* ↗

☐ Chinese   ☐ Vietnamese   ☐ Native Hawaiian
☐ Filipino   ☐ Korean   ☐ Samoan
☐ Asian Indian   ☐ Japanese   ☐ Chamorro
☐ Other Asian – *Print, for example, Pakistani, Cambodian, Hmong, etc.* ↗   ☐ Other Pacific Islander – *Print, for example, Tongan, Fijian, Marshallese, etc.* ↗

☐ Some other race – *Print race or origin.* ↗

FIGURE 5.2 US census form

the historical impact on the perception of the two terms. Dr. Brody tries to simplify the understanding of these complex concepts this way: "Race is something we believe to be heritable, and ethnicity is something learned."[15] In reality, it is not that easy. This simplification masks the history of how race has been used to advance social and economic power for one group over others. And throughout history, the tides of racial classifications have changed several times. This is the case with Irish immigrants for example. The history book *How the Irish Became White* by Noel Ignatiev delves into how Irish immigrants in the early nineteenth century fled their homeland, only to be discriminated against in the United States because of their country of origin.[16] Over time, the tides turned, as their skin color (the primary physical attribute US institutions wield to sort people into racial categories) gained them the social acceptance that was denied Blacks from the diaspora and African Americans.

At the end of this fruitful exploration of ethnicity prompted by three business professionals taking the ASI and sharing observations, here's where we, the authors of *The Business of Race*, have landed: The ASI is a stellar educational tool. Both authors learned much from taking it—several times. Its questions exposed us to ideas and history previously unknown to us, such as the differences in, and relationships between, the concepts of race and ethnicity. Also, neither of us was familiar with the term "housing covenants," a question on the ASI. That unfamiliarity prompted more research. Our understanding gained further traction when our colleague Rochelle Newman-Carrasco shared the racial exclusion language in the deed to her home (Figure 1.1 in Chapter 1). For topics such as these, the ASI is an excellent point-in-time awareness gauge of societal dynamics that perpetuate structural racism. And, it is a practical tool for advancing individual conscious competence through changes in knowledge, patterns, and habits.

DEI Conferences Aren't Immune

Lorie Valle-Yañez (you may remember her from Chapter 3), now chief diversity and inclusion officer at MassMutual, grew up in the multicultural state of Hawaii. Her father was Filipino and her mother Nicaraguan. Also, she has Chinese and Native American ancestors. "Even people in my field try to put me in a box," Valle-Yañez shared with us. "I was at a DEI conference, and somebody comes up to me with the clipboard and asks, 'How do you self-identify?' I replied, 'Oh, I'm multicultural or multiracial. And he says, 'No, I mean, how do you actually self-identify your race?' And I reply, 'I'm very comfortable being multicultural.' And he replies, 'Well, I can only write down one thing.' And that's when I said, 'It sounds like a personal problem to me.'"[17]

We hope that now you have a better understanding of your antiracist functioning style and racial identity. Also, that you recognize the need to become more culturally competent. We recommend one more type of inner work to facilitate dialogue on race and cultural differences: identification of your individual strengths, which will lead to a better understanding of the strengths of others you work with.

DISCOVER YOUR STRENGTHS

"Assume positive intent" is a tenet of positive psychology, and not one that many workplaces would attach to race talk. Yet that is precisely what we suggest. The best way to cultivate a positive mindset is to start with individual strengths. The US culture—from primary school to the workplace—tends to focus on what's missing or broken. This "fix-it" preoccupation is not unique to the US. And also predates modernity. For early humans to survive, we had to be on the lookout for a saber-toothed tiger, not a beautiful sunset. Our brains are hard-wired to perceive threat, real or imagined. This *fight-or-flight response* is what psychologists call "negativity bias." That's why we are keenly aware of and ruminate over insults and microaggressions. Yet rarely do we bask in praise or recognition from our boss or colleagues. The human habit of "fixing" left many of us to grow up not knowing our unique gifts. It's difficult to apply strengths to any situation, race talk included, if you don't believe you or others have any.

Constructive race talk is more likely when the people involved come to it ready to contribute their strengths rather than ideas for "fixing" others. Another benefit? When we can name and acknowledge the strengths in others, what positive psychologists call "strengths spotting," the receiver feels "seen" and valued. This is a foundation for building stronger bonds, a progression toward a coalition of "we."

To discover your strengths, we recommend the VIA Character Strengths Survey. It is available in 40 languages and free of charge from http://businessofrace.pro.viasurvey.org. This 96-question assessment takes less than 15 minutes to complete. It identifies your natural strengths, and through a common language, helps you to apply them to all facets of life, including the workplace. Individual strengths such as *bravery, forgiveness, love of learning, curiosity, perspective*, and *social intelligence* are only 6 among the 24 universal VIA Institute's strengths. These 24 strengths, once identified and explored individually, provide the needed self-awareness and confidence to enter into race talk and other difficult conversations. In a team or organizational setting, create a group strengths profile by asking employees if they are willing to share their top five strengths. This is a concrete way to explore an asset-based coalition of "we." Ruth Pearce, from the VIA Institute, explains a strengths-based dialogue "is about gaining the trust you need and finding out what you have in common, before you get to those tough topics like race. . . . It's a safe way to explore differences, potential isolation, and exclusion." In her project and client work, Pearce, who self-identifies as a White American originally from the United Kingdom, has experienced how the VIA Character Strengths "transformed people's appreciation of each other through recognition of the strengths that they brought to the table."

Race talk can be emotionally charged with an us-versus-them perspective. Or the belief, "If someone else gets, then I lose." Enter race talk with this deficit mindset, and it almost guarantees a downward spiral in dialogue. Instead, take the first step in developing an asset mindset: Identify individual strengths.[18]

Strengths in Action

Members of a project team responsible for implementing a new technology at a Fortune 500 financial services company were not collaborating productively, and it was impeding the project's success. The company appointed consultant Ruth Pearce (quoted above) as the new program manager to help. She implemented a variety of team-building approaches—including the VIA Character Strengths

Survey—to reestablish engagement, teamwork, and trust. Here's her own account of the experience:

> There were 45 people on the US team. Two-thirds of them were from India, on a two- to three-year contract, and the other third were predominantly White Americans. We also had another 65 people in three locations in India. Throughout our time as a team, the Indian caste system impacted the interactions between team members in ways many of us Americans did not understand.
>
> On the project was a design team made up of three designers and a design lead. All four were from India, but from different regions with different value systems. We started to notice that the design team wasn't designing anymore. Everything was coming from the design lead. When we did the VIA, we learned that his top strength is judgment. This was not a top strength for the other three designers. Their strengths were honesty, perspective, and forgiveness.
>
> The designers would say, "Look, we've got this great design. It's fantastic," and the design lead's immediate response was to balance that enthusiasm with judgment.
>
> He would say, "No, that won't work, and here's why." Through the VIA the designers recognized that they could be more effective as a team if they got the design lead's feedback earlier, when their ideas were more nascent. And the design lead recognized how he could better support the designers by acknowledging both the positives and the negatives of their ideas.
>
> I used the VIA because as people look at their character strengths, they begin to realize there's commonality. You may share character strengths like kindness or fairness; though each culture may express them differently. The common language of VIA also helps balance overuse

and underuse of character strengths to promote constructive group dynamics.

Finding common ground and gaining a greater understanding
and appreciation of each other's strengths will foster teamwork, cohesion, and a sense of belonging. In addition, we were curious if project
teams exposed to character strengths led to improved business outcomes. It had. The technology project team transformed the way it
conducted backups and testing by reducing task performance time
from a week to 24 hours. Can this improvement be attributed solely
to the VIA? Probably not. Pearce had implemented "a variety of team
building approaches." However, the VIA figured prominently in the
project team's discussions well beyond the introductory session on
strengths.

THE FINE POINTS

- Assimilating the conscious competence learning model will help you to possess more compassion for yourself and others as you pass through each stage of developing new skills and behaviors.

- Understand your antiracist style. Explore your racial identity. Identify your character strengths. Think of these assessments as the foundation for your inner work. They will shape the questions you will ponder and the additional resources you will explore on your race journey.

REFLECTION

- How do you self-identify?

- How would you define your racial identity in six words?

- Given where you are in your own race journey, which assessments described in this chapter are you most curious about? If you have already taken one or more of these assessments, what did you learn about yourself and others?

- What has been your experience with *color blindness* and *color awareness*?

- How might you introduce one or more of these tools to your colleagues, team, boss, board, students, people management/HR, or others?

CHAPTER 6

THINKING ABOUT HOW YOU THINK

Five Core Muscles

The world is intertwined today, much more than it was when I was coming out of school. Because of that, you really need to have a deep understanding of cultures around the world. I have learned to not just appreciate this but celebrate it. The thing that makes the world interesting is our differences, not our similarities.

TIM COOK
White American businessman and CEO of Apple[1]

Some team members may not believe that tackling race and racism is salient in the workplace, that it will "distract" from business operations. Other team members may feel the organization must speak to and openly address race and racism. Otherwise, the proverbial elephant in the room will continue to undermine business goals. Some people are flat-out fearful. Of conflict. Making mistakes. Of how race work will change the organization and their place in it, especially if they've benefited from the status quo. Still, others may be eager to talk about it in the wake of violent attacks against Black people from the diaspora, African Americans, and Asian Americans and Pacific Islanders in 2020. And especially because the attacks continue today and are escalating. Those hoping for a discussion don't want race talk to occur in a vacuum. Rather, they crave this exploration in a safe work environment, one that will enable constructive progress. Whatever your individual perspective on addressing race and racism in the workplace, the world's increasing multiculturalism demands that organizations begin their race work journeys or advance those already in the making.

Talking about race in the workplace has been taboo for so long, we must first prime ourselves before diving headfirst into this complex and emotionally charged work. If you haven't prepared the culture with the necessary tools and mindsets, then the more equitable norms you are attempting to cultivate in your business practices will not stick. Race talk is heavy lifting for sure. You must be fit. A body-builder physique is not required, but it does mean hitting the proverbial gym. Let's look at the five core muscles you must build and strengthen to prepare for, advance, and sustain this work: They are change readiness, cultural curiosity, empathy, growth mindset, and spectrum thinking.

READY, SET, GO: CHANGE READINESS

Readying an organization for any change requires effort, be it moving your data to the cloud, encouraging employees to adopt a new benefits plan, or motivating executives to delve into a new performance management system. So does race talk. After studying 30,000 smokers who successfully kicked the habit, University of Rhode Island's psychology professor Dr. James Prochaska developed a model for how people make positive, lasting changes in their lives. One of his most significant findings is that people wanting to make a change ("I will quit smoking tomorrow") often rush into action (throwing away all their cigarettes) before laying the necessary groundwork.

The consequence of this "rush into action" is the same when applied to race work. For example, a leader eager to demonstrate that he's advancing racial diversity, hires an external consultant to conduct unconscious bias training for the entire organization. The leader's intention is sincere, but without the necessary forethought and planning, the chances of sustainable change are small. We could describe this leader as having an *overfunctioning antiracist* style, which you learned about in the last chapter. Prochaska's model shows that before taking *action* and sustaining change (what he calls *maintenance*), you must pass through three stages: *precontemplation, contemplation*, and *preparation*.

The conscious competence learning model (CCLM) we introduced you to in the last chapter focuses on the stages we pass through as we *learn*. Prochaska's model focuses on *change readiness*. While there is overlap between the two models, together they provide a more robust view of how we create and sustain changes in our lives. Figure 6.1 presents the five stages that make up Prochaska's change readiness model.

Prochska's *precontemplation* stage is similar to the CCLM's *unconscious incompetence*: *you don't know what you don't know*. Someone at this stage could be the executive who consistently confuses the names of the only two Asian American women that work in his organization. Or the manager who believes racism is a relic of the past, now let's all get back to work. *Contemplation* recognizes that there is a problem. This mirrors the *conscious incompetence* stage in the CCLM. Finally, *preparation* focuses on readying ourselves for action. We do this through self-education. All change is a nonlinear process that unfolds over time. When we can recognize where we and others are in the change process, we are more likely to be successful.

Maintenance

Action

Preparation (Ready)

Contemplation (Getting Ready)

Precontemplation (Not Ready)

FIGURE 6.1 Prochaska's change readiness model.
(*Courtesy of Pro-Change Behavior Systems, Inc. 2021.*)

Race work readiness is not specific to hierarchical leaders and White people. If you are an individual contributor or frontline employee you must ready yourself to engage in dialogue with people different from yourself—be they coworkers or customers. If you are a person of color, you, too, must ready yourself to collaborate with others to propel the company in a more racially equitable direction.

Some people of color shared with us that they are tired of doing this work, notably, educating their White colleagues. We are also hearing from some of our White colleagues that they don't want to "bother" their Black colleagues. The Black director you first met in Chapter 1, Erneshia Pinder, has felt the fatigue herself. However, she has a different perspective, one she admits may be unpopular: "A lot of the Black fatigue that we're feeling is self-inflicted," she says, "because we've been carrying this burden for years. If you're tired, ask yourself what you've done up to this point to be part of the solution. The answer might be you haven't done a lot and that's why you're fatigued. While this isn't a Black person problem to solve, we do have to be actively involved in the solution. Part of that is speaking up. If we don't, nothing's going to change."[2]

Pinder has received some flak from friends and colleagues. They question why she still "works for the man," meaning corporate America. Her answer is this: "Not everyone can or wants to go out on their own and do their own thing. If we do, we'll never correct the misguided thinking that people have had all these years about our capability. I'm content to work from the inside out to make it better for the next person. Maybe they won't have to use their voice quite as much or as forcefully as I've had to."

> "While this isn't a Black person problem to solve, we do have to be actively involved in the solution. Part of that is speaking up. If we don't, nothing's going to change."

CULTURAL CURIOSITY

The second muscle that must be strengthened is cultural curiosity. The world is shrinking. On a given workday you may interact with coworkers, colleagues, and customers from many different races and ethnicities. Add the pervasive use of digital technology, and we may connect with exponentially more people from different countries around the world.

Growing up in a predominantly White suburb of Hartford, Connecticut, Heather Bodington, enterprise digital strategic planning manager at CVS Health, could count the number of her classmates of Asian descent on one hand, and three of them were her adopted brothers.[3] Also adopted at birth from Korea by White parents, she self-identified as White and had little experience with diverse cultures and racial identities. It wasn't until Bodington took a job at Aetna (now a subsidiary of CVS Health Corporation) that she became exposed to a wider community of Asians and came to self-identify as Asian.

In 2015 she "built the courage" to apply for a "once-in-a-lifetime opportunity" to work in South Korea on a discovery deal between Aetna and Samsung. That seven-month experience sparked her interest in learning more about her country of birth. She studied the language ("less proficient than a toddler," she jokes), watched Korean television miniseries (or "K-dramas," as they are called), and experimented with traditional Korean foods.

Today Bodington is a member of one of the company's colleague resource groups called the Asian Professional Network Association

(APNA). "Being an APNA member has helped me grow and embrace my heritage. I'm proud to be a Korean American," Bodington says. She's met colleagues who are Indian, Japanese, Chinese, Korean, Vietnamese, and Thai. "Even one group of Asians has so many different cultures within itself. Working in technology, I actually have a lot of Indian colleagues, and I realized that many states within India even have their own language and customs. So even among a single population like India, there are so many differences."

Bodington says the reward of building your cultural competence is learning how best to work with your colleagues who are different from you. Understanding cultural differences is a twenty-first-century competency for all employees. This includes learning about deep norms surrounding what is considered the appropriate time to express opinions, or being aware of dietary traditions that can influence what foods to order for your next lunchtime meeting.

"You can't treat everyone who is of a certain racial or ethnic background the same," says Bodington. "For example, there's a stereotype of Asians that they are heads down, work really hard, and are very modest about their accomplishments. You have to get to know them as an individual and at least broaden your perspective."

Our Mind's Eye

The stories we tell about people who are different from ourselves have to do with the texture of our exposure. Just because you work around, with, and for people of backgrounds different from your own doesn't guarantee cultural competence. Some of that exposure is transactional. For true engagement, seek depth of interaction. Earlier in this chapter, we mentioned an executive who consistently confuses the names of the only two Asian American women who work in his organization. You may have rushed to judgment ("Is he *that* underexposed?") or identified with him ("I sometimes can't tell people apart either"). Let's dig deeper.

Research finds that the dynamic of "You all look alike to me" is hardwired in each of us. In one experiment, 17 White participants studied both White and Black faces on a monitor while lying inside a functional MRI scanner, which identifies changes in brain activity. Psychologist Brent Hughes from University of California, Riverside, and his team of researchers looked at the White participants' high-level visual cortex to see whether it was more tuned in to differences in White faces than Black faces.[4] The visual cortex is the first stop for processing impulses from the eyes; the high-level visual cortex specializes in processing faces.

Their findings affirmed those of previous studies: participants showed a greater tendency to individuate—recognize differences in—own-race faces and less for other races. Some call this the "other-race effect." Easily differentiating between the faces of one's own race but not other races is profound. The implications can range from embarrassing (such as the executive who can't differentiate between two Asian American employees) to life-changing (selecting the wrong individual from a criminal suspect lineup).

Previous studies have found the other-race effect in populations besides Whites. But Hughes isn't comfortable extrapolating his findings to Black people—that they also "deindividuate" (do not recognize differences in) White faces via the high-level visual cortex. The reason: dominant-group versus nondominant-group perceptions. Members of nondominant groups have more exposure to members of the dominant group than the other way around. Hughes says, "It could be that exposure to individuals of different groups may help the visual system develop expertise that reduces this effect."

Hughes cautions that the study results should not be used as an excuse for "You all look the same to me." We can override our mind's eye, but only with intentionality to really "see" people who are different from ourselves, especially if we are members of a country's dominant group.

Grow Your Network

Prudential's CMO Susan Somersille Johnson's recommendation for developing cultural curiosity and appreciation of others is so obvious that it is often overlooked: "Widen your social network," says Johnson "because proximity is everything. If you don't have proximity to the issue, you don't care about it enough. When you have to make the hard decision, you're not going to do it unless you really feel the pain of the situation."[5]

She advises, "If you want to integrate your organization, integrate your life." The first time she suggested to an executive that he widen his network, he was taken aback. "'How do I do that, Susan?' He started describing his network, his church, his friends, his family. It was not integrated. It was not diverse."

Johnson explained that many executives have good intentions. They make time to have lunch or meet with racially diverse, high-potential employees, but it's only once a quarter. These interactions are transactional, rather than rapport-building over time. It's hard to appreciate differences and find commonality when your social circle is just like you. "It's a real challenge for corporate executives to get close enough to the issue to do what it takes because it is hard work," Johnson says. "Widening your social networks is a big ask, but we have to get there. They really want to change but often don't know how."

> If you want to integrate your organization, integrate your life.

Travel the World

Another way to build your cultural curiosity is by traveling. Between late 2008 and early 2009, Joanna Barsh, the McKinsey director whose quote began Chapter 5, took a group of McKinsey women from multiple offices around the globe to Uganda.[6] The purpose of the trip was to assess the economic impact of The Hunger Project—a humanitarian effort that combines the development of agency with microlending practices to help people eliminate poverty. Out of the 150 women who applied for the pro bono project, 5 were selected to accompany Barsh on the trip. It would also be a great opportunity for these women to apply their skills in a new way while learning about another culture. The group visited with the Ugandan women. Barsh recalls:

> We sang, we danced, and it was all very romantic. And then I met this one woman. We were sitting on the ground in front of her house, and she was showing me her two chickens, and then she said, "I'm just like you." And I was thinking, "I'm this hoity-toity senior White woman from McKinsey, in New York City." I said, "You're just like me? Really?"
>
> She said, "My hope is that someday soon I can come to your house and visit you."
>
> And I thought, "You are so right, lady. Who the hell am I to think that this is a one-way thing? If we are partners in this Hunger Project, then I have to accept that you feel equal to me. That was a huge lesson for me. I told her that it would be our greatest dream for her to travel to New York and visit me at my house and that I would welcome her.

Barsh related her Ugandan epiphany to how she perceives her role in the workplace. She shared with us that influencers throughout the organization, and particularly those with positional hierarchy, will want to check their beliefs. For example, thinking that you have "made it" doesn't mean you are inherently better than others and that they are in some ways deficient.

Ask Questions

Build your cultural curiosity by showing genuine interest in your colleagues and asking thoughtful questions.

Rajesh Ramachandran, executive director at CVS Health who now leads the company's integration with Aetna, has an impressive LinkedIn profile. He began his career at the National Institute of Information Technology (NIIT) in India. He worked for the Internal

Revenue Systems in Singapore, then moved to the United States and worked as a contractor for UPS, IBM, and then Aetna before becoming a full-time employee at what is now CVS Health. We were curious how Rajesh came to live and work in the United States. So we asked. Here's what he said:

> I was one of those Indian kids who thought I'd grow up and play the famous sport cricket for the Indian team. But my dad gave me a reality check. "No," he said, "that's not going to put food on the table. You need to focus on your studies." I was very interested in biology and chemistry at the time so I majored in chemistry. One day I was driving with my uncle on a bike and saw this huge poster about computer science and computers.[7]

It was 1996 or 1997 when Rajesh saw that billboard. Computers were in the early stages. After graduation he was trained by Asia's only IBM-recognized training facility in Trivandrum, Kerala. Not only was his decision to take the job at NIIT an opportunity to work in this new field of computers, but at the time, computers had to be housed in an air-conditioned environment. Living in a tropical climate, Rajesh figured, "Why not? I'll get to work in air conditioning." There he gained programming and mainframe experience, which led him to work in Singapore and later the United States with one of the big consulting firms. He joined Aetna as a contractor in 2004.

"I really loved the people I worked with at Aetna," Rajesh says. "They never saw me as a vendor. I was one among the community. I think at Aetna I was shielded. People like Lisa, Kathy, Jim, Louie, and Jay saw my performance; they didn't judge where I was from. I felt like they were genuinely interested in me and gave me good opportunities to work on complex projects. One day my boss took me aside and said, "Rajesh, you're shaking like an elephant."

Rajesh demonstrated by shaking his head from side to side. He explained to his boss that in his culture you showed agreement by nodding your head from side to side, not up and down.

"We would share pictures of our families, talk about what marriages look like, what life is like," Rajesh said. "The funny thing is when you sit down and talk about your differences, you find out that some of your core principles are the same. We all want to be recognized by our parents; we all want to have good opportunities."

> Show interest, ask questions and celebrate differences.

We were also curious about Rajesh's cultural viewpoint on skin color. "It plays a big part in Indian culture, and it starts out in school with kids saying, 'I'm fair skin, and you're not fair skin,'" says Rajesh. "In India, where marriages are mostly arranged, some ads read 'looking for a fair skin girl,' and then you look at the guy and you can barely make him out because he is so dark. Whenever there is a racial inequity conversation here [the United States], it brings back some of those old memories of India and our caste system. We were exposed to it, and it was not right."

After our interview with Rajesh, we learned something else about his cultural heritage. We shared by email that we were going to include his story in this book. We explained that we would introduce him to readers by his full name and subsequently refer to him by last name only. He asked if we would use his first name, Rajesh, instead. He explained that in the southern part of India, where he is originally from, people usually take on their father's name as their last name. To distinguish himself from his father, he preferred we use his first name. We both found it satisfying that the topic we were writing about, cultural curiosity, led to another cultural discovery. Cultural competence is no longer optional. It is a twenty-first-century success mandate in the workplace and beyond. Show interest, ask questions, and celebrate differences.

WALK IN THEIR SHOES: EMAPTHY

This next muscle to develop for effective race talk and race work is empathy, or what we call walking in someone else's shoes.

All people suffer. Put racism aside for the moment. Today it is likely one of your coworkers is suffering. For example, the suffering may arise from sources outside of work, such as concern for a sick child or elderly parent. A spouse, partner, or friend may have just lost her job. Perhaps you or one of your colleagues are suffering from work itself. Do you feel pressure to deliver more with fewer resources? Overwhelmed by aggressive deadlines? Frustrated by being passed over again for a promotion, or hurt by team members or a supervisor who ignores your contributions? Or perhaps you or someone you know is struggling with the challenges of working from home. At work suffering can present as missed deadlines, errors, mood swings, and sick days. Sometimes these behavioral changes trigger judgment on the part of coworkers, rather than compassion and empathy. University of Michigan Ross School of Business researchers and professors Drs. Monica Worline and Jane Dutton in their book, *Awakening Compassion at Work*, write, "Empathy is feeling what another feels; imagining oneself in another person's circumstances; feeling concern for another person's suffering."[8] There is also a leadership component to empathy. The Center for Creative Leadership has found that empathetic bosses earn the trust of their employees, who are, in turn, more productive.

Effective relationships, both inside and outside of work, require empathy. Productive race talk requires empathy, too. We most often recognize empathy when it is absent, such as the doctor whose lack of bedside manner detracts from how her patient perceives her medical care. The question becomes, can you learn to be more empathetic? The good news is you can. Research by Helen Riess, MD and associate professor of psychiatry at Harvard Medical School, shows that empathy is both an automatic feeling and also a conscious choice. Humans have the capacity to turn on and turn off feelings of concern for others. Since we can choose empathy, we can also grow it to connect

> Nourishing empathy lets us help everyone we interact with, whether for a moment or a lifetime, thereby also nourishing ourselves.

with people more deeply. "Nourishing empathy lets us help everyone we interact with, whether for a moment or a lifetime, thereby also nourishing ourselves," writes Dr. Riess.

> We cannot expect to understand and grow from each other's lived experiences if we cannot listen and communicate with empathy.

Harvard Medical students, trainees, and physicians nationally and internationally are now learning how to grow their empathy in Riess's Empathy and Relational Science Program. You can, too. When you engage other people, pay attention to the components of Riess's seven-step model E.M.P.A.T.H.Y.* as you do: eye contact ("E"), muscles of facial expressions ("M"), posture ("P"), affect—the scientific term for emotion—("A"), tone of voice ("T"), hearing the whole person ("H"), and your response ("Y").[9]

The science of compassion shows us that if we are physically present but psychologically absent, we telegraph our lack of interest through our posture, body language, lack of eye contact, and failure to ask questions. We cannot expect to understand and grow from each other's lived experiences if we cannot listen and communicate with empathy.

GROWTH MINDSET

The fourth muscle that you will want to flex in your race work is *Growth Mindset*. Stanford University psychologist Dr. Carol Dweck has spent 30-plus years researching how people face challenges.[10] In over a hundred studies that have been replicated in both sports and business, Dweck found that how we perceive challenges, mistakes, setbacks, and risks—all things that likely happen every day in our jobs and especially when engaging in race work—determines if we will persist or give up.

People with a fixed mindset believe their abilities are unchangeable traits—one is born with a certain amount of skill, intelligence, and creative ability that can't be improved upon. For instance, someone with a fixed mindset might say, "I'm a natural-born soccer player." Or "I'm just no good at soccer," believing that one's athletic sales can't be developed. In the workplace a fixed mindset might show up as, "I'm a natural-born salesperson" or "I'm just not good at spreadsheets." Those with fixed mindsets may avoid challenges, give up easily, when faced with an obstacle or difficulty, and ignore constructive feedback.

People who possess a growth mindset believe that their successes and failures are not based upon their abilities—how smart they are, the skills they possess—but are attributable to how much effort they put in. Along the way, they expect to make mistakes and understand that they are part of the learning process. Think of your brain as a muscle: the more effort your brain exerts, the more it can grow and undertake new learning. As Dr. Carol Dweck says, "a growth mindset is not a declaration, it's a journey," one that involves small, progressive shifts in thinking, rather than huge leaps. Human beings rarely operate in an either/or world. As go humans, so goes mindsets. Depending on the circumstance, you likely operate somewhere in between Fixed and Growth.

The route along this journey has been skillfully rendered in an easy-to-understand chart by James Anderson, an Australian-based educator who is a Certified Growth Mindset Trainer.[11] He calls the chart, The Mindset Continuum, originally published in the book, *The Agile Learner: Where Growth Mindset, Habits of Mind and Practice Unite.*[12] Before you continue reading, take a moment to access Anderson's Mindset Continuum. We've included the link to the PDF in the Additional Resources, organized by chapters. It will be a helpful reference as you read the next section that describes it in more detail. "One of the biggest myths about Mindsets is that there are only two: the Fixed Mindset and the Growth Mindset," writes Anderson. "This confusion has led to many misapplications of psychologist Carol Dweck's work. While Dweck herself typically talks about Mindsets as being either Fixed or Growth, this juxtaposition is simply to help contrast the difference between the two extremes. Throughout her research, she recognizes that we fall along a continuum." Dweck notes that none of us has a Growth Mindset in everything all the time. You could have a predominant Growth Mindset in some areas, and in others, express more Fixed Mindset traits.[13] Anderson's Mindset Continuum shows this well. With Fixed Mindset at one extreme, and what he calls "High Growth" Mindset at the other, the continuum also depicts in between, the Mindsets of Low Growth, Mixed, and Growth. Anderson's Mindset Continuum helps us understand the nuances of Dweck's work. This includes the beliefs and disciplined thinking involved to journey along the continuum in each of eight different domains: (1) worldview; (2) challenges; (3) encountering difficulty and obstacles; (4) effort; (5) feedback and criticism; (6) success of others; (7) making mistakes; and (8) offered help and support.[14]

As we better understand how our abilities change (from "born this way" to invested effort), we travel along the continuum. We become increasingly aware of our capacity for growth. As a result, our responses to these eight domains such as challenges, feedback and criticism, and making mistakes slowly shift. Let's explore an example using Anderson's Mindset Continuum language. (Now is a great time to have the chart handy.) Let's say you hold a Mixed Mindset around the domain of Effort. Such a mindset believes that "effort is necessary but not usually enjoyable." And though this Mixed Mindset recognizes when "effort is being ineffective" it is "likely to prefer to do it easily."[15] How does a Low Growth Mindset respond to the domain of Effort? It recognizes that effort is sometimes required, but believes that sustained effort is undesirable. This mindset does not understand that "not all types of effort produce growth." A High Growth Mindset understands the Effort domain as "a path to mastery, and actively works on developing strategies to produce more effective effort."

One of the themes in this book is that race work is a journey. And part of that journey is making mistakes and learning from them. Our mindset at a given point along the Fixed to High Growth continuum will determine how we respond to the stumbles we will make on this journey. Let's reflect on one more example in the domain of Making Mistakes, using the language of Anderson's Mindset Continuum. In this domain, a High Growth Mindset "deliberately stretches themselves so errors have high learning potential to facilitate further growth." A Growth Mindset "recognizes mistakes made are signposts for learning opportunities." How does a Mixed Mindset respond to making mistakes? This mindset "expects to make mistakes and understands they can be corrected." A Low Growth Mindset "makes excuses for mistakes and looks for quick fixes." This mindset may even blame others for their mistakes. And a Fixed Mindset "actively hides or ignores mistakes."

Reflect on Dr. Dweck's Growth Mindset model, and based on her research, James Anderson's Mindset Continuum. Take a break from these pages and contemplate this practical and skillfully documented framework. See where you sit on the Mindset Continuum in the eight different domains. When you encounter difficulties and obstacles, do you give up immediately? Do you persist only when you see progress? Or do you persist for long periods of time, even in the face of setbacks? Do you learn from feedback when you receive it? Do you ask for feedback proactively? When other people succeed, do you feel threatened? Or do you celebrate the masters and experts and ask, "How did you do that? I want to learn." Remember, as Dr. Dweck notes, we are a *mixture* of Fixed and Growth mindsets. With five mindsets on the continuum explored in relation to the eight domains listed above, we suspect you will find, upon reflection, that your mindset shifts in different circumstances. None of us has the same mindset in all domains all the time. The point of this tool, and this chapter overall, is to prepare ourselves to be more mindful about how we think, and become *disciplined* thinkers when collaborating with our peers in race work.

Developing a Growth Mindset requires deliberate practice and active nurturing over time in small, targeted steps. Here are two approaches we use in our coaching practices to help business leaders make gradual progress along the Mindset Continuum. One is to recognize your inner critic and then dispute it with evidence to the contrary. The other is to play. Yes, play.

Recognize Your Inner Critic and Dispute Negative Thinking with Evidence

Say you're learning something new such as understanding racial differences. Your inner critic may pop up and say, "Talking about race is a can of worms. You'll never grasp this." First, recognize that this is your inner critic seeking to disempower you by keeping you comfortable and resistant to change. The next step is to challenge that voice. You might say to yourself, "Wait a minute. I learned how to use our new performance management system. I can learn how to have productive discussions around race, too." Or "I was able to have a tough conversation with my boss about my role, and it strengthened our relationship. Or, "Race talk feels scary. I'll probably make mistakes, but that's how I'm going to learn and build relationships."

Play: Create–Dismantle–Re-create

Another way to develop a Growth Mindset is to play with an approach to experimenting, called "Create–Dismantle–Re-create." Gina first experienced this technique in a one-on-one coaching session 20 years ago. The coach was Brianna Rush, a painter who conducted art workshops in corporate settings in Connecticut and who now lives and paints full-time in Arizona.[16]

First, gather some random art materials. If you don't have any, borrow some from your kids. If you don't have any kids, collect items from around the house or office such as napkins, loose change, rubber bands, paper clips, Post-it Notes, markers, duct tape, catalogs, wrapping paper, or just about anything you were getting ready to toss into a junk drawer; you get the picture. Spend 30 minutes creating a collage (two dimensional) or assemblage (think sculpture). Afterward, observe your creation with a five-minute "freewrite." Set a timer for five minutes and write about whatever pops into your mind. Write the old-fashioned way, using paper and pen only. No digital devices to distract you or ensnare you into overthinking. What's next is key to the "free" in freewrite: keep your hand moving; no stopping, no crossing out. If you get stuck on a word, leave a space and keep going.

Next, dismantle or destroy what you've just created.

Yup, you read that correctly. You kind of choked, didn't you? Why would you take apart or destroy something you've just created? Oh, so many reasons. For now, take apart your collage or sculpture.

You won't need the same 30 minutes it took to create it. Don't let that stop you from getting imaginative. Tear it. Stomp it. Dunk it in . . . whatever. Shred it with scissors. Toss it into the microwave (if no metal is involved in the construction). See what happens.

Freewrite again for five minutes on what is now before you. And if you feel something deep that asks for expression, then allow psychic space for it to surface. Maybe silence. Tears. Anger. Regret. Fear. Uncontrollable laughter. Maybe more than five minutes of writing to excavate an old memory.

Next, take 45 minutes to re-create something new from what you've just taken apart. We have no idea what that will be, and at the moment you begin, neither will you. That's why this part of the practice is the longest. You'll need time to be with what's in front of you, to let your brain wander. This is key to breakthrough thinking. And thanks to MRI technology, neuroscientists have cracked that code.

"The secret to breakthrough thinking lies in our ability to switch between [two modes], the focused and the meandering," write researchers and leadership experts Olivia Fox Cabane and Judah Pollack in *The Net and the Butterfly: The Art and Practice of Breakthrough Thinking*.[17] The focused mode is the one you use to get things done. The one we are all too familiar with in the business world. "Executive network" (EN) is what Cabane and Pollack call the part of your brain's wiring that is responsible for this operating mode. They describe the EN as being "goal-oriented and deadline-focused. It's a champion at making lists, following timelines, and coming in under budget."

Focus is only half the story when developing strategy, managing projects, and experiencing breakthroughs. The other half of that story requires you to periodically step away from the EN. Research shows by doing that, you drastically improve the quality of your ideas, your work, and your productivity. This mind wandering state is what Cabane and Pollack call the "default network" (DN). Unlike the inner critic we described a few pages ago, "think of the DN as a council of breakthrough geniuses inside your brain. The geniuses talk and exchange ideas, half-baked theories, and wild speculations. The DN is the source of all our creativity, all our invention. . . . If the EN gives us the ability to accomplish a task, the DN gives us the ability to look through the complexity of the world to see the patterns underneath." This is why we do not rush the re-create segment of create–dismantle–re-create. The DN, however, is not a resting state. Under the brain's conscious radar, it activates old memories, toggles back and forth between the past, present, and future, and recombines different ideas. Using this new and previously inaccessible data, you develop enhanced awareness and can imagine creative solutions leading to better decision-making. Tapping the DN also helps you tune into other people's creative genius.

What do we especially love about create–dismantle–re-create? It is a practice of releasing perfectionism. It helps you view "failure," so deeply unsettling for many, for what it truly is: iterative learning. This is a key feature of a growth mindset. Throughout the book we will revisit create–dismantle–re-create, and focus on it through the lens of prototyping in Part V: New Policies, New Practices. For now, make something. Break it apart. Reassemble it in a new way. Your re-creation will reveal your next steps much faster than a stymieing plod toward the "perfect" plan.

Play at Work

Let's see how one midsize private company, in the urban development luxury apartment industry, applies the create–dismantle–re-create model to race work.

"I'm a huge fan of breaking things and putting them back together," says Nina Davis, VP of people and culture at City Club Apartments.[18] "Let's look at what our competition is doing. Let's look at what another industry is doing. How do we create fair and consistent practices that really get us the diversity that we're looking for?"

"It doesn't always take reinventing the wheel or doing something extraordinary that's going to cost a ton of money," says Davis. "You can begin by just looking at the current things that we have that are variables and not fixed and then ask, 'How can we change these variables to show more of a spectrum?' And then for the things that are fixed, ask, 'Are they really fixed, or can we break them and restructure them?'"

Davis shared how City Club Apartments approached grand openings from a diversity and inclusion perspective when a new property was near ready to debut on the market. Prior to her joining the company, there was little thought of who would be on the preopening team.

"Anybody that was in the area or was willing to travel would go, and often it would be one demographic with no thought to diversity and inclusion," says Davis, who self-identifies as Black. "Now we've implemented an opening task force. We're identifying individuals before we're even done breaking ground on construction. We're being very mindful of who will represent a particular discipline or knowledge and being very inclusive to be sure our property task force is diverse."

Change readiness, cultural curiosity, empathy, and growth mindset—all skills that will facilitate productive race talk and race work. And there's one more muscle you'll want to develop, and it has to do with *thinking about how you think*.

SPECTRUM THINKING

Workplaces do not operate in a dynamic of polarized extremes: Black or White, male or female, introvert or extrovert. Humans, like the rest of nature, exist on a spectrum, not in dichotomy. We made this point earlier when we examined fixed and growth mindsets along a continuum, not as immovable extremes. We understand, appreciate, live, think, work, and communicate along a spectrum. What we call "spectrum thinking" is the ability to remain open to wide-ranging, new ideas to make sound business decisions.

Dichotomous thinking creates a polarizing dynamic where "either/or" extremes exist with no possibilities along the spectrum in between. "My way or the highway" thinking shuts down discourse. It's impossible to appreciate differences, practice cultural curiosity, be empathetic, and find common ground when we approach race work from this place. This yes-no, winners and losers approach is what dominates when people bring what they believe to be *the* answer to an issue solely based on their perception of reality. Spectrum thinking invites dialogue through exploring common ground. The ability to think along a spectrum of wide-ranging ideas is a skill that can be cultivated. Moreover, it is necessary for the complexity of race work. Six Thinking Hats is a tool your organization can use to practice and become more disciplined in this skill.

The Six Thinking Hats® model was first published in 1985 by Edward de Bono,[19] physician, psychologist, author, inventor, and philosopher. Six Thinking Hats is a muscular technique that facilitates decision-making by encouraging exploration of different points of view in parallel, rather than in opposition.[20] It helps us to move beyond our habitual thinking styles to widen our perspective, and also inhabit that of other people. During an argument, people withhold information if it does not support their point of view. Rather than walking into a room with the intent of reinforcing what we already believe and needing to be "right," the Six Thinking Hats tool helps us to operationalize how we think regardless of our preferred styles. This allows our discussions, exploration, and the actions that flow from them to be more effective: specifically, to design new possibilities, not argue between two existing possibilities.

How does it work? James P. "Pat" Carlisle, president of the de Bono Group, describes the Six Thinking Hats this way. "Typically, when we think, we try to juggle too much at once," says Carlisle. "We may be looking at the information, judging it, and forming new ideas all at the same time. The Six Thinking Hats allows us to unbundle and separate out the different aspects of thinking, one mode of thinking at a time." If you don't like an idea, you are not going to spend much time thinking about its benefits. If you do uncover good points, you would have to accept that you "lost" an argument. Which brings us to our old ways of thinking: dichotomous arguments focused on winning or losing. This lacks creative energy. Six Hats opens up new worlds.

"It's a tool set," says Carlisle. "When you play golf, you have in your bag several different clubs or tools for playing the game. For making long shots, you use a driver tool. The putter tool is for hitting the ball into the hole on the green. Similarly, each of the six hats is a tool with a specific function. Just as you select a golf club, so you would select a thinking hat." To be clear, the six hats are not descriptions or categories of thinkers. Every thinker should be able to use each hat just as every golfer should be able to use each club. It is true that some people may be more adept at using one hat than another. And some people may also prefer to use one hat rather than another. However, the hats do not represent types of thinkers. Rather, they serve as a direction and focus for thinking. Understanding this distinction is key to using Six Hats effectively.

Let's look at each hat, which represents a particular *mode of thinking*:

White hat—the factual hat. White hat is informative. It is all about data. What you have, what you need, and, if you don't have what you need, where to get it.

Red hat—the hat for the heart. Red hat honors intuition and feelings. Invested in instinct, red hat invites feelings without justification.

Yellow hat—the value hat. Yellow hat is always on the lookout for benefits and values. Yellow hat holds the positive view in any situation.

Black hat—the judge's hat. This hat invites us to explore with caution. Black hat offers logical reasons for concern. One of the most powerful hats, it encourages us to identify, consider, and weigh risks.

Blue hat—the conductor's hat. This is the control hat, thinking about and managing the thinking process. This hat sets the agenda, focuses, and sequences it.

Blue hat ensures that guidelines are observed. It asks for summaries, conclusions, decisions, and action plans.

Green hat—the creative hat. Green hat is a fount of new ideas. It poses alternatives, possibilities, and new concepts.

You are probably aware of how you and others tend to inhabit the roles on the teams or groups you belong to. Maybe you are the one who always keeps an eye out for risk and challenges using a black hat perspective; or maybe you are the red hat passionista, excited about the possibilities, and who plunges forward indifferent to potential blind spots. Maybe it is you, always crunching numbers in her head underneath her white hat; or perhaps you are the blue hat wearer, holding the big picture, and keeping the group's focus on track. All these different roles are valuable. If, however, the same person always inhabits those roles, then the group's ideas and operational dynamics follow a predictable pattern.

The Six Thinking Hats are designed to help people to step out of their usual role, to deliberately adopt modes of thinking that broaden their perspective. By extension, this helps them remain open to exploring previously unimagined possibilities in service of the idea at hand. Thinking in parallel, not in opposition, allows us to investigate every idea to its fullest, without one mode of thinking dominating the proceedings.

Imagine a company that only looked at the financials (white hat) and not the emotional payoff of a new customer service initiative (red hat). Conversely, imagine one that cared solely for the feelings of stakeholders with little regard to profit. How about strategy discussions that are all blue hat, hovering at 50,000 feet with no white hat—facts and figures—perspective? How many meetings have you attended where the talk is filled with green hat possibilities and no one asks, "How do we actually do this? Where do we start, and who is doing what?" In those instances no one is wearing the blue hat. Or meetings where a green hat–dominated discussion energizes the room with fresh ideas but with no input from the black hat to consider potential obstacles? We've all been there. And we all know that without the diversity of multiple perspectives, homogenous strategies often lack substance, stakeholder engagement, and, by extension, staying power.

Let's consider a cross-functional team with a mix of managers and sole contributors. In these instances the managers, those with positional power, and who may have low self-awareness, might dominate the proceedings with their thinking focused in a direction everyone in the group has come to expect. Let's say a manager tends to focus his thinking in a yellow hat direction. Everything is unicorns and rainbows with this employee who also has hierarchical power. He pleasantly dismisses thinking in the direction of the white hat (facts and figures) or black hat (consideration of potential challenges). In this scenario, guess who misses out? *Hint:* not employees. Rather, it's the project at hand and the company attempting to bring it to life but can't due to the lack of multiple perspectives. This manager is not incapable of switching hats. He might prefer not to, but he can. That's the beauty of the tool.

Six Hats is also a common language that helps us to accomplish this ourselves and invite others to join us. For example, a thinker is asked to speak to yellow hat benefits, regardless of whether or not the person likes the idea. Euphoric supporters are, in turn, asked to outline black hat cautions for their ideas. If you say to someone, "Don't be so negative," you are judging and "calling out." But if you ask, "What is your yellow hat thinking?," you are calling people in. Six Thinking Hats helps us all to learn, practice, and cultivate the skill of switching the direction and focus of our thinking regardless of our personal preferences.

Using the designated hat. It is essential when engaging Six Thinking Hats for everyone who is participating to use the same hat at the same time. When different modes of thinking conflict, the tool's common language and boundaries are designed to invite team members who might otherwise be reluctant to contribute with a particular mode of thinking, to do so. And without judgment or attack. For example: Sanjay doesn't want to wear the green hat (contribute while the group is focused on that particular mode of thinking) when it's time in the discussion to do so. Three options are available for folks who don't want to play by the rules—rules that require each of us to wear the same hat at the same time, so that we are thinking in parallel not in opposition. Recall from Chapter 1, the discussion of coalition building. Thinking in parallel (same hat at the same time) helps us to become "we" and not separate "I's."

> **Option 1.** If Sanjay has nothing to say under the green hat, then that means Sanjay has nothing to say.

> **Option 2.** Sanjay may leave the group discussion (of his own volition, he is not asked to do so by others).

> **Option 3.** The facilitator invites Sanjay to stay and observe the process. We don't call Sanjay out; we call him in so he can see how the discipline of changing our direction and focus in thinking works. This is one way to encourage fresh vantage points for those not accustomed to inhabiting perspectives outside their comfort zone.

Encouraging all to participate. Sometimes there is a dynamic whereby a person who considers himself or herself to be the wearer of a particular hat will keep quiet when the other hats are in use. Then he or she will only take part in the meeting during the assigned hat period they prefer. One way to shift this energy of speaking only to particular hats: Rather than wait for volunteers, ask individuals specifically for their thinking under each hat in use.

Facilitation. With the exception of the blue hat, interruptions are not permitted when each hat is in use. The rules do not allow for a meeting participant to say, "Putting on my black hat . . ." Were it permitted, then the hats would simply become a description of what people were going to say anyway, and the whole point of the hats discipline would disappear. The cautious people, for example, would constantly be putting on their black hats and interrupting with risks. Without such a deliberate thinking model as this one, emotionally charged race talk and race work are likely to devolve into arguments, silence, and standoffs. Which is one of the reasons so many of us are fearful of this work at work. And the reason we, the authors, share this powerful tool: it provides clear boundaries for constructive, collaborative discussion. And goes a long way toward establishing psychological safety (don't worry; you'll learn how to build this, too, in the next chapter).

Explore Race Work with Six Thinking Hats

The thinking used in a meeting for race work can be organized with a sequence of hats. Remember that everyone uses the same hat at the same time. Ask everyone to contribute under each hat. If someone wants to use another hat, ask the person to wait until the designated time for that hat.

Note that the blue hat is an opportunity to set the focus for the discussion, without getting into the discussion yet. If there are multiple agendas, use the blue hat to recognize and then schedule when they will be discussed. The blue hat also ensures that everyone is playing by the rules—wearing the same hat at the same time, for a specific period of time, as some people will require more discipline to stay active while thinking under certain hats. It also ensures that adversarial discussion does not take over.

The red hat is used for sharing a feeling or hunch without justification. It is not for determining truth but for understanding what is influencing someone's thinking. The red hat is important to race work because it is what's underneath the feelings that will surface in discussion sequences for black hat (risks and concerns) and for yellow hat (benefits and values). Also, feelings can change in response to new or additional facts (white hat). "Good idea!" is not yellow hat. It's red hat: emotion with no justification. Yellow hat needs a plus point: "It's a good idea because . . ." Red hat is also a great hat for a process check. Or a quick survey of the room to get a feel for an idea. That gut feel can later contribute to the white hat discussion for the data needed or a green hat discussion to generate ideas. Time. Focus. Direction. These are the core disciplines of Six Thinking Hats.

> Better decision making depends on how people discover, discuss and develop ideas together. It is possible to have diverse representation and still suffer from poor decision making due to a culture of exclusive thinking. Six Hats is a mechanism that respects and values diversity of ideas and makes for better decision making as those ideas are more fully explored.
>
> —*James P. "Pat" Carlisle, president, the de Bono Group*

When we use the discipline of Six Thinking Hats, we:

- Separate ego from performance. Through a common language, we request a switch in thinking without inciting combat or having to win.

- Explore topics in parallel—all parties use the same mode of thinking at the same time to explore the pros and cons in a constructive way, express fact and opinion separately, and apply judgment to ideas after the ideas have been developed and assessed for benefits.

- Encourage everyone to use all six thinking modes and prevent the dominance of a few preferred modes.

- Recognize that we are all capable of using each mode of thinking, regardless of our habitual preferences.

And this focused, disciplined direction in thinking opens up new possibilities for advancing your organization's race work.[21]

THE FINE POINTS

For so long, race was an undiscussable in the workplace. Today many companies recognize that they must address race if they want to remain competitive. However, without preparation, diving into race work can backfire, potentially causing more damage than good. You must begin by building five core muscles:

- Change readiness
- Cultural curiosity
- Empathy
- Growth mindset
- Spectrum thinking

REFLECTION

- Specific to race work, where are you on the change readiness continuum?

- How might you use the create–dismantle–re-create exercise to give yourself permission to play and experiment with diversity, equity, and inclusion?

- What's one small step you can take to become more curious about people who are different from you?

- Who among your friends and/or colleagues are suffering from racial injustices you see in the media or racial inequities in the workplace? How might you reach out to them like you would if they were experiencing a loss, illness, or any other challenging situation?

- In which situations might you first practice using Six Thinking Hats before applying the discipline to race talk?

- Which core muscle do you most want to build? What's one small actionable step you can take to begin?

PART IV

CULTURE AND LEADERSHIP

Conventional notions about leadership tend to place high value on decisiveness, confidence, and extroversion. However, in the VUCA (volatile, uncertain, complex, and ambiguous) environment we are living and working in today, we need to expand our skill sets beyond those longstanding norms. Today leaders must cultivate a growth mindset, be as intelligent emotionally as they are technically, and all the while demonstrate transparency. This includes humility—acknowledging mistakes and demonstratively growing from them.

To help companies come to terms with inherent biases embedded within their organizations, they must shift how they lead. That includes appreciating and enabling leadership beyond the hierarchy. We (the coauthors) never held a position at the vice president level or higher in those years we were employed by large corporations and midsize companies. That was intentional. We did not wield influence from positional power. Rather, as individual contributors and midlevel managers we were able to navigate organizational dynamics and drive change through engagement, curiosity, and empathy.

Companies must also recognize that sustainable improvements in racial diversity, equity, and inclusion are core to their business operations. And, treat it as they would any other strategic priority. In the next two chapters, we expose you to leaders with this mindset. They are comfortable with uncomfortable truths; willing to fail publicly; have the courage to name the proverbial elephant in the virtual meeting room. Also, they know when to hold the reins and when to pass the reins. And they recognize resistance simply as part of the process. We also look at the changing expectations for boards and of customers, the import of psychological safety, and the science of small wins. And we introduce you to SOAR (strengths, opportunities, aspirations, and results). This is a tool for collaboratively engaging people at any level of your organization in the development of your company's racial diversity strategy.

CHAPTER 7

UNCOMFORTABLE TRUTHS AND FEARLESS LEADERS

Lessons from *The Matrix*,
Singapore, and Texas

But the real world doesn't go away. Racism exists. People are getting hurt. And just because it's not happening to you, doesn't mean it's not happening.

TREVOR NOAH
Black South African actor, writer,
international stand-up comedian,
comedy show host, and author of
Born a Crime: Stories from a South African Childhood[1]

n the science fiction action film *The Matrix*, the main character Neo is offered the choice between a red pill and a blue pill by rebel leader Morpheus. The red pill represents an uncertain future—it would free Neo from the enslaving control of the machine-generated dream world and allow him to escape into the real world, though living the "truth of reality" is harsher. The blue pill represents a beautiful prison—living in confined comfort, no want or fear, within the simulated reality of the Matrix. "You take the blue pill . . . the story ends, you wake up in your bed and believe whatever you want to believe," says Morpheus. "You take the red pill . . . you stay in Wonderland, and I show you how deep the rabbit hole goes." Neo chooses the red pill and joins the rebellion.

"Red pill" leaders take risks, listen to employees rather than think they must have all the answers, and share what they learn from their own personal journey. This open embrace of the unfamiliar demonstrates courage, humility, and vulnerability—key attributes of a fearless workplace, which is a requirement for constructive race work. A fearless workplace has many Neos, people who are unafraid to take the red pill—the one that reveals uncomfortable truths.

In the late summer/early fall of 2020, we (the coauthors) took the red pill and started writing this book. We didn't want to confine our writing about race solely to our Black and White lived experiences, so we surveyed a cross-section of more than 50 racially diverse professionals.[2] We asked them to share their most burning questions related to race and racism in the workplace and what they struggled with the most. We learned some "uncomfortable truths." For example, Black, Brown, and other people of color have asked for decades, if not centuries, "What about me? Why can't I get ahead in this world?" Today, some White people are asking the same question, creating a new kind of tension in the workplace. A White woman with nearly 10 years of working experience wrote, "Sometimes I feel like being a White, middle-class woman makes me less competitive for a workplace promotion or getting hired for a new job."

Another survey participant, a Black female leader with nearly 20 years of business experience, was both "surprised and saddened" by some of the "noise" she heard and read on the company's intranet: "There's been a transfer of emotion in some respects. The fear that I, as a Black woman, have felt about my place in society has started to shift to some of our White colleagues. There's a fear of 'what about me?' From where I sit, I question that thinking. When I look at our leadership team, it's predominantly White. If I look at most leadership across the country, even from a government perspective, it's mostly White. So for me, I struggle with people questioning if this [focusing on racial equity]is the right thing to do."

A professional with more than 30 years of business experience shared: "As a White man, I struggle with the notion that to defeat racism or discrimination against a minority many advocate discriminating against the majority. This just doesn't seem right—to fight an evil with that same evil."

One of the business leaders we interviewed, law professor and DEI consultant Kathy Taylor who self-identifies as Black, also shared an uncomfortable truth: "There's this notion that if we are committed to equity and inclusion then that means 'our whole board will be Black and Hispanic, and White people will be missing from the equation.' That's not always articulated because it's not the politically correct thing to say."[3]

Encouraging people to discuss an undiscussable, such as race and racism, requires risk taking. It requires being a red pill leader. A prime example of a red pill leader is chairman emeritus of Starbucks, Howard Schultz. When Schultz was CEO, he thrust himself into the spotlight of the emotionally charged issue of racism when he launched Starbucks's Race Together campaign in 2015.[4] The media, his peers, and scholars criticized him

> You cannot expect 400 years of racially unbalanced norms to be overturned in one financial quarter.

for it and declared the initiative a "failure" and "superficial gesture."[5] No points for trying. No acknowledgment for moving the needle.

A few weeks later during a panel discussion at Spelman College, a historically Black college for women in Atlanta, Schultz tells the audience that he's not backing down. "I feel we've been called to do this," Schultz said on stage. "Along the way, there are going to be some mistakes."

Of course, there will be.

You cannot expect 400 years of racially unbalanced norms to be overturned in one financial quarter. Black people make up 13.4 percent of the US population and account for only 3.2 percent of the senior leadership roles in large companies.[6] As a red pill leader, Schultz recognized that, but Starbucks isn't a one-man show.

In September 2017, Starbucks announced the appointment of Rosalind Brewer to the role of group president and chief operating officer, making her the first Black leader and the first female leader to hold the position. With years of leadership, including her most recent position as CEO of Sam's Club, Brewer was well positioned to help the ubiquitous $84.6 billion coffee brand continue to grow. Before stepping into her role as Sam's Club CEO in 2012, Brewer served six years in executive roles with Walmart and 22 years at Kimberly-Clark, where she worked her way up from research technician to president of manufacturing and operations.

During her time at Sam's Club, Brewer connected with Starbucks's then CEO Schultz when he visited Walmart's Bentonville, Arkansas, headquarters in 2016 for a panel discussion with Walmart CEO Doug McMillon. McMillon canceled at the last minute and called on Brewer to stand in (Sam's Club is owned by Walmart). Schultz and Brewer continued to build their relationship over the years. Brewer and her team visited Starbucks's flagship roastery in Seattle, where Schultz asked Brewer to consider joining the company's board. She accepted. In a *Fortune* magazine article, Kevin Johnson, the current CEO of Starbucks, said that Brewer's impressive work as a board member is what made him consider her for the COO role. Other board members agreed that she would be a great addition to the Starbucks executive team. After two years in the COO role at Starbucks, in March 2021, Brewer assumed the role of chief executive officer of Walgreens Boots Alliance Inc. and also joined the Walgreens board of directors.[7]

ANOTHER FIRST FOR
A BLACK WOMAN, PART I

A few years out of graduate school, in 1992, a young professional living in Baltimore and working at Johnson & Johnson (J&J), had an opportunity to live overseas in one of her favorite continents: Asia. Her chances for the J&J account manager role in Singapore were looking great. She had jumped through all the corporate hoops including going through internal interviews and submitting an updated résumé and other documents required for this overseas opportunity.

Then, . . . nothing. A big blank space. A dearth of sound. Eerie quiet.

What was going on?

She wanted to know, but didn't want to look desperate or be perceived as not concentrating on her current client account. So she discreetly called colleagues at J&J's world headquarters in New Brunswick, New Jersey.

More quiet. Then . . . the *call.*

It was from Diane, a White senior executive at the J&J operating company that employed the young professional. Diane was affable, smart, articulate, and humane, and she got right down to business.

"I suspect you must be wondering what is going on," Diane said.

"Yes," Gina responded with a nervous giggle in a weak attempt to sound nonchalant. "The thought has crossed my mind." Her heart was pounding.

"Gina, a couple of weeks ago, senior executives, middle managers, and technical folks were in a meeting at our Santa Monica office. Senior officials of the Singapore government were on speakerphone. When the conversation turned to the specifics of account management, one very high-ranking official said, 'Of course, the person you send will be White.'"

Diane paused. Gina didn't fill the silence. She listened. She controlled her breath so Diane couldn't hear it reverberating through the phone.

"That was an uncomfortable moment in the room for everyone on our side of the table, Gina, because everyone in that room knew that you are the person being considered to fill the first account management slot. I wasn't at the meeting, but afterward everyone was wondering, 'What did that mean?' Was the government official making an assumption? Was it a specific request? The folks in the meeting didn't know what to make of it."

Gina still hadn't said a word.

"As you can imagine," Diane continued, "we've been going through a lot of machinations over here in New Brunswick."

Courage is but one character strength that this story will highlight. We'll get to what ultimately happened in Chapter 8, but first consider this: When the people on the conference call heard the client say, "Of course, the person you'll send will be White," should someone have spoken up? Why or why not? If yes, what might have the person said? Would you have spoken up?

In addition to the five core muscles outlined in the last chapter (change readiness, cultural curiosity, growth mindset, empathy, and spectrum thinking), our interviews revealed five more skills that leaders at all levels need to develop to advance race work. As shown in Figure 7.1, they are humility, courage, listening, failing well, and resilience.

FIGURE 7.1 Five skills to build. (*Illustration by Lucy Engelman.*)

HUMILITY, COURAGE, AND LISTENING IN ACTION

Eight years before the death of George Floyd, another George, George Zimmerman, fatally shot 17-year-old high schooler Trayvon Martin. The year was 2012. CEO Ben Hecht, whom we introduced you to in Chapter 2, was already five years into his tenure at Living Cities, an urban development organization whose mission it is to close racial income and wealth gaps. One of Hecht's employees, Nadia Owusu, now author of *Aftershocks*, a memoir of her own struggles with racism, came into his office. Hecht shared with us the details of this pivotal moment in his race journey:

"'I'm here on behalf of the other senior leaders of color,' Nadia said to me. 'Nobody feels like they can talk about Trayvon Martin's death in the office. We talk about [Living Cities] being a place that fights poverty in US cities, but we don't see race anywhere in the work we do. People think we're not even allowed to talk about it.'"[8]

"I just listened," said Hecht, "but in my head I was thinking, 'Who the hell do they think they are? I've been doing this work for

> Churning through talent, no matter the size of your company, cuts into profitability and productivity. When talented employees leave an organization because they don't feel like they are valued and appreciated, it's the company, not the employee, who is the big loser.

25 years, and they've been doing it for 5 or 10.' And then I came to the conclusion that they were right." Right? Wrong? It sounded like Hecht was polarizing rather than practicing spectrum thinking. "I thought, are these six or seven people of color who I know and respect right? Or is the one White guy, me, right?," Hecht said. "I came to the conclusion that they had to be right because I didn't know enough." This is humility in action—the first strength of a Red Pill leader.

Hecht and the organization have been on this journey for nearly a decade. Milestones include an annual racial equity audit that now has four years of data to measure progress, identifying and screening for racial equity competencies during the hiring process, and requiring all new hires to undergo a multiday training. On a grading scale from A to F, Hecht gives himself and the organization a C. "We're trying," says this red pill leader. "This is lifelong work. You do your part in the organization and try to make it a better place for people of color to work. We are at the early stage of racial equity. If you think of it as a hockey stick," Hecht demonstrates with his arms, "we're nowhere near the neck."

Companies rely on data to make sound business decisions, from what to outsource and invest in, to which product and services to develop. Creating and sustaining an antiracist workplace is no exception. Only when Nadia Osuwu confronted Hecht did he closely look at the data. "It showed people of color, especially women of color, churning through organizations. You have to ask yourself why. Every person of color who had left the organization seemed to have a good reason," Hecht told us. Only when he looked at Living Cities' attrition data did he see the pattern. Churning through talent, no matter the size of your company, cuts into profitability and productivity. When talented employees leave an organization because they don't feel like they are valued and appreciated, it's the company, not the employee, who is the big loser.

Hecht admits that sometimes for-profit business leaders dismiss Living Cities' racial equity journey and don't see the connection to their own organization. They point out that Living Cities is a social change organization, so of course it must focus on racial equity. Hecht offers another view. "Every company is affected by America's changing demographics, and yet none of us were trained to do this work. When you look inward, it's ugly."

In this story Nadia Owusu, one of Hecht's employees, demonstrated a second strength of a red pill leader; *courage*. She could have chosen the do-nothing strategy, and so could have Hecht. It would have been easier, but it would not have advanced positive change in the company's racial diversity. Courage is required at all levels in an organization to advance race work.

"If leaders don't have the courage to stand up for what is an ethical and a business imperative, then the rest of the organization won't stand up for it," says Prudential's CMO Susan Somersille Johnson.[9] Johnson has a deep appreciation for racial, ethnic, and cultural diversity from her years working in countries around the world. She was often the only Black woman, American, or native English speaker. "My hope is a world where people appreciate and value diversity, which will give business leaders the courage to stand up for what's right and to crush racist policies. Because it takes courage to do that, and so you have to really want it and value it."

> "You also need to be thankful that folks are sharing how they feel, and you can't take it personally. Look at it as an opportunity to learn, grow, and move your organization forward and move our country forward, too."

Hecht and Osuwu's story also demonstrates a third strength besides humility and courage that red pill leaders must cultivate: *listening*. Had Hecht dismissed Osuwu's feedback and tried to explain away his actions, the organization would not be where it is today. The significance of listening also showed up in several other interviews for this book, including the one with EVERFI's cofounder and president Ray Martinez. We first introduced you to Martinez in Chapter 2. He describes the company's race work as a "journey" that required introspection and the deliberate seeking of feedback from employees. "You need to be able to listen, really listen," Martinez explains. "You also need to be thankful that folks are sharing how they feel, and you can't take it personally. Look at it as an opportunity to learn, grow, and move your organization forward and move our country forward, too."[10]

STUMBLE AND HUMBLE—ACCEPTING FAILURE AND RESILIENCE AS STRENGTHS

As a society, we are often obsessed with perfectionism and catastrophize our failures. Luckily, failure does not result in the end of the world, and we can bounce back from setbacks if we can learn to accept failure with humility. This is especially important in race work, because you will get some things wrong. We must learn how to fail well in race work, in all of our work, and in life. "It's not easy to falter in front of people," says Kathy Taylor, the law professor and DEI consultant whom we quoted earlier in the chapter.[11] "You can't do this work without bumping your head, particularly when many of us were taught not to talk about race."

Taylor says if we're open to making mistakes, then we'll be more prepared when it happens and better able to process the lessons learned. "Missteps will not be the reason to say, 'I shouldn't have done this.' Missteps must become the reason we do this work, and why we must do it better."

Failing well is a prerequisite to red pill leadership. Comfort with uncomfortable truths demands wearing egg on your face and extracting your foot from your mouth with grace. No way around it. When Olympic ice skaters land double toe loops and triple Salchows during competition, it is because in practice they've fallen over and over and over again. You know that. And yet you imagine you will never fall flat on your behind undertaking race work. Hahaha! That's the laughter of love, empathy, and compassion. We've been there. And we're certain we will be again.

Consider this: on the first pages of this book, we shared the story of the phone call that sparked the idea to collaborate on this book about race and racism. Here's what happened after Margaret left a voicemail for another Black client–turned–friend, Mhayse Samalya, to see how he was doing in the days after the murder of George Floyd.[12] The next day Samalya returned Margaret's call. They swapped stories about their families, shared how they were adjusting to the pandemic, and discussed the latest act of racism, George Floyd's death, and the ensuing protests to end police brutality.

"One more thing before we hang up," Samalya said. "I have to tell you this because we've known each other a long time and I value our friendship." He and Margaret had met more than 25 years earlier while employed at the same company. Ten years later, when Samalya became president of his own company, Margaret consulted with him and his leadership team. They stayed in touch ever since, visiting each other when their work travels brought them to opposite coasts where they lived. Margaret couldn't imagine what her friend and colleague was about to share with her.

He told her, "I appreciated you calling me the other day and leaving a voicemail. When you said you were 'calling all of your friends of color to see how they are doing,' I was taken aback. I thought I was your friend, not a friend that is in some folder on your desk marked 'Black friends.'"

Like anything else in life, people perceive and react to the same situation

> "I've been seeking a directive about what I need to do to get it 'right' when there is no right way. Explicitly telling folks, 'you will get this wrong and you need to try anyway,' is a message that is missing from the conversation right now."

in differing ways. People who identify as Black, Indigenous, or a person of color are no more homogeneous than White people. Margaret kept listening. She didn't defend the voice message she left. Instead, she wanted to understand Samalya's perspective, which was so different from the response Gina had to her phone call.

"Imagine," said Samalya, "if I said to you, 'I'm calling all of my friends of Whiteness to see how they are doing.' See how that sounds?"

Margaret recalls talking to Samalya about race only twice in their 25-year relationship: first when the Democratic Party nominated its first Black presidential candidate, Barack Obama, and then when he won the election. Clearly, race had been an undiscussable between them. It took courage for Samalya to broach this sensitive issue with her. It took openness on Margaret's part to listen and not defend.

Conversations like those Margaret had with Gina and, later, Samalya are strong beginnings for race work in organizations across the United States and around the world. Risking that phone call over remaining silent can be less fraught with fear. *Failing well* is another twenty-first-century competency.

Another salient race work skill is the ability to bounce back from failure. One of our colleagues, Meghan Donahue, a learning and professional development manager at a global law firm who self-identifies as White, wrote to us after reading an early draft of *The Business of Race*. She said she felt a sense of relief when she learned that making mistakes and failing well are part of the race work journey. "I've been seeking a directive about what I need to do to get it 'right' when there is no right way. Explicitly telling folks, 'you will get this wrong and you need to try anyway,' is a message that is missing from the conversation right now.

> You won't risk change if you focus on what you have to lose. The more productive question is, what do I have to gain?

The expectations are so high and everyone is afraid to fail, be 'canceled' or decried 'tone deaf.'"[13]

Donahue's relief is palpable. We live in a culture that automatically dismisses anyone who says or does something perceived as wrong. So we fear taking action, risking mistakes. And when we do, we are more likely to defend, disengage, or browbeat ourselves. Instead, like Olympians, let's practice failing well: act, learn, listen, and persist. The practice of failing well helps us to build one more strength: *resilience*.

Resilience is the ability to get back up after you've been knocked down, the capacity to recover quickly from difficulties, not wallow in them. In race work, that guarantees the proverbial foot in mouth. No worries. We've all eaten foods that didn't agree with us. That doesn't mean we stop eating. After your digestive flip-flop, make peace with the discomfort. Go a step further and own it publicly because you will be modeling what everyone on this journey will encounter. You show that you get to live another day. Motivational speaker and self-improvement guru Iyanla Vanzant who self-identifies as Black, says, "You can feel bad and recover."[14] This makes it safe for others to do it, too.

> By adopting a growth mindset, we accept that our ability to grow isn't the result of having won a talent lottery. Rather, mistakes are necessary milestones on the journey of learning and growth.

The ability to "fall, learn, and get back up" is what resilience is all about, says executive coach Karen Senteio, who self-identifies as Black. "White women [and men] need to understand that being an ally may cost them something," she says.[15] You won't risk change if you focus on what you have to lose. The more productive question is, what do I have to gain? "It might cost you a relationship, one that no longer serves either of you," says Senteio. "But the benefits far outweigh the costs. What is gained is the sharpening of your values." And the strengthening of a core muscle that allows you to stand firm in service to those values. Senteio explains: "You're going against a system designed to keep many silent. Be prepared for people to say, 'How dare you rise up and tell us our system is wrong?'" People of all races and ethnicities will benefit from building their resilience. If you need help, go back to the previous chapter and spend some time reviewing the material on growth mindset. By adopting a growth mindset, we accept that our ability to grow isn't the result of having won a talent lottery. Rather, mistakes are necessary milestones on the journey of learning and growth.

KEY STRENGTHS OF RED PILL LEADERS

- **Humility.** Acknowledge that you don't know everything and don't have all the answers.

- **Courage.** Speak up even when it's uncomfortable to do so.

- **Listening.** Have patience to hear someone out. It means being able to restate someone else's words, thoughts, and opinions, even if you may not agree with them. Express gratitude for the open sharing.

- **Failing well.** Recognize that mistakes are inherent to learning and growth.

- **Resilience.** Grow the capacity to recover quickly from difficulties and setbacks.

PSYCHOLOGICAL SAFETY

Even if you already possess the five core muscles you learned about in Chapter 6 and the five strengths described in this chapter, race work still is not easy. Conversations on race and racism will *not* be comfortable, but they must be safe.

Research by Harvard Business School professor Dr. Amy Edmondson, who self-identifies as White, has found that psychological safety must be present, especially when grappling with emotionally charged topics such as race and racism, because such topics insist on vulnerability.[16] Before you make yourself vulnerable, you must first feel safe. Google conducted a massive four-year study to find out what differentiated great teams from not-so-great teams. The biggest differentiator by far of excellent teams at Google was psychological safety.[17] Dr. Edmondson said in an interview that was music to her ears.[18] Similarly, Christine Robinson, a senior advisor to philanthropic foundations such as the Ford Foundation, also confirms that psychological safety is key to what makes the world's top-performing teams. It's the bedrock, Robinson explains. "First of all, it makes

> Conversations on race and racism will *not* be comfortable, but they must be safe.

everyone feel welcome, listened to, and appreciated. People are free to ask questions, to raise concerns, to pitch ideas without unnecessary repercussions."[19]

Answer these questions through the lens of your organization. Specifically, how can you create a more courageous company culture? How are mistakes looked upon? What happens when people risk something new, speak up, or are the lone voice that says "no" when everyone else is saying "yes"? Are the "yes" people rewarded while those who challenge the status quo are sidelined and silenced?

> Absolutely critical to race work is the ability for people to come to their jobs and speak up with impunity about what they know, what they don't know, what they see, what they're worried about, and what they aspire to be.

The diverse ideas people bring to organizations also bring value to the marketplace. And yet in many companies as much as half the employees report that they don't feel safe speaking up. That means we're losing enormous value. If we aren't hearing from people, we may be missing out on a game-changing idea that could improve quality, shorten turnaround time, or invent a new product or service. We might miss an early market opportunity that someone saw but felt unable to share with their team or manager. Or a perspective that would advance the company's race work. We need to start "calling people in" to race discussions, as Smith College professor and activist Loretta J. Ross says, rather than "calling people out."[20]

Absolutely critical to race work is the ability for people to come to their jobs and speak up with impunity about what they know, what they don't know, what they see, what they're worried about, and what they aspire to be. Hecht from Living Cities sums it up this way: "As long as most companies are White led, then if you're at the top of the organization, you have to create the space and safety. You have to make sure you're creating an environment where everyone can contribute from wherever they're sitting and not to be afraid to speak up."[21]

Let's do another deep dive into one more organization, the Transportation Department of Austin, Texas, to see how psychological safety and the five red pill leader strengths play out.

In August 2019, Austin's Transportation Department required its employees to attend a one-hour diversity and inclusion training.[22] In all, 272 employees—more than three-quarters of the department—participated in the workshop. A week after the training, nearly two-dozen unnamed employees emailed a 13-page memo to executives. They detailed how the presentation was offensive, entirely inaccurate at times, and "emotionally and professionally damaging." Experts on race and gender who reviewed the training feedback reacted with disbelief.

"As someone who does this type of training and who has taught these issues for over 20 years, I am absolutely flabbergasted that a diversity and inclusion training could be so poorly executed," a professor in the College of Liberal Arts at UT Austin wrote in an email. "This training was so bad that it almost appears to be a parody on diversity training gone wrong."

What exactly was "so bad," and how did the Austin Transportation Department recover? Let's do what businesses do after implementing any initiative: a project review. Let's practice *failing well* and see what we can learn from the experience.

What Went Wrong and Lessons Learned

First, the vendor was outside of its bailiwick. It was an EAP (employee assistance program) consulting company that provides mostly one-on-one counseling for employees. And for those services, the EAP vendor, which had a longstanding contract with the Austin Transportation Department, had already received close to a million dollars. However, department heads could reach out to the vendor for specialized training on various topics, including diversity and inclusion.

Second, when the Transportation Department heads reached out to the vendor to provide diversity and inclusion training, apparently it did so with no connection to an organization-wide strategy.

Third, when approached by the two department heads, the vendor decided to fulfill the request itself rather than refer a consultant with more experience in delivering these kinds of workshops. This lack of DEI acumen resulted in the 13-page, 30-point bulleted list from Transportation Department employees about everything that went wrong with the training. This included inaccurate references and vocabulary—conflating "race" with "nationality"—and open ridicule and inflammatory remarks about particular groups of people.

The fourth misstep was how management responded to the failure. When employees approached HR after the training with their feedback, it was downplayed with comments such as, "It wasn't that bad!"

Let's reframe these missteps into lessons learned and actionable steps you and your organization can take. We uncovered four:

First, rather than handing race work over to whoever raises their hand, create a group of racially diverse employees, with executive sponsorship, to work collaboratively and to advise the company's leadership. That's what nearly every company we interviewed has done to provide input into strategy and crisis management. As examples:

- Living Cities built its D&I strategy shortly after Nadia Owusu had the courage to approach CEO Hecht. "We created an internal team of people that we call C.O.R.E.— colleagues, operations, and racial equity," Hecht told us.[23] "That group has been critical for our ongoing work. They make recommendations to our leadership team on what our priorities should be for the year." Hecht went on to explain that C.O.R.E. members meet with every business team, both internal- and external-facing, to check in on progress, as well as conduct an annual racial equity audit. As mentioned earlier in the chapter, Living Cities now has four years of data and uses it to adjust for continuous improvement.

- CFRA Research, one of the world's largest independent research firms with offices in New York, London, Kuala Lumpur, Charlottesville, and Washington, DC, began using a similar approach in June 2020. The catalyst? The public outcry of the murder of George Floyd and the protests that followed. "We have an employee resource group that we call our Social Justice Task Force," Heather Thomas-McClellan, global head of talent, shared with us. "The idea came as we were sitting in one of our senior leadership team meetings talking about the recent events and how we, as a company, should respond. We decided that we shouldn't be the ones determining how we respond. Instead, we came to a consensus that we should put together a team of employees to share their ideas, just like we would for any large, complex initiative."[24]

Thomas-McClellan explained that the team of volunteers was made up of four women and two men, all from racially and culturally diverse backgrounds, herself the only White woman, and who also served as the team's sponsor. "The team came up with a list of recommendations and first presented them to our senior leadership and then to all of our employees at a Town Hall meeting," she said. "We agreed that the focus this year would be on helping people understand unintended or unconscious bias and things that happen in the workplace that they may be missing."

Since then, CFRA Research has begun implementing the team's recommendations, which included modifying the company values to make a stronger statement about diversity; cascading unconscious bias training first to the senior leadership team, then managers, and then all employees; starting a book club; and creating a dedicated channel in Microsoft Teams to share educational materials. It's an effective way for a medium-size company to start. "We also want to get involved in volunteer events to show commitment to our communities," Thomas-McClellan said "However, we haven't figured out the best way to do this yet with everybody working from home and the Covid-19 challenge."

The second lesson from the Austin Transportation Department training is to connect the dots between tactical actions and how they align with your racial diversity strategy, rather than offering one class here and one class there. The city of Austin, Texas, recognized that its next steps must be a systematic approach to shifting cultural norms for how the city operates and conducts business. Simply putting out a public #BlackLivesMatter statement can actually do more harm than good. "When you do these periodic interventions, without people understanding that it's part of something bigger," Living Cities CEO Ben Hecht told us, "it has no credibility and can actually do more damage. It's like putting lipstick on a pig."

Third, if a company sponsors a training that is poorly designed and executed, it's imperative the company's leadership acknowledges the mistake. This requires that leaders actively listen and publicly commit to educating themselves before making another knee-jerk reaction. "There's no playbook," says Hecht. "Like the adoption of anything new, you have to have early adopters who are going to be public about their work, knowing that they will make mistakes and not be the most successful. We need leaders to acknowledge the risk of doing this isn't as great as they fear. Unfortunately, courageous leaders are in short supply."

In the hopes of sharing some best practices with other leaders, in June 2020, Hecht authored a *Harvard Business Review* article, "Moving Beyond Diversity Toward Racial Equity."[25] An anonymous group of former Living Cities employees wrote a scathing public rebuttal to Hecht's article. Hecht shared his perspective with us:

> Some people probably thought, "Who is this White guy? He's sanding all the rough edges and not acknowledging the harm experienced by staff, past and present. He's making it sound like he's got it and did it all himself." My whole reason for writing that article was to tell people at least what I have seen, and it's a ton of work, and I don't have all the answers. When you put yourself out there,

you're going to get beat up, but you have to do it anyway. You have to have the courage, or else nothing will change.

Hecht then shared a conversation he had with another senior executive years before in a small conference room over lunch:

I said to him, "You're one of the most respected CEOs in the United States. Why don't you stand up more forcefully for what's right when it comes to poverty and racism?"

And you know what he said? "Every time I do, I get the crap beat out of me, so why do it?"

I said to him, "With all due respect, because you're getting paid $35 million a year. Of all people, you can get the crap beat out of you. That's part of your job. It's the social contract if we want to have responsible capitalism."

And he says, "I do it more than most leaders, but you have to understand, I get very little gratification for doing the right thing." I know he's right, but we have to do it anyway. And we have to do it in a public way and with humility, and hopefully enough people will give them grace, too.

The fourth and last lesson learned from the Texas Transportation Department's experience is to hire or contract with experienced professionals to help you. If you don't have internal resources dedicated to diversity, equity, and inclusion, then build or buy this competency. Depending on your company size, you might hire one or more full-time professionals, develop internal talent, or vet external consultants. Don't expect that your lead trainer or professionals in your learning and development department are skilled in designing and delivering this type of training. Or consulting with organizational leaders to develop a racial diversity and inclusion strategy with clearly defined metrics. They can, however, help you evaluate whom you might contract with or hire to do race work.

FOUR LESSONS LEARNED FROM THE AUSTIN, TEXAS, TRANSPORTATION EXPERIENCE

- Create a group of racially diverse employees, with executive sponsorship, to work collaboratively to advise the company's leadership.

- Connect the dots between your company's racial diversity *tactical actions* and how they align with your racial diversity *strategy*.

- If a training or other educational event goes poorly, publicly acknowledge the mistake, share lessons learned, and apply them to your next steps.

- If you don't have internal resources dedicated to diversity, equity, and inclusion, then determine which strategy will work best for your company: build or buy.

Workplace diversity programs and training have their origins in protecting management against individual and class-action discrimination lawsuits. This is why for decades HR and legal departments have discouraged managers from talking about race, religion, politics, sexual orientation, mental/emotional/physical/cognitive disabilities, and other sensitive topics.

Today, managers who have been shushed are expected to act beyond compliance box-checking and facilitate meaningful dialogue about race and racism with their employees. Few are equipped to do so. Even if they naturally possess emotional intelligence skills—such as empathy, compassion, and listening—few have explored their own biases and mindsets to be able to confidently lead a discussion on these intense and complex topics.

CFRA Research's global head of talent Thomas-McClellan explained to us, "I cringed at the idea of where these conversations could lead, having never broached these conversations with managers before. It always seemed safer to just tell managers to avoid these conversations. I'm not saying we shouldn't do it going forward; I'm just saying we have a lot of education and development to do first."

Before you jump into race talk (an *overfunctioning* antiracist if you took the ASI described in Chapter 5), it's important to undertake your own inner work and learn from others. While we have a deep belief that mistakes and failing well are a necessary part of this journey, avoiding common pitfalls is always a good practice.

THE FINE POINTS

Let's look at what these stories from red pill leaders have in common:

- Facing uncomfortable truths and acting with courage.

- Taking risks and embracing the unknown.

- Persisting despite stumbling.

- Learning from mistakes and growing from them—individually and organizationally.

- Communicating with transparency.

Creating and sustaining an antiracist workplace will not be a straight line, or smooth sailing; however, it can be less choppy if you:

- Learn from the experiences of others.

- Show how your initiatives tie to a larger business strategy.

- Publicly admit your mistakes and grow from them.

- Actively listen. You don't have to have all the answers. Instead, hold the space to let others express their feelings and ideas.

- Foster a culture where all employees feel safe and supported.

- When racist jokes or sentiments are expressed, rather than remaining silent, speak up. Let it be known why it is harmful to individual employees and to the organization as a whole. This is a teachable moment. Take a risk and enlarge a micro-opportunity.

REFLECTION

- Have you ever remained silent when you've heard a racist comment? Have you ever spoken up? How do you feel about those experiences now? What might you do differently the next time?

- What is one uncomfortable truth you learned, and how have you grown from it?

- Specific to race and racism in your workplace, what does "taking a risk and embracing the unknown" look like for you?

- When was the last time you gave yourself permission to fail?

- Think of a misstep you or your organization made in race work. What did you learn from it?

- Would you describe yourself as a red or blue pill leader? What about your manager?

- What's one small step you can take to become more of a red pill leader, regardless of where you sit in the hierarchy of your company?

CHAPTER 8

LIKE ANY OTHER STRATEGIC PRIORITY

Commitment, Specificity, and the Science of Small Wins

Every moment is an organizing opportunity, every person a potential activist, every minute a chance to change the world.

DOLORES HUERTA

Hispanic American labor leader and civil rights activist who, with Cesar Chavez, is a cofounder of the National Farmworkers Association, which later became the United Farm Workers[1]

Black guy, a White guy, and a White woman walk into a bar. Well, not exactly. They met while working at a startup, Linden Labs—a San Francisco–based internet company best known as the creator of the 3D virtual world, Second Life. Together this trio cofounded Truss, a software development company, in 2011.

The Black guy, Everett Harper, is Truss's chief executive officer; the White guy, Mark Ferlatte, is the company's chief technology officer; and the White woman, Jen Leech, is the chief operating officer. Go to Truss's website, and you'll see racial diversity in action. Click on "Meet the Team," and you'll see a photo and bio of every single member of their 40-plus team. Click on "Jobs," and the first thing you'll see are the words "In search of an inclusive and transparent workplace culture that encourages you to be your best self."

> "We are already on the edge of the norm, and being on the edge means that we see the assumptions that are often in the center. That's what made us a great founding team."

The tech industry is not known for its gender diversity, let alone its racial diversity. Yet here is a company that was started by a diverse trio. We wanted to learn more, so we reached out to one of the cofounders, Everett Harper.

"Walking into a room, we do not look like the Silicon Valley standard," says Harper.[2] We are already on the edge of the norm, and being on the edge means that we see the assumptions that are often in the center. That's what made us a great founding team."

So Harper and his cofounders asked themselves, "What other contrary, data-driven beliefs could we instill in our company right from the beginning?" One notion: there are lots of people outside the Bay Area who are never thought of as potential employees of a startup company. This "what-if" exploration led to the idea of structuring Truss as a fully distributed company—where all employees work entirely remotely. What the Covid-19 pandemic ultimately forced many companies to do, Truss has been doing for over a decade. "We knew there are great women engineers, but they're not on anybody's typical list," said Harper. The question for the three founders then became, "How do we find them?"

Most startups are running so fast, they often forgo the traditional business exercise of developing a vision, mission, and values. Not Truss. The company builds infrastructure for its clients—systems, software, and operations. So the three cofounders thought, why not apply this same thinking to building their company? A lot of people advised, "Don't waste your time on core values; just get stuff built." Harper disagrees: "Writing down our commitment to being a diverse company set into motion an investment in our infrastructure that made things easier, faster, and simpler later. That was one of the better business decisions we've made."

Harper offered five pieces of advice:

First, "Declare it. Diversity doesn't matter if everybody quits, right?"

Second, it has to come from the top. "The executives don't have to carry out all the work, but they have to be accountable, because culture change needs authority to drive it."

Third, it needs to have a purpose, or what Harper calls a "why." "Be clear on how it connects to the business. We believe it is the right thing to do, but it's not a moral issue." Rather, Harper says, "It will enable us to hire better-quality people with diverse backgrounds and ensure they stay because they are embedded in a system that is fair."

Fourth, "Get feedback from the people most affected by the system. If it becomes a siloed project owned by one part of the organization and silent to everybody else, I predict it will fail."

Lastly, Harper is a huge proponent of experiments. Fundamental to experimentation is making mistakes and learning from them. This is one of the core competencies you learned about in Chapter 6 where we introduced create–dismantle–re-create. You'll also learn how Harper experimented with pay transparency in Chapter 11.

We encourage older, more traditional businesses or ones that have historically excluded non-White workers to experiment with Harper's suggestions, too. The difference is that no two businesses will approach race work in the same way. Harper's five pieces of advice are neither

> The executives don't have to carry out all the work, but they have to be accountable, because culture change needs authority to drive it.

formulaic nor linear. But they are not random either. They are strategic. If you think they can only work at a startup in the high-tech industry, think again. This next company we're going to explore is in an industry as old as the Bronze Age.

ADAPT OR PERISH

It's neither the businesses with the deepest pockets, nor those with the deepest experience, that survive when faced with uncertainty. We've seen it time and again: businesses that are able to adapt, not only survive but also thrive. Most recently we've witnessed this adapt-or-perish mindset firsthand when some of our favorite restaurants closed their doors, while others transformed themselves into catering/takeout businesses in response to Covid-19 restrictions. Let's see how some other companies have adapted to the VUCA environment we are all living and working in.

Cranes reaching into the sky indicate a strong economy. They nearly disappeared in US cities during the Great Recession of 2008–2009. So did the talented professionals in engineering and construction management jobs who left the construction industry to find employment elsewhere. Construction firms that did survive the Great Recession began ramping up again in 2010 but were faced with a labor shortage.

One such firm was Shawmut Design and Construction, a Boston-based construction management firm. The leadership decided the best way to solve the labor shortage was to "cultivate our early-in-career talent," says chief people officer Marianne Monte, of both the firm's existing workforce and recent college graduate recruits.[3] Shawmut advanced that decision by developing an in-house Construction Management Skills Training (CMST) program. "A great training ground for people of color and women coming out of construction management and engineering degree programs," says Monte. "Today we have our first two VPs who graduated from our CMST program."

In 2015 Shawmut, 100 percent employee-owned, declared its aspiration to be the employer of choice for women. Shawmut's declaration and subsequent actions "were a business decision to mirror our clients," says Monte. "They are not only White men. They are women. People of color. Gay and transgender people." She says it enables Shawmut to speak the language of "different perspectives." This recruitment approach also helps Shawmut strategically partner with key community constituents who are also clients. In addition to managing the construction of complex, multimillion-dollar building projects such as luxury apartments and retail stores on New York City's Fifth Avenue and in Beverly Hills on Rodeo Drive, Shawmut works with clients that include hospitals and academic institutions. As a general contractor, Shawmut has made it a strategic priority to partner with small businesses owned by women and people of color. Employing more diverse subcontractors in the local community helps Shawmut win business with large clients that also have diversity as a strategic priority.

Historically, the construction sector in general, and Boston in particular, has been especially challenging for people of color. According to the Economic Policy Institute (EPI), a DC-based think tank that conducts economic research, "Construction is a sector that has historically excluded Black workers—including the unionized portion of the industry.[4] Giving people of color access to good jobs is an important part of closing our large and persistent racial wage inequities." EPI reports that only 13.8 percent of the nonunion jobs in the construction industry are held by Black workers.[5] The US Bureau of Labor Statistics cites that women hold less than 10 percent of these jobs.[6] Since

Shawmut began its race and gender journey more than a decade ago, it has raised those numbers to 20 percent people of color and 35 percent women. The company recognizes that it still has a long way to go.

Shawmut's story is one of adaptation. Adapting to a seismic change—a recession—was how the company survived. Many of its competitors that failed to adapt did not. In 2020, two societal events—the pandemic and the Black Lives Matter movement—collided, prompting businesses around the world to adapt.

THE PANDEMIC, PROTESTS, AND PIVOTS

You probably recall the exact day in 2020 when your company announced you would be working from home due to the pandemic. You also probably recall how you felt when you watched the 9-minute, 29-second video of George Floyd pinned to the ground by a White police officer with his knee pressed into Floyd's neck.

In the spring of 2020, in response to the murders of unarmed Black people, attacks on Asian Americans, and the ensuing protests, companies that have been involved in diversity work for decades and others that have traditionally remained silent put out public *statements* condemning the violence. Prudential went a step further and made a public *commitment*. This included nine specific actions to advance racial equity. Five of the commitments are to its people, two are specific to the products and services it designs and delivers, and the other two are specific to society at large. Prudential's chairman and CEO Charlie Lowrey went further still and built *accountability* into these commitments by tying executive compensation to diversity and inclusion goals. This was nothing new for Prudential. The company has been at this work for decades. Lowery joined Prudential in 2018. Within the first four months of his new role, he declared four major priorities—not unusual for a senior executive to do in his first 100 days. What was unusual is that being a fully inclusive company was on this White CEO's short list. As Lowrey says, himself, "Driving progress toward racial equity is a moral and business imperative that aligns directly with our company's purpose to solve the financial challenges of our changing world."[7]

Current events always inform a company's business strategy. The pandemic and protests precipitated many companies undertaking a hard pivot—from a strategy focused on all-encompassing diversity to one focused on *racial* diversity.

Another way companies pivot is when they bring in new talent. One company that has done this effectively is McCormick & Company. Its iconic red-capped, plastic jars may be a staple in your kitchen. And also a staple in your great, great grandmother's kitchen, too. Some of your favorite restaurants use the company's products in nearly every dish. From its humble beginnings in the basement of a Baltimore home, the spice manufacturer and distributor has grown into a global company with $5.5 billion in annual sales. McCormick has also been on its race work journey for more than a dozen years. When Nereida Perez first joined the company as global head of diversity and inclusion at the start of 2019, the company was still doing what she calls "first-level" work, meaning awareness building. "One of the first things I did was review the company's global diversity and inclusion strategy," she says. "I then restructured the Global Diversity Council, pulling together employees from across the company. Together we developed and proposed an enterprise strategy that focused on three areas: workforce, work environment, and marketplace."[8] The workforce piece of the strategy included talent acquisition and talent development. The work environment component began with an employee engagement survey to understand how included people felt. This gave Perez the information she and other leaders needed to delve deeper. And the marketplace review included answering questions such as, How accessible were its products and services? What did its community relations profile look like? How was it engaging in and standing up for social justice?

When Perez joined McCormick in 2019, it had already established employee resource groups in each of the 27 countries it operates in. The focus, however, in many countries was on the advancement of women and the issues they face. Over the last two years, McCormick has reshaped its ERGs to focus on each country's needs from a diversity and inclusion perspective. Nereida explains:

> The employee groups that were established to focus on women's efforts wanted to do more. They started having conversations about people with disabilities and the inequalities they and other groups faced. Our women's groups in France, Italy, and in the UK decided that they wanted to focus on broader issues. And so the group in Europe launched an initiative called Emb-RACE to talk about racial differences and inequities that might exist. We have a group in Poland that's primarily focused on women's initiatives and then one in South Africa still focused on women's initiatives, but that may change over time. It's just where they are on their journey.

What started as an enterprisewide approach to diversity and inclusion has now become embedded into the company's line of businesses. To better understand the needs and issues of its Black employees, McCormick formed an executive advisory group that included its first Black female division president, three VPs, and one senior director who was very involved with the Black Employee Group (ERG). "We conducted focus group meetings with the Black employees to find out what was on their mind," says Perez. "That conversation got positioned as a discussion with our CEO and our management committee to talk about unresolved issues the organization needs to work on."

No matter your company size, no matter if you have dedicated DEI professionals, no matter your industry, you need a strategy.

An outgrowth of the executive advisory group's work, and subsequent presentation to CEO Larry Kurzius and the management committee, was a letter Kurzius sent to its operations around the world. The letter outlined the commitments the company would make to remove any perceived or real barriers to hiring and advancement. The letter also outlined the three pillars of the D&I enterprise strategy: workforce, work environment, and marketplace. Executing on these commitments would not be formulaic. Instead, each line of business would be responsible and accountable for developing its own country-specific action plans. This approach "shaved years off" McCormick's readiness. Perez, who is no newcomer to the diversity and inclusion space, told us, "What I thought would take three, maybe four years to get each business line ready to have their own diversity action plan happened practically overnight."

The companies we highlighted above in this chapter—Truss, Shawmut, Prudential, and McCormick—could not be more different from one another. One is a Fortune 500 company, and another has fewer than 50 employees. Two have a dedicated DEI office, and two do not. They also represent four different industries. What they do have in common are red pill leaders who are open to developing and refining their racial diversity strategy. No matter your company size, no matter if you have dedicated DEI professionals, no matter your industry, you need a strategy. Diversity and inclusion are not standalone, HR-specific priorities. They are at the core of your business. Business leaders will need to come to grips with this reality before any meaningful change can occur. This is not a program you can opt out of. Pull out the tried-and-true business tools you use for other strategic priorities—focus groups, internal and external scans, planning templates, surveys, and project management matrices—and apply them to race work.

SOAR; DON'T SWOT

A powerful business planning tool you can use to develop your racial diversity strategy is SOAR. As we noted in the introduction to Part IV, SOAR stands for strengths, opportunities, aspirations, and results (see Figure 8.1). This simple yet powerful tool comes from the field of Appreciative Inquiry (AI), which takes a positive, strengths-based approach to organizational change.

Unlike the traditional SWOT (strengths, weaknesses, opportunities, and threats) that focuses 50 percent of your time on *deficits*, SOAR uses an *asset* approach. This doesn't mean that SOAR ignores weaknesses and threats. Instead, it prompts leaders to reframe them into opportunities, aspirations, and results, creating a more empowering, energizing, and actionable discussion. Neither does SOAR ignore difficult conversations. Rather, it provides space to reimagine what is possible. Create–dismantle–re-create, the process you learned about in Chapter 6, can help you to play and experiment with what you identify when using SOAR.

SOAR Analysis

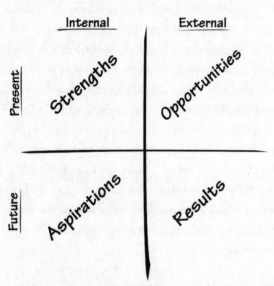

FIGURE 8.1 The SOAR framework. (*Illustration by Jaime Raijman with permission from Profit from the Positive, LLC.*)

SOAR comes from research conducted by business professor Jackie Stavros, at Lawrence Technological University in Michigan, for her doctorate of management two decades ago.[9] Since then, it has been used by microbusinesses and global businesses, the US Army, and nonprofit organizations. Use SOAR for a strategy you want to develop, including race work. A discussion using SOAR helps put our brains in a more positive emotional state. This allows us to connect with others and be more creative—two important conditions to cultivate for any kind of work, and especially race work.

All emotions, positive and negative, affect our ability to think creatively. Have you ever tried to brainstorm with a friend or colleague who is in a negative mood? It can't be done. When we are in a positive emotional state, we are more open to novel ideas and possibilities. This is what Dr. Barbara Fredrickson, from the University of North Carolina at Chapel Hill, calls the "broaden and build theory."

When we kick off meetings by asking people what's wrong or identifying weaknesses or threats, we inadvertently trigger people's protection mode. When we ask people to talk about their strengths instead, their brains launch into what Stavros calls the "connect mode." For example, if a threat to creating a racially diverse and inclusive workplace is that you're afraid of losing talented employees to your competitors, SOAR reframes that threat. Ask instead, "What marketplace opportunities might arise from creating an environment where racially diverse employees can contribute fully?" What are the recruitment, retention and productivity opportunities? Reframing doesn't mean avoiding difficult conversations or speaking in euphemisms. Rather, it articulates what you want to have happen, which "broadens and builds" discussion in an actionable direction.

When we focus on opportunities and aspirations, we can uncover what people care deeply about. "It's not about telling people they need to create a diverse, inclusive and equitable organization," says Stavros. "It's asking them."

Use SOAR, a process inquiry tool, no matter where you are in your race journey. SOAR questions guide you in recognizing the positive actions already embedded into your culture and strategy. A tenet of behavioral change is this: people are more willing to venture into the unknown when they can bring to a new creation, the positive aspects of an existing dynamic. This tool helps you, your organization, and team discover a shared vision for the future. In Table 8.1 are sample questions you may wish to explore. And likely you will have others.

TABLE 8.1 SOAR in Action: A Sampling of Questions You Might Ask

Strengths	Opportunities
What are we already doing well?	What opportunities do we see?
What are we most proud of?	What have other companies done?
Aspirations	**Results**
What do we want to be known for?	How will we know if we are successful?
What impact might we have in the world?	How will we measure progress?

How diverse and inclusive is your company's strategic planning process today? Is it primarily held at the senior leadership level, or does your company bring in other voices? The first step is to have your internal stakeholders—your employees—represented on the strategic planning team. At some point you may also want to bring some of your customers and suppliers into the process. In Chapter 12 we'll share some of these partnership models. Lastly, when implementing your racial diversity strategy, approach it as you would for your other business strategies: with clear accountabilities and measures, and a process for communicating and reporting progress.

"Taking a project approach is how we execute and make an impact," says Heather Thomas-McClellan, global head of talent at CFRA Research, whom you first met in the last chapter.[10] "Rather than some sort of theoretical framework that's floating around, we break things down into bite-sized and meaningful actions you can actually bring to completion. Just like any project, we'll assess and review the impact to the organization. I think that's the only way that diversity, inclusion, and racial equity will actually get integrated into the business."

ORGANIZATIONAL READINESS

In Chapter 6 you learned that *readiness for change* is a core muscle individuals must flex or build as part of their own race journey. Organizations must do the same. Assessing organizational readiness can serve as a guidepost for how to approach race work, and then you can measure your progress over time. If you are a people development, DEI, or HR professional, or a senior leader or board member, take a look at the Annie E. Casey Foundation's "Race Matters: Organizational Self-Assessment" report.[11] The Organizational Self-Assessment (OSA) is free and one that leaders with positional hierarchy in your organization can take. This 28-statement assessment gauges the current state of your organization and identifies what your next steps might be. The assessment is based on a continuum of four organizational approaches, as shown in Figure 8.2.

Color-blind • Diversity-only • Race-tentative • Equity-focused

FIGURE 8.2 A learning continuum for race-focused work.
(*Courtesy of the Annie E. Casey Foundation.*)

Let's look at some of the characteristics of the four organizational approaches: color-blind, diversity-only, race-tentative, and equity-focused. In Chapter 5 you learned why claiming you are *color-blind* shrinks opportunities for discovery among employees and for the organization. It can also fuel animosity by denying the history and culture of nondominant groups.

When embarking on any large initiative or strategic change, it's a good idea to examine your current state. You may not know at the outset what to do, but knowing your current state will help pinpoint where to start.

If you still need a business case, try this: when we take a *color-blind* approach, we fail to see opportunities to grow market share in underserved populations. What does *color-blind* look like from an organizational perspective? A *color-blind* organization

> Disruption is a 180-degree turn from a longstanding norm that requires necessary growth-producing upheaval. It requires an organization to reinvent itself by reimagining its existence. If implemented constructively, disruption often results in cataclysmic innovation, creating a new standard against which entire industries redefine themselves.

avoids or shuts down conversations about race, and believes it will only create unmanageable discord. A *diversity-only* organization proposes universal strategies that are presumed to work for all employees. A characteristic of a *race-tentative* organization is one in which employees or management has gone through antiracism or unconscious bias training, but the organization is still unclear about what to do next. Lastly, an organization that has taken an *equity-focused* approach has put measures in place for management accountability.

Individuals do not come to race work from the same starting place. Neither do organizations. Benchmark where your organization is today and then repeat this process annually to measure progress toward goals.

HOW TO USE THE OSA

- Give as prework before bringing a business unit, senior team, or board together for a virtual or in-person meeting. Remember to set context: Why are we doing this?

- Using a skilled facilitator, go through each of the four approaches (color-blind, diversity-only, race tentative, and equity-focused) and discuss how each person scored the organization.

- Most likely, people will see things differently. Get curious and find out why.

- Identify where the greatest opportunity for progress can be made by looking at the quiz's statements that were not checked.

- Assign accountabilities and agree to follow up on progress at least quarterly.

- Retake the assessment annually to continue your journey.

When embarking on any large initiative or strategic change, it's a good idea to examine your current state. You may not know at the outset what to do, but knowing your current state will help pinpoint where to start. The results of your OSA are a pulse on whether your organization's current race work is interrupting or disrupting the status quo. Workplaces interrupt all the time: leadership, customers, or an external force such as a global pandemic or recession requires a reengineering of a product cycle, marketing strategy, team, or department. Disruption is a 180-degree turn from a longstanding norm that requires necessary growth-producing upheaval. It requires an organization to reinvent itself by reimagining its existence. If implemented constructively, disruption often results in cataclysmic innovation, creating a new standard against which

> Building and sustaining an antiracist workplace requires daily practice.

entire industries redefine themselves. Companies notable for disrupting entire industries include Amazon (mail-order/home-shopping business), Netflix (movie rentals), Craigslist (newspaper classifieds), Uber (taxi), and Airbnb (hotels). As for the tech industry, disruption is an innovation standard other industries regularly attempt to emulate.

Interrupting institutional racism encourages us to name, constructively and with care, what's unspoken. We consider changes to our internal policies and practices, but we don't necessarily shift them to create new norms, hold people accountable for those new norms, or influence industry standards.

Disrupting institutional racism fundamentally questions how we operate. Our values align with our business operations, and when they don't, we hold systems and people accountable. Disruption is a game changer characterized by learning iteratively and embracing uncertainty through experimentation. Disrupting the status quo views the discomfort of not knowing through the asset lens of discovery and possibility, all while building on successes. Building and sustaining an antiracist workplace requires daily practice. It is intentionally created, consciously monitored, and sustainable beyond a budget line item or the whims of a particular CEO. There is no end. Only opportunity and continual growth. No different from a company's commitment to profitability, productivity, growth, innovation, and talent.

Disruption is what the mammoth pharmaceutical retailer CVS did when in 2014 it reimagined itself as a health services company. CVS Health knew it couldn't present healthy living as a key value proposition if it sold cigarettes. (The Centers for Disease Control reports that cigarette smoking is responsible for more than 480,000 deaths per year in the United States, including more than 41,000 deaths resulting from secondhand smoke exposure.) So it stopped selling them. And took a $2 billion hit in lost revenue. What more than compensated for that loss was improved relationships with customers, employees, and health industry partners that recognized CVS Health's larger commitment to healthcare over short-term profits. It wasn't painless, but it was a necessary game changer for the company's new direction and growth. As we now know, that included acquiring mega health insurer Aetna in 2017, transforming CVS Health into a Fortune 5 company.

Speaking of healthcare, Covid-19, the latest pandemic (yes, there will be others, as there were others before this one), has been a catalyst for many businesses to adapt (interrupt) or reinvent (disrupt) how they operate. Interruption and disruption are lenses through which workplaces can begin or continue their race work journey. Remember, no two journeys will look alike, because no two organizations are alike.

PUTTING A STAKE IN THE GROUND

Helping people become comfortable with discomfort is no easy task. It requires courage, persistence, and a willingness to take risks, as this next story demonstrates.

After her tenure at LLNL and six years at ESPN, Lorie Valle-Yañez assumed a new role at MassMutual: diversity and inclusion officer. "At MassMutual, we've been working at this for a long time, and it continues to evolve," says Valle-Yañez.[12]

MassMutual had been training its workforce in what Valle-Yañez called "foundational" diversity education for years, focused on understanding the business case and leader roles and responsibilities. Yet the organization's complexion hadn't much changed during those first several years. People of color were on the payroll, but their representation in leadership roles was minimal. Valle-Yañez was perplexed. Rather than withdraw to her office and ponder in isolation, she convened a group of leaders from across the company to deliberate. After a series of difficult discussions, the group landed on the root cause: The company's leaders were not culturally competent or inclusive. The work of the group then shifted: what next? Valle-Yañez and her team began researching programs to identify those with transformative depth. Considerable vetting resulted in identifying a four-day immersion experience.

Scheduling senior leaders to attend a two-hour workshop can be tough for any business; having them participate in a four-day learning experience triggers conversations about justifiable expense. After much feasibility discussion among the executive team, one leader acquiesced. He would attend with this caveat: he had to leave early. The CEO stepped in, and made his expectations clear. Every executive on the team would pilot the program. All would attend the entire four days. And *no one* would be leaving early.

Courage isn't fearlessness. Courage is taking action despite fear. In the lead-up to the four-day event, Valle-Yañez had her doubts. The program she recommended might not work. "I said to myself, 'If it blows up and I get fired, I'll go happily because it tells me that they are not ready.' We were already six years into the journey, and I thought, 'If they are not ready now, then they'll never be ready and I couldn't help them.'"

The learning experience kicked off with the entire executive team, some of their direct reports, and Valle-Yañez. Each daylong session ended with a cocktail hour—a key design feature that allowed participants to gather and talk about what they experienced that day. On the second evening, one of the senior execs approached Valle-Yañez. "He comes over with his cocktail in hand and sits down next to me and says, 'Lorie, congratulations. I commend your courage, because this was potentially a career-ending or career-limiting move.' I nodded. I already knew that going in."

Fast-forward to the fourth day. Like any well-designed off-site event, time is set aside on the last day to identify next steps. The conversation was filled with debate, just as it was when deliberating whether the entire executive team should participate in the training to begin with. This time the questions were, who in the organization should participate next and how? Some of the senior executives who had just gone through the four-day immersion thought all leaders should have the same experience. Others thought minisessions might work better. Aligning all parties in decision-making may be the pre-ferred model for many organizations. Sometimes that isn't possible or desirable when leading transformation. And that was the case in this concluding decision: All MassMutual leaders would attend this four-day immersive experience, said the CEO. And he charged Valle-Yañez with figuring out how to make that happen. Recognize when your team is not completely aligned. Engage your intuition to know when to cut off debate. Then publicly make the decision. That it will likely be an unpopular one is a hallmark of red pill leadership.

CONSENSUS DECISION MAKING

Don't confuse consensus with a unanimous decision. They are not one and the same. Unanimity equals everyone on the same page with unwavering commitment. Decision by consensus means all participants have had an opportunity to share their perspectives, but not necessarily agree with the final decision. However, consensus still requires active support of the final decision, not sabotage. It's fairly easy to spot a saboteur: the person who, when questioned about an unpopular decision, responds, "Well, that's not what I would have done. That was [insert the senior leader's name] decision."

Some employees will appreciate race work, race talk, educational opportunities, and meaningful change. Not everyone will. Expect resistance. It's part of the process. Your company may decide to focus on the low-hanging fruit. That can be a great place to start, as we describe below. If that's where the organization chooses to *stay* on its race journey, own that position with transparency. If you are a leader with positional power, respect your employees enough to be authentic about the degree of your commitment. Employees will know when you are window dressing. When you are straightforward, employees may not agree with your position, but at least you've not misrepresented it.

THE SCIENCE OF SMALL WINS

Low-hanging fruit *can be* a starting place to demonstrate action, catalyze engagement, and build momentum while your organization is building the ladder to climb to the top of the tree where discovery and voluminous opportunity await. Behavioral psychologists call this the "science of small wins." It's an effective approach for sole contributors and managers alike. "Small wins have a transformational power," says Vancouver-based educator Mehrnaz Bassiri.[13] Here's how it works: You, your team, or your organization experiences a small win. Rather than skipping over it, you notice it. Maybe it gets implemented. Then another small win happens and then another. Each small win builds upon the former. Small wins add up, which lead to greater and greater accomplishments.

If you're waiting to implement your racial diversity and inclusion strategy until there is no resistance, then pull up a chair; you will be waiting forever. Change requires letting go of the status quo. Specifically, what you learned about in Chapter 6: create–dismantle–re-create. Dismantle what exists today to examine its parts; keep what works well, toss out what doesn't, and introduce new components. You will need to look at your organization and ask, what will it take to move from where we are today to where we aspire to be? "It's a stairstep, not a single jump," says consultant Christine Robinson. "A process. It's going to take their leadership, embrace, constant shepherding, their ability and willingness to listen, and to be questioned."[14]

ANOTHER FIRST FOR
A BLACK WOMAN, PART II

In the last chapter we promised we would tell you how this story turned out.

We left off with Diane telling Gina (yes, this book's coauthor) that the Singapore government official had said "Of course, the person you send will be White." And how the folks at the J&J Santa Monica office were stunned into silence.

Diane continued talking. She described what happened in a later meeting with only J&J employees in attendance: "Since we didn't know what the government official meant when he said, 'Of course, the person you send will be White,' I said, 'I think we need to simply ask him.' So, Gina, I did that."

Gina listened intently. If the Singapore government was not interested in having a Black manager run its account, now would be the time to know before she boarded a plane and uprooted her life.

"Gina, I told the official that this account was important to J&J. It was the first time we were taking the Live for Life program overseas, and we were heavily invested in our collaborative success. In part, that means we would only send to manage the account someone whose skills and abilities were exceptional and whose project management experience was deep. I told him that person had already been identified. And she is a Black woman. Then I asked him directly, Gina, 'Is she going to have problems working and living in Singapore?'"

At the time, Singapore had three distinct cultural groups: The Chinese were the majority population in both numbers and power. And the Malays and Indians made up the two other large cultural groups. Singapore also was home to large communities of European, United States, and Australian expatriates. What the high-ranking Singapore government official told Diane was this: "In Singapore, when a dark skin person says something, it carries little weight. When a Chinese person says something, it carries stronger weight. And when a White person says something, people sit up and listen." That said, the Singapore government was interested only in the successful implementation of J&J's technology for the island nation. "It would be good for my people to see a Black person in a position of authority," the official told Diane. "It would be important for their growth."

Diane's bottom line: "Gina, only you can decide whether or not you feel comfortable moving to Singapore based on what I just told you. Know that J&J supports you. We would never ask you to live or work in a place where you felt poorly treated. If you decide to accept the position, know that at any moment, if you feel uncomfortable and want to come home, We. Will. Bring. You. Home."

Gina has never told this story before. To anyone. She's sat with that conversation and that decision for nearly three decades. She was a young professional at the time and longed for expat experience. She also wanted to be the kind of person her late father was fond of encouraging her to be, one who doesn't make "fear-based decisions." That telephone conversation with Diane felt like the trajectory of her life would be forever cemented based on which path she chose.

Of course Gina would go! What did she have to lose? She could always come home.

THE FINE POINTS

Workplace racial diversity and inclusion is like any other business priority. You need a strategy and specific plans to execute on it. To do this work, it's important to:

- Make it part of your business operations, not an HR or L&D (learning and development) initiative.

- Consider replacing your traditional SWOT analysis with a strategic conversation using the SOAR framework.

- Listen to your employees and engage them in the process.

- Be willing to experiment.

REFLECTION

- What's your "why," and where will you begin?
- How is your organization interrupting and/or disrupting the status quo?
- What kind of commitment have you and/or your organization made to dismantle and re-create a racially inequitable workplace?
- How can you demonstrate courage?
- What are some small wins you can highlight to continue the momentum you have created thus far?
- How involved are you and other key stakeholders in your company's strategy? Do you have a voice or role in its development or execution? How might you influence this process to make it more inclusive?

PART V

NEW POLICIES, NEW PRACTICES

ndividual decision making by leaders who embrace a diverse and inclusive workplace is admirable, but the real work must be undertaken at the institutional level.

"I appreciate that you don't want to dismiss or be overly critical of anything that has happened before," Prudential's chief marketing officer Susan Somersille Johnson shared with us in an interview, "but last year I had a real wake-up call when a CEO said to me, 'I've been going to diversity training for 30 years, and it's not working.' We've been trying to change people, which is important too, but it's only part of it."[1]

In Chapter 3 you learned that diversity, equity, and inclusion have evolved since the 1960s. And, much of the focus has been on education, training, and awareness building.

What organizations haven't devoted equal attention to is how to change the system of work—business policies and practices—to create a racially diverse, inclusive, and equitable workplace. That is the focus of the next four chapters.

Joanna Barsh, who self-identifies as White, has worked with hundreds of corporations during her 32-year career at the global consulting firm McKinsey. She's interviewed over 500 men and women at more than 100 companies since 2004. "Have we inadvertently or explicitly created policies, practices, and structures that consistently make it harder for some people than others to get ahead at work?," asks Barsh. "Almost every company I've ever visited has embedded in the institution things that make it harder."[2]

Executive coach Leslie Ashford, referring to her role as head of talent for a global financial services company before she retired, said,

"DEI consultants did a good job explaining the business case, but they didn't tell you about the difficult and raggedy things you need to know and will encounter. They would do the workshops, but they didn't dig in to assess where our culture is today and where we are going, and they certainly didn't look at our policies and practices."[3] In this section we share some of the best practices we learned from our research and interviews with a broad swath of chief executive officers, chief DEI officers, and other business leaders who have been at this work for decades, as well as others who are newer to the scene and are challenging old assumptions.

We've organized the chapters by the life cycle of the workforce: from where we recruit, who moves on to the interview phase, and who is ultimately offered a position and for how much, to onboarding, professional development, and promotions. We also examine how you can engage in the company's race work, multiple stakeholders—your board, community, suppliers, customers, and employees. Finally, we show how seemingly simple actions, such as selecting employees to participate on high-profile panels and projects, and in professional development programs, send powerful messages that no words, public statements, or philanthropy can adequately convey.

"You can't just stop at programmatic efforts," advises EVERFI's CEO Ray Martinez, whom we introduced you to in Chapter 2. "It needs to be a part of our institutional framework so that we're constantly reviewing policies that drive equitable opportunities for everybody."[4]

There's a lot to unpack. Let's get started.

CHAPTER 9

RECRUIT LIKE BILLY BEANE

Look for Talent
Where Others Are Not

Please help others rise. Greatness comes not from a position but from helping build the future. We have an obligation to pull others up.

INDRA NOOYI
Indian American businesswoman,
former CEO of PepsiCo
and now Board Director[1]

Savvy sports coaches don't recruit solely from top college programs, expensive camps, or well-known high schools. They head out to the public playgrounds and recreational fields to scout their next talented players.

Billy Beane, executive vice president of the Oakland Athletics, revolutionized methods of evaluating Major League Baseball (MLB) players and recruits. The subject of Michael Lewis's book *Moneyball: The Art of Winning an Unfair Game* and the Academy Award–nominated movie *Moneyball*,[2] Beane pioneered a new way to build a winning organization. He applied a unique lens to a game played the same way for over 100 years because he was looking where none of his competitors were willing to look.

"One of the best hires I ever made was a Harvard Econ major who didn't play sports, and was able to come in and look at things with an eye that wasn't biased," Beane has said in numerous articles about his recruitment approach. "You take a blind eye from the start. No assumptions. Ultimately we wanted to take all the emotion out of our decision making, which comes with your own experience."[3]

Beane competed for talent with baseball clubs that invested millions of dollars in player evaluation and salaries. His modest budget forced him to think differently about talent recruitment and management. He used objective data instead of traditional statistics and gut instincts, to make his baseball hires.

This pioneering recruitment approach ensured Beane had cognitive diversity in the recruiting room—people who wouldn't normally be there—who would serve as a built-in check for biases. Also, they had the willingness to challenge traditional models and long-held assumptions to imagine new possibilities. Unconscious bias hardwired into recruitment practices is difficult to overcome without education and training. Beane's education came from reading the academic work of Bill James, Pete Palmer, and other proponents of "sabermetrics," which is the application of statistical analysis to baseball records. You already know about *unconscious incompetence* from Chapter 5—we don't know what we don't know. That's where Beane was before he started researching sabermetrics. All he knew at that juncture was that the Oakland A's were losing and he couldn't compete using conventional wisdom.

Studying sabermetrics was Beane entering the learning stage of *conscious incompetence*. He now knew what he didn't know. Recall from Chapter 5 that this is often the most difficult stage of learning because we are aware of our knowledge gaps and that feels uncomfortable. In the next stage, *conscious competence*, we've assimilated what we've learned, feel more competent, and now want to apply that proficiency to close the gap.

Conscious competence came in the form of Beane's "best hire," Harvard-educated statistician Paul DePodesta, who was skillful at analytics and familiar with baseball statistics. Beane said, "I wanted somebody who could make sense of all of this data. Simply put, someone who enjoyed doing math."

The two mined data on hundreds of individual players, and discovered statistics highly predictive of how many runs a player would score. Though these numbers weren't traditionally valued by baseball scouts, Beane realized this meant that players who scored high on these statistics were likely to be undervalued by the market. That's where he went looking, where his MLB competitors were not—players whose stats suggested they would score runs but who were under the radar of other teams. As Beane began to acquire such players, the A's started to win, often beating teams with much bigger salary budgets. By "turning a baseball team into a mathematical formula," in 2002 the A's won the American League West division and had a 20-game winning streak, setting what was then an American League record.

The last stage of the conscious competence learning model— *unconscious competence*—is where Beane lives these days. The A's have been among the most efficient winners in baseball under Beane. Between 1999 and 2016, the A's won 1,547 games, among the most in baseball, according to Baseball Reference, a website that provides baseball statistics for every player in Major League Baseball history.[4] The only team to win more was the New York Yankees with 1,690 wins. However, each Yankees win cost $2 million on average, according to Beane, based on the team's payroll, whereas each A's win cost just $760,000.[5]

In the *unconscious competence* stage, we become so competent that we no longer have to think about our actions or behaviors. They become second nature. This is certainly true for Beane, whose life changed after author Michael Lewis penned *Moneyball*. Beane is internationally recognized and a sought-after speaker, not as a baseball executive but a business leader.

"We didn't invent anything," Beane notes. There were no "secrets." The MLB culture was so insulated, nobody was willing to use the ideas of the sabermetrics pioneers that had been published since 1977. Based on detailed data on baseball players available since the 1800s, for decades these pioneering academics had been publishing about inefficiencies in the game that included evaluating skills that were not essential to winning. The regression analysis used by the Oakland A's was a 150-year-old technique that could have been easily calculated with 1980s' computers.[6] More than Beane looking where no one else was looking, he had the courage to use what he learned. The analytics advised against the conventional wisdom of how to run a successful baseball team. As a result, Beane met with enormous resistance as he changed recruitment approaches within his own organization. Moneyball "succeeded for the Oakland A's not because of data analytics but because of a leader who understood the analytics' potential and changed the organization so it could deliver on that potential."[7]

It's not only MLB. For example, many business recruiters regularly tap from four-year, predominantly White institutions (PWIs), as they have for decades. When asked why there are no BIPOC candidates for a particular position, recruiters often respond with "We couldn't find any for this position."

Company executives often perpetuate this myth. For example, in a company meeting and later in an email, Wells Fargo chief executive Charles Scharf told employees that the bank had trouble reaching diversity goals because "the unfortunate reality is that there is a very limited pool of Black talent to recruit from."[8]

That's not true. Ted Fleming, head of talent development for a Fortune 5 company and bestselling author of *Develop: 7 Practical Tools to Take Charge of Your Career*, tells recruiters and executives, "You couldn't find anyone for this position because you don't have an expansive network."[9]

Kenneth J. Bacon, a former mortgage industry executive who is on the boards of Comcast Corporation, Ally Financial Inc., and Welltower Inc., was more direct in a CNBC report: "There is an amazing amount of Black talent out there. If people say they can't find it, they aren't looking hard enough or don't want to find it."[10]

If you are under the impression that there is a lack of BIPOC talent, next time you look at your roster of interviewees, ask yourself, "Does it look like the United States?" That's the question a retired director of human resources, also from the mortgage industry, suggested organizations ask to create more racially diverse candidate pools. "We did this before we sent the candidate slate to the hiring manager for further consideration, a retired HR director told us. "That mantra, 'Look like the United States,' encouraged us to dig deeper and expand our network."[11]

Here are suggestions for how you can begin to do the same. Have you searched LinkedIn for groups? The Society of Hispanic Professional Engineers has its own LinkedIn page. It was founded in Los Angeles in 1974 by a group of engineers employed by the city. Their objective was to form a national organization of professional engineers to serve as role models in the Hispanic community. Maybe your business is embarking on succession planning for your senior legal counsel or needs an attorney for your board. Tap into NAPABA, the National Asian Pacific American Bar Association. NAPABA is the preeminent professional development organization and voice for 50,000 Asian Pacific American attorneys, judges, law professors, and law students. The organization has chapters across the United States, each with its own web presence.

Another way to expand your pipeline and find more racially diverse candidates is to conduct a Google search by profession. For example, the term "Black Accountants" led us, the coauthors, here: "In December 1969, nine African-American men met in New York City to discuss the unique challenges and limited opportunities they faced in the accounting profession," begins the formation history of the National Association of Black Accountants (NABA) on its website.[12] "In that year, there were only 136 African-American Certified Public Accountants (CPAs) out of a total of 100,000 in the United States." Today, NABA represents more than 200,000 Black professionals in the fields of accounting and finance.

Whatever the particular training required for a professional trade, there is likely to be a Black, Brown, or people of color organization that supports it. Black accountants, engineers, lawyers, and architects all have their own associations. The National Society of Black Engineers (NSBE) was founded in 1975 at Purdue University, in West Lafayette, Indiana.[13] With more than 30,000 members worldwide, NSBE is one of the largest student-run organizations in the United States. Its activities center on improving the recruitment and retention of Black and other engineers of color in both academia and industry. In 1990, the Society of Black Architects launched in the United Kingdom. There are professional associations for Black journalists (need a talented professional for your corporate communications team?) and Black doctors (seeking a medical director for your insurance corporation or hospital board?). Graphic designers, chemists, filmmakers, psychologists, geophysicists, and every other profession imaginable has its own association for nearly every BIPOC group. We've listed more than a dozen in the Additional Resources section of this book to give you a jump-start.

Black professionals are everywhere. Tenured Wall Street professional Lauren Holland chairs a word-of-mouth network called "Wall Street Friends," which has its own website.[14] It includes 8,000 members from communities of people of color. In 2020 she sent out more job posts to those professionals than in the last five years.

Today, just 1 percent of venture-backed startups are founded by Black entrepreneurs.[15] For years, venture capitalists (VCs) and founders have asked Kobie Fuller, general partner at Upfront Ventures, a Los

Angeles–based venture capital firm, for advice about where they can find amazing Black talent. His answers were limited to people in his network and a few associations. As a Black VC, he wanted better visibility into his own community and couldn't believe that a centralized network of Black professionals didn't exist yet. So he cofounded one.

Valence is an online network of 10,000 Black professionals concentrated in the tech industry.[16] "Despite an increasing focus on representation across industries, only 3% of Silicon Valley's workforce population is Black," writes the Valence team on its website.[17] Valence's stated mission is to "create new paths to success for Black professionals." Its vision: "Generations of Black Professionals skilled in the art of business; closing the racial wealth gap."

Also, check out OneTen: "A coalition of leading executives who are coming together to upskill, hire and advance one million Black individuals in the United States over the next 10 years into family-sustaining jobs with opportunities for advancement."[18] They connect employers with talent partners and leading nonprofits that support development of diverse talent. The multiracial founding leaders include Ken Frazier, former chairperson and CEO of Merck; Kenneth Chenault, former chairperson and CEO of American Express; Ginni Rometty, executive chairperson at IBM; and Ken Sharer, former CEO of Amgen. The nearly 50 companies participating in the OneTen coalition include Target, PepsiCo, Merck, Northrup Grumman, Berkshire Hathaway, Cargill, HP, Lowe's, Whirlpool, J&J, and Synchrony. As noted on its website, "OneTen is not just philanthropy. Rather it is a coalition of leaders across industries who are committed to ensuring that Black talent with the skills and aptitude to earn success also have the opportunity to achieve success."[19]

Black professionals. Asian professionals. Latino professionals. Multiracial professionals. They are omnipresent. It's OK if you have only one fill-in-the-blank-with-race friend. Ask that friend about the countless professional organizations, clubs, networks, sororities, and fraternities that they are either a member of or know about. Then reach out. Embrace the possibilities. Expand your networks beyond the transactional. Deepen your engagement through lived experience.

Seeking assistance in racially diversifying your senior executive recruitment? Bridge Partners can help. Bridge Partners is a BIPOC-owned retained executive search firm that engages an inclusive search process from start to finish. In short, it purposefully brings diverse leaders to the table.[20] The racially diverse team of partners have unique, varied backgrounds and extensive global networks. They are able to maximize coverage of the current marketplace to swiftly locate, engage, and assess highly skilled executives.

Looking to recruit from diverse colleges and universities? Seek out those institutions with the designation MSI and HSI.

"MSIs are institutions of higher education that serve minority populations," writes the US Department of the Interior on its Office of Civil Rights page.[21] "They are unique both in their missions and in their day-to-day operations. Some of these colleges and universities are located in remote regions of the country; others serve urban neighborhoods. Some are only a few decades old, others have been striving for more than a century to give their constituents the social and educational skills needed to overcome racial discrimination and limited economic opportunities."

MSIs include Historically Black Colleges and Universities (HBCUs), established prior to 1964, for the primary purpose of educating African Americans. There are 91 four year and 17 two year HBCUs in the United States.

Also, there is a plethora of BIPOC sororities and fraternities you can tap into for talent. For example, Zeta Phi Beta, is a 101-year-old Black sorority. Yes, it's a professional network and potential source of a more diverse candidate pool. It is also historically significant. Zeta Phi Beta is one of the "Divine Nine," so nicknamed because it consists of nine historically Black sororities and fraternities that form the National Pan-Hellenic Council founded at Howard University on May 10, 1930. The university was established in 1867, two years after the abolition of slavery.[22]

Founded in the years after the American Civil War and concentrated in the southern United States, HBCU sororities and fraternities help members land the best internships that lead to the best jobs after graduation, just like Ivy League sororities and fraternities do. These sororities and fraternities also work to advance the opportunities of future generations through community service and philanthropy.

The existence of these networks that descend from HBCUs is important because for a century after the end of slavery in the United States in 1865, most colleges and universities in the South prohibited all Black and Brown people and African Americans from attending. In other parts of the country, the majority of higher education institutions were predominantly White. Formed during the period of segregation in the United States prior to the Civil Rights Act, PWIs limited the admission of Black students.[23]

Workplace comments such as "Slavery was 400 years ago, get over it" show a need for employees to educate themselves beyond the singular United States narrative that obscures racism within collegiate institutions meant to educate. In reality, they preserve the racially inequitable status quo.

Hispanic-Serving Institutions (HSIs) are another example of MSIs. HSIs are accredited, post-secondary, higher educational institutions with at least 25 percent total full-time enrollment of Hispanic undergraduate students. HSIs include four-year and two-year, public and private educational institutions, and enroll 40 percent of all Hispanic American students of higher education. There are 274 institutions of higher education defined as HSIs using the criteria defined by the White House Hispanic Prosperity Initiative.[24]

Another example of MSIs are Tribal Colleges and Universities (TCUs). Presently, there are 32 fully accredited TCUs in the United States.[25] Located mainly in the Midwest and Southwest, TCUs service approximately 30,000 full- and part-time students.

The Asian American and Native American Pacific Islander-Serving Institutions (AANAPISIs) program[26] is a federally designated MSI program. "The AANAPISI program provides grants and related assistance to AANAPISIs to enable such institutions to improve and expand their capacity to serve Asian Americans and Native American

Pacific Islanders and low-income individuals. To qualify for an AANAPISI grant, an institution must have at the time of application, an enrollment of undergraduate students that is at least ten percent Asian American and Native American Pacific Islander."[27]

SPIKING BEANE'S RECRUITMENT STRATEGY

He holds a master of fine arts from New York University's Tisch School of the Arts. He also teaches a master's series there in directing strategies. His undergraduate degree is from Morehouse College, an HBCU located near downtown Atlanta. "The House," as alumni collegially refer to it, was founded in 1867. Notable Morehouse graduate and Oscar-winning director Spike Lee ran into "We can't find any" during the production of his 1992 film *Malcolm X* starring Denzel Washington.

"We were crewing up and I had my meeting with the Teamsters," Lee shared in an online directing class one of the coauthors, Gina, participated in.[28] On movie sets, Lee explained, Teamsters Union members drive the production trucks. "I said, 'Do you have any Black Teamsters?'" When the Teamsters representatives said no, Lee indicated he had contacts who could and would be ready to drive the trucks on the day the movie shoot began. "A week later, miraculously, they found some Black Teamsters," Lee laughed. He advises, "We, as a people, underestimate our power. When you're in a position to give a qualified person a gig in an industry that's not set up for them to be in, you've got to do that." Lee would not make a movie about a Black activist without Black Teamsters. He made it happen by leveraging his power as a well-known movie director. Nearly 30 years after the production of *Malcolm X*, we wondered if the racial makeup of the Teamsters Union, which is now 1.4 million strong, had changed. What we learned is there are thousands of Black members; however, there is a dearth of Black leadership. As of November 2019, Teamsters for a Democratic Union (TDU) reported that out of the 400 locals, "only 17 are led by African Americans. Teamsters deserve leadership that looks like the membership and a union that fights for social and economic justice for all workers."[29] We visited the Teamsters website and also learned that of its 24 executive board members, only one is African American.[30]

And speaking of organized groups, lots of professional networking happens on the green. If you're a golfer, think Augusta National Golf Course in Georgia, home of the prestigious Masters Tournament. It was 11 years after the passage of the Civil Rights Act that was supposed to end segregation that the club allowed its first Black competitor. Another 26 years would pass before admitting its first Black member.

The myth of "There aren't any" and overt bias during the hiring process (as you will see in Chapter 10) cause some professionals of color to get creative about getting their foot in the door.

WHAT'S IN A NAME

In her 2018 memoir, *I'm Still Here: Black Dignity in a World Made for Whiteness*,[31] US author Austin Channing Brown writes, "In this society where we believe a name tells us everything we need to know about someone's race, gender, income, and personality, my parents decided to outwit everyone by giving their daughter a White man's name." At age seven, after a librarian hadn't believed Austin's library card belonged to her—"Are you sure this is your card?"—Austin insisted her mother tell her why she and her father gave her that name.

"We loved it," Austin's mother told her seven-year-old. "One day you will have to apply for jobs. We knew that anyone who saw it before meeting you would assume you are a White man. We just wanted to make sure you could make it to the interview."

Dr. Katherine DeCelles, who is the James M. Collins Visiting Associate Professor of Business Administration at Harvard Business School, found that some African Americans toned down mentions of race when applying for a job. For example, dropping the word "Black" from a membership in a professional society for Black engineers. Others omitted impressive achievements altogether, such as nixing the mention of a prestigious scholarship in a résumé for fear it would reveal race. In DeCelles's two-year study, she found that different groups used different Whitening techniques.[32] For example, Asian applicants often changed names to sound more Western, like substituting "Luke" for "Lei." Some concealed their race because they worried that employers might be concerned about a language barrier. DeCelles noted that applicants can't prove their English proficiency on a résumé scan but can do so at the interview.

DeCelles and her coauthors found employers whose job postings included words like "equal opportunity employer" or "minorities are strongly encouraged to apply" can give BIPOC candidates the impression that it's safe to reveal their race on their résumés.

To test whether BIPOC candidates Whiten less often when they apply for jobs with employers that seem diversity-friendly, the researchers split participants into two groups. They asked one group to craft résumés for jobs where the ads included pro-diversity statements. The other group wrote résumés for ads that didn't mention diversity.

The researchers found BIPOC candidates were half as likely to Whiten their résumés when applying for jobs with employers who said they care about diversity than with employers who did not explicitly mention diversity in the job posting. However, applicants who disclosed their race hurt their chances of being considered. A major outcome of the study found that employers claiming to be pro-diversity discriminated against résumés with racial references as much as employers who didn't mention diversity at all in their ads.

> Organizations may value diversity, but those values haven't been translated from the person who writes the job description to the one screening the résumés.

"So much of what takes place, I believe, is unconscious," says project manager Cyndy Woodman at biotech firm Genentech.[33]

Woodman took an unconscious bias workshop that she found "*Very eye opening!*" During a group breakout, participants evaluated résumés to determine whom they'd hire. What they didn't know: every résumé was the same; only the names were different. The wide range of responses to each résumé was prodigious.

DeCelles agrees that organizations may value diversity, but those values haven't been translated from the person who writes the job description to the one screening the résumés.

LITTLE THINGS ADD UP TO BIG RESULTS

"Above the glass ceiling is a concrete ceiling," say architects Elsie Owusu and Shawn Adams.[34] Only 1 percent of British architects are Black. Elsie Owusu was born in Ghana, and co-led the refurbishment of the United Kingdom's Supreme Court and London's Green Park tube station. Advice given to her in the 1970s by a mentor: when asked what she would do once qualified, she must reply that she's going home to Africa to help her people. Owusu reminded her mentor that Brixton (a UK city) was her home. Her mentor's response: "If they think you want to stay here as a qualified Black architect and work in the United Kingdom, they'll be less likely to give you a place, because they'll think you're going to compete with 'home students.'"

Millions of young people, especially in communities of color, are often written off for jobs because they don't, won't, or can't conform to the mainstream status quo. Yet they possess qualities businesses seek such as innovative thinking, risk taking, and initiative. Look to organizations that mentor middle schoolers and high schoolers to fuel your recruitment pipeline. If you want to attract and retain talent, look where your competitors are not. Think like Billy Beane.

That's what Nereida Perez did when developing McCormick's global diversity and inclusion strategy. To recruit candidates that look like the markets they represent means stepping beyond the usual pipeline and not "recruiting for one position, seven candidates who look alike or all graduated from similar schools."[35] Beane articulated his strategy to key stakeholders in his MLB organization with metric specificity. Perez emphasizes the importance of creating strong partnerships between all parties involved in the recruiting and hiring process: "Your talent acquisition and talent management teams and your HR folks must ready themselves for conversations around goals and objectives with hiring managers."

Everett Harper, Truss's CEO and cofounder, sums up recruiting efforts this way: "It's a whole bunch of simple little things that do take some investment, but tend to pay off because you have built trust with these networks."[36] These "simple little things" include appearing on panels and sharing articles and job postings on special networks including Slack groups, Facebook, and LinkedIn. These "little things" add up to big results. Currently Truss's workforce is 55 percent women, and over 35 percent are BIPOC employees and people who identify as LGBTQ+. Those are impressive numbers, particularly for an industry that is still predominantly White and male. When you break down those metrics, you also discover that 33 percent of the ownership and 20 percent of the leadership team are Black.[37]

We were curious if working from home due to the Covid-19 pandemic presented an obstacle for people in expanding their networks. We learned that as workers are becoming more adept at using digital technology like Zoom, Microsoft Teams, and WebEx to connect with coworkers, in some ways it has made it easier to expand professional networks. "In the past, the people you met and socialized with at work were the folks confined to the space at your office," says Heather Bodington of CVS Health,[38] whom you met in Chapter 6. "Now, by leveraging these digital tools to communicate with each other, we're broadening our reach. I've met people in Denver, Phoenix, and Chicago that I probably would not have interacted with or even met without these types of platforms," says Bodington, who prior to the pandemic worked out of CVS Health's office in Burlington, Massachusetts. The pandemic may have isolated us physically, but we are more connected digitally, which expands our networks.

No one is a prophet in one's own land, goes the saying. Not because employees lack the wisdom or skills that an organization seeks. Rather, the organization is blind to their gifts because the package is familiar. That's what happens with insular networks. The people in them don't know what they don't know. Move yourself along the conscious competence learning continuum. Expose yourself to new and different communities to know what you don't know and ultimately know well what you now know. This will enhance your ways of seeing uniquely, like Billy Beane.

THE FINE POINTS

We don't know what we don't know. Until we expose our unconscious biases, hiring racially diverse candidates will remain elusive. However, before you can hire racially diverse candidates, you must find them first, which requires you to look where others may not:

- Search beyond your own social clubs and circles to get referrals for more racially diverse candidates.

- If you typically recruit from PWIs that are four-year private colleges and Ivy League schools, be sure your internal and external recruiters establish relationships with HBCUs, MSIs, HSIs, and two-year community colleges.

- Tap multicultural professional societies both inside and outside the university setting.

- Advertise in multicultural media outlets instead of those in the mainstream.

- Branch out on LinkedIn. LinkedIn has advised for years to "connect only with people you know." Huh? How on earth are you going to expand your network if you do that? Networking is not solely a numbers game. The point of networking is to grow your professional and social communities along lines that expand your perspective and worldview.

- Contribute to racially diverse forums by writing articles about your company's inclusive culture and goals to bring more racial diversity to the table.

- Start an internship program for college students and also for middle schoolers (yes, you read that correctly—some of them have their own businesses) and high schoolers to serve as a pipeline for racially diverse talent.

- If you are able to recruit racially diverse candidates but find that they don't have the years of experience you are seeking, start an apprenticeship program for early-in-career employees.

- Tap your frontline and plant operations staff such as housekeeping, dining services, facilities, and customer service. There's a tendency to overlook these areas when searching for talent within organizations. This in turn, preserves the status quo. Potentially viable candidates will forever remain invisible to you if you believe that the only ways of getting ahead in life are through a college degree, shiny résumé, and an old-boy network.

REFLECTION

- What are you or your company already doing well to recruit and hire more racially diverse employees?

- What else can you do to tap into more racially diverse networks?

- The next time you hear "We couldn't find any people of color" to fill a particular position, will you remain silent, or will you be brave, seize the micro-opportunity and turn the discussion into a teachable moment?

- Whom do you need to collaborate with to be sure your recruiting process is racially equitable?

- If you live or work outside the United States, identify as recruitment sources schools, associations, and networks outside the norm.

CHAPTER 10

HIRING MADE VISIBLE

Individual Decisions, Institutional Changes

We have to stop believing it when people say "Black women or women of color can't be aggressive in the workplace." That's a dog whistle for us to be quiet. What we are is passionate. We have to be done with being quiet and start defining what it means to show up and take up space in a meeting, on a project, and in an organization. We have to be bold. We have to be courageous. We have to stand and make a clearing for us to create, whether it's within an organization or we decide to move out and start our own business.

KAREN SENTEIO
Black American, Executive Coach[1]

On the southwest side of Boston lies Roxbury, one of the twenty-three official neighborhoods in the city. It is predominantly Black. The year was 1988. Gang members. A stray bullet. A murder. An all-too-familiar story in US cities. Only this time the stray bullet killed 12-year-old Darlene Tiffany Moore. One eyewitness placed 23-year-old Shawn Drumgold, a Black man, at the scene of the crime but was unable to identify his photo out of a lineup. At trial, however, the witness identified him after images of Drumgold's face spread throughout the media. A jury convicted him of first-degree murder and sentenced him to life in prison.[2]

After 14 years behind bars, Drumgold was released, not for good behavior, but wrongful conviction. His exoneration followed the discovery that police failed to share key pieces of investigative information with the defense. This included compensating a witness in exchange for his testimony, and having identified a viable suspect after Drumgold's arrest.

In the previous chapter you learned about how unconscious bias plays out in the recruiting process. Now imagine the job search hurdles facing a Black man who was wrongly accused of murder.

Jim Ansara, who at the time was CEO of Shawmut Design and Construction, saw Drumgold's case on the news. Ansara reached out to Drumgold and said, "If you want to work, you can come work here." And he did.[3]

Manuel Meza, whom you met in Chapter 5, leads a 200-person global markets organization for one of the biggest banks in Mexico City. Meza also believes in giving people a chance. Similar to some companies in the United States that tend to favor Ivy League graduates, Meza explained the bank favors knowledge workers hired from private universities. When checking the company statistics, Meza noted that "only 20 percent of our hires came from public universities, and they are hard workers."[4] That percentage was "not acceptable," Meza told us, and he set out to deliberately hire people from previously untapped backgrounds and universities. "I wanted more diversity on the team and to provide opportunities to people who don't typically have access."

In addition to attending public universities, many of the new hires also come from social environments where they've been under-exposed to different worldviews. So Meza lobbied for a six-month internship at headquarters in Europe, to expose them to new experiences and expand their networks.

Upgrading business skills and social and cultural exposure are core facets of many leadership development programs in companies around the world. Rather than provide this exposure to people who already have access to it, Meza made the invisible visible—the bias toward new hires from private universities and whose life experiences were typically associated with private education—and hired outside the box.

We wondered, if hiring people from public universities wasn't a parent-company initiative, what motivated Meza? "Why not stick to the way things were always done?" we asked.

"Now we're getting more philosophical and personal," he responded. "My dad comes from the north of Mexico, on the Pacific coast, in a town called Mazatlán. He is the oldest of nine brothers and sisters, and they come from, well, let's say they were not wealthy. When my dad turned 18, he moved to Mexico City to study architecture on a scholarship, and specialized in maintenance. He became a successful career professional who made his way up the social ladder." Meza's father was at one time in charge of Mexico City's entire subway infrastructure.

> Racial identity, which is part of our lived experience, matters in the workplace. It shapes nearly every interaction, conversation, and business decision whether or not we are aware of it, whether or not it's visible.

"Some of my uncles who stayed in Mazatlán drove a cab. Now there is nothing wrong with driving a cab," Meza said. "But I saw how people can progress and change status and be better than their parents. I saw that my dad did it—to study on a scholarship and work, work, work. Because of that he was able to give my brother, sisters, and me better opportunities. That is something I've always had in mind. That is what has moved me ever since I've had the chance to hire people, starting 10 years ago."

Our lived experiences don't remain at home when we go to work. They infuse our being. As you read in Chapter 5, racial identity, which is part of our lived experience, matters in the workplace. It shapes nearly every interaction, conversation, and business decision whether or not we are aware of it, whether or not it's visible. It certainly shapes decisions such as the one Jim Ansara made to hire Shawn Drumgold, and Manual Meza's decision to hire graduates from public universities and provide them with professional development opportunities.

In Chapter 9, you learned how to broaden your network to find racially diverse talent. In this chapter you've thus far read about an atypical hiring decision (by a CEO) that affected a single employee. And you've read how lived experience inspired a single manager to recruit outside the norm and lobby his employer to establish a unique internship.

Now let's examine how you can *institutionalize* racially equitable hiring practices. Experiment with the six practices depicted below (see Figure 10.1). The first (1), *The Voice* method shows how to screen résumés to minimize bias. The next five are about making the invisible visible: (2) assemble diverse interview panels, (3) ask value-based questions, (4) solicit additional input from frontline employees, (5) keep your diversity values and goals top of mind when making your final hiring decision, and (6) "get loud" if you need to. The first practice: screening résumés.

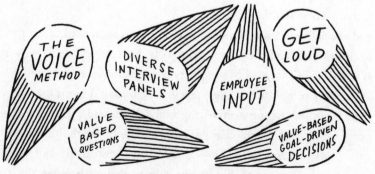

FIGURE 10.1 Six strategies to make hiring racially equitable. (*Illustration by Lucy Engelman.*)

1. USE *THE VOICE* METHOD

Have you ever seen the talent show *The Voice?* On *The Voice*, aspiring singers audition for judges whose chairs face away from the stage. This permits the judges to evaluate the artists solely on talent, not appearance and the myriad biases that stem from the lightning-fast box-checking that humans do when first meeting someone new. So what does this show have to do with hiring? *The Voice* method makes what is visible on a résumé invisible to interviewers and hiring managers.

It works like this. If you are an internal or external recruiter, remove names, gender, college name, and other identifiers from résumés before turning them over to the hiring manager to begin the interviewing process. Recruiters call this "blind recruiting." The purpose is to minimize biases by focusing hiring managers and teams on evaluating candidates' skills and work experience.

2. ASSEMBLE DIVERSE INTERVIEW PANELS

In the last chapter, we focused on ways to broaden your candidate pool to create a racially diverse slate of interviewees. You want to be sure your interview *panels*, the people who are interviewing candidates, are diverse, too. Panel members can include the staff who will be reporting to whoever is hired, peers, and other strategic partners. If you don't yet have racially diverse employees, tap into external networks to serve on your panel. Review the last chapter for where to find them. Building relationships with racially diverse professionals outside of your organization to serve on your interview panels can lead to unimagined opportunities for all parties. If you are not a hiring manager, volunteer to be a part of the interview process.

3. ASK VALUE-BASED QUESTIONS

"Without using the word 'different,' what's your definition of diversity?"[5] That's the question Fractured Atlas asks when interviewing candidates. Fractured Atlas is an organization that provides fundraising tools, educational resources, and personalized IT support to help individual artists and arts organizations.[6]

The company's ongoing work is ensuring that all employees and artists in their membership reflect the diversity of the arts community and society as a whole. Every Fractured Atlas job description includes its antiracist and anti-oppression values statement. By the time applicants get to an interview, they should be prepared to have a conversation about diversity, equity, and inclusion. "Antiracism is not just a policy, it's a set of principles against which we measure every aspect of our work," says Lauren Ruffin, Fractured Atlas's co-chief executive and external relations officer. Specifically, the organization has found that asking the question "Without using the word 'different,' what's your definition of diversity?" can be an effective way to gauge whether a job candidate is willing to commit to the collaborative effort of creating and sustaining an antiracist workplace.

Ruffin, who is Black, and Fractured Atlas co-CEO Tim Cynova, who is White, are trying to discern whether the candidate has researched the company's values. If the candidate, for example, pushes back to say they're asking the wrong question about diversity, this could be a sign of aligned values. For example, instead of *defining* diversity, the candidate may wish to discuss *how* diversity has or has not operated in his or her previous work environments. Vague responses filled with alphabet soup or no grasp of diversity as a concept does not outright disqualify the candidate at Fractured Atlas. The candidate might still show promise as an employee based on training, education, and experience specific to the desired position. There is no plug-and-play response to that question.

Rather, a strong-skilled candidate with limited understanding of diversity might still advance to second-round interviews at Fractured Atlas. In these conversations, hiring managers will ask how the candidate has promoted diversity and inclusion at previous workplaces. If the candidate is unable to share actions they've taken to interrupt systems of oppression, Cynova says it's usually a sign that there is a values misalignment between the candidate and the organization. "When an employer starts talking about racism and oppression in the workplace," Cynova says, the employer has "changed the unwritten employer-employee contract. People will say, 'I signed up to work for an innovative arts organization, and now they're requiring meetings to talk about racism.'"[7] This could cause job seekers not to apply. Also, current employees may feel like they're being asked to take on values in the workplace that they don't personally believe in.

The risk, Cynova says, is that you'll lose employees, donors, customers, and board members who are not aligned with your clearly stated workplace antiracist values. But you will lose those who are aligned if you don't. Be clear. Stand strong. Attrition will happen no matter what. Attrition incurred from clearly articulated values will benefit your business.

Similarly, keeping résumés colorful, rather than Whitening them as you read about in the previous chapter, is one way job seekers can evaluate if an employer's values are aligned with their own. Some students interviewed for DeCelles's résumé Whitening study were staunchly opposed to it. They intentionally retained racial references as a way of potentially identifying employers who might not welcome people of color.

For 30 years now, Living Cities, which you are now well acquainted with, has had the mission to improve low-income communities and the lives of people who live there. However, it has only been in the last decade that the organization has purposefully added racial equity to its competency framework. "We forced ourselves to really describe and articulate the competencies needed to do racial equity work. Now we search, recruit, and interview candidates based upon those competencies," says CEO Ben Hecht.[8] And one of these competencies is "an understanding of the role of history and its impact on the work we do." Living Cities has always asked job seekers to share what they know about the company's mission to see if they have done their homework. Now they also ask a specific question about why the organization's work is so important.

"Their knowledge of racial inequity in the United States doesn't have to be deep," says Hecht. "However, the candidate needs to display a clear willingness to learn concepts and history." This is a concrete expression of educating ourselves, introduced in Chapters 4 and 5. Self-education demonstrates commitment to doing our own inner work.

Hiring mistakes can cost a company more than six times the job's salary after calculating eclipsed expenditure of onboarding and training. That's why involving team members and business partners in the hiring process has become commonplace. Regardless of which side of the desk you are on—interviewer or interviewee—a more racially equitable interviewing process requires that we become better skilled at asking questions.

4. SOLICIT EMPLOYEE INPUT

Also, we need to dig deeper. Take your interview process a step further and solicit input from the employees the candidates interacted with during the hiring process: the employee who arranged the interview schedule and the one who greeted the candidates upon their arrival. If travel was required, seek input from the employee who met the candidates at the airport or train station. Why? To find out how the candidates treated them. Of course, candidates will present their best selves during interviews with the hiring manager and other formal interviewers, but it is when no one is looking that it matters most. How candidates engage with people of different racial and gender identities, and levels within the organization, can tell you a lot about their values and how they will lead.

> What once was a "policing exercise after the fact," says CFRA's Heather Thomas-McClellan, "is now a values exercise conducted at the moment of decision."

5. MAKE VALUE-BASED AND GOAL-DRIVEN DECISIONS

When making the final hiring decision, keep your diversity goals and values top of mind. What once was a "policing exercise and done after the fact," says CFRA's Heather Thomas-McClellan, "is now a values exercise conducted at the moment of decision. Instead of asking ourselves 'Will we be compliant at the end of the year?,' we're asking, 'Does this decision align with our diversity and inclusion values?'"[9]

6. GET LOUD

Blind recruiting. Racially diverse interview panels. Input from employees beyond the direct hiring parties. Asking value-based questions, and making value-based hiring decisions. You may face some challenges institutionalizing these racial diversity hiring practices. If so, you may need to take a stand and "get loud."

Martinez of EVERFI says, "I've personally been very loud about making sure we're taking an equitable approach when hiring and filling vacant positions. We started by letting everyone know that this is an institutional-wide priority."[10] "Everyone" meant fostering a better connection between EVERFI's senior vice president of DEI, the HR leadership, and the hiring managers to be sure they were all aligned. Next came training—on how to screen résumés to remove bias; about universities and other institutions that were recruitment feeds; on deeper questions to ask during the interview; and about the interview process itself to ensure multiple points of view. Martinez says, for EVERFI, "that's been step one in our journey."

Being "loud," as Martinez advises, can look like this: You're about to make a hiring decision for a _____ [insert any job, from frontline staff to C-suite executive]. After much vetting and multiple interviews, you've narrowed the candidate pool to two strong finalists. One is a Black female, and one is a White male. You and your interview panel believe that both candidates are equally qualified. Either one could be successful in this role at your company. To whom do you offer the job?

Let's first look at the composition of the existing team that the new hire, no matter who it is, would be joining. Is the team racially and gender diverse, or is it more homogeneous? Is this an opportunity to bring more diversity to your team? Have specific and measurable goals been set to increase the number of racially diverse employees at your company?

From our coaching experience and interviews we conducted, we know many hiring managers wrestle with decisions like these. If they offer the job to the Black woman, they worry that others will think their decision was a "diversity hire" and automatically assume that she is less qualified. If they offer the job to the White man, they worry that others will think they are perpetuating the "status quo."

What's required is putting a stake in the ground. If your company doesn't have racial diversity goals or clearly articulated values, people positioned to make hiring decisions can still create a more racially diverse and inclusive workplace. For example, say you are a coffee shop supervisor. You need to hire another barista. You recognize the business benefits of having a racially diverse workforce. Be willing to stand firm in your choice of hiring a person of color and clearly articulate it. When we can explain our decisions with candor, regardless of how popular or unpopular they may be, that's authentic leadership. And if you are not a hiring manager, you can still influence the hiring process, but only if you're willing to speak up. It's easier to sit on the sidelines and critique the lack of racial diversity than it is to "get loud." However, as we've said before, we can't solve what we don't talk about. The next time there's an open position on your team, be sure to remind your manager that he or she has an opportunity to bring more racial diversity to the organization, and offer to help source candidates.

The six companies we've featured in this chapter—Shawmut Design and Construction, a global bank in Mexico City, Fractured Atlas, Living Cities, CFRA, and EVERFI—all perform their work in an office environment. What does the hiring process look like in other work environments? Many job seekers often begin their search online. Some also go door-to-door to ask if the company is hiring. They'll have résumés in hand, or request an application to fill out. While the candidate is able to walk in the door, what happens next rests on the hiring manager who has the decision-making power.

When Canada-based journalist Andray Domise, who is Black, wrote about the 2018 arrests of two Black men at a Philadelphia Starbucks, he also shared a personal hiring story.[11] In his early twenties he worked at a cell phone shop in a local mall. One afternoon, while he and his manager worked on a sales report, a young Black man dressed in slacks and a "too-large blazer" came into the store and asked if they were hiring. "We were," recalls Domise. The manager was interviewing on average two people a day in the food court. "But as my White manager looked up at the young Black man in front of him, his eyes lingered for a moment on the man's cornrows before saying, 'Not now, but I'll take your résumé.'"

The young man handed over a résumé from the stack he carried, and thanked the manager. As the applicant turned his back to leave, Domise's manager removed a pen from his shirt pocket and marked the numbers "110" in the corner of the résumé. "When I later asked what '110' meant, my manager drew a diagonal line between the two ones, changing the three-digit code to the word 'NO.' Nothing more needed to be said between us." The company they worked for took pride in its "commitment to diversity," painstakingly outlined in the employment contract both Domise and his manager had signed, and heavily implied in its television and print marketing. "But despite all of that, I'd just watched my White manager profile a Black youth out of a job."

> It's too easy to scapegoat an individual. In doing so, we let the institution and its practices off the hook and nothing changes.

It's tempting to point to a single person—the manager in this story—as the villain. If it weren't for him, that young man might have had a chance. Or point to Domise: What do you mean "Nothing more needed to be said between us?" Why didn't he speak up? It's too easy to scapegoat an individual. In doing so, we let the institution and its practices off the hook and nothing changes. This story is not about the manager. Rather, it highlights the need to examine a *system*, one that hired and retains a manager in a position of power to racially profile prospective employees unchecked.

WHEN YOU'RE A COMPANY OF ONE

Say you are an independent consultant, a microenterprise with one employee—you. You might be thinking "creating a diverse workforce doesn't apply to me." But it does. As a small business owner, you wear many hats and perform myriad tasks yourself. However, you probably outsource some of your auxiliary functions. For example, how racially diverse is your accountant or financial advisor? Your IT support or web designer? Your digital marketing professional?

THE FINE POINTS

Businesses have made some progress since the Jim Crow era of 1877 to 1964[12] when Black, Brown, and people of color were by law denied jobs in the United States. Today, newspaper ads no longer read "Blacks Need Not Apply." And violence is not openly exacted against BIPOC job seekers. However, the US workplace has shifted from conscious forms of racism to unconscious biases on the part of individuals who craft the policies and practices within the institutions they uphold. Ensure your hiring practices don't inadvertently limit your candidate pool. Reimagine them to create and sustain a racially diverse and equitable workplace:

- Train the people who are screening résumés for conscious inclusion to eradicate decision-making based on a quick skim of a résumé or group stereotypes.

- Consider removing information about race, age, gender, and other demographic identifiers from résumés before sending them to interviewers and hiring managers.

- Include one or more questions about diversity, history of race/racism, and company values.

- Use objective data collected during the interview process, and be sure to review your diversity goals and values before making a hiring decision.

- No matter your position, speak up when you notice unfair hiring practices. And if need be, *get loud* to ensure hiring a racially diverse workforce remains a priority for your business.

- Don't make hiring decisions in a vacuum. Involve members of the team they will join if hired, and other department employees who will work with them. Also, be sure to include feedback from employees of all hierarchical levels whom candidates interact with at each stage of the process.

REFLECTION

- What are you or your company already doing effectively in your hiring process?

- Given your role, what's one actionable step you can take to create a more inclusive hiring process and guard against conscious or unconscious biases?

- Who is someone you want to give a chance to? Someone in whose life you could make a truly positive difference—by hiring them?

- If you are seeking a new job yourself, what question(s) will you ask to uncover if the hiring manager and company share your values?

- If you are an independent consultant or other small business owner, what can you do to hire racially diverse suppliers?

CHAPTER 11

NO SECRETS IN PAY AND PROMOTIONS

Close the Wage Gap; Crack Open the Concrete Ceiling

The reason why we conducted salary transparency was a diversity issue.

EVERETT HARPER
Black American, a cofounder and the CEO of Truss[1]

What do a multinational supermarket chain, industrial machinery company, software developer, and social media innovator have in common besides high profitability? They've all implemented pay transparency, which is the professional way of saying everybody knows everybody else's salary.

Like race, compensation is yet another *undiscussable* in the workplace. We were all taught that it's impolite to talk about money. And certainly not to share information about how much we earn with others, especially coworkers. Why? Salary discussions may expose gross inequities that have nothing to do with our experience and knowledge, and instead have more to do with our race, age, gender, ethnicity, if we are disabled in some way, and/or our ability to negotiate. Companies that have performed compensation due diligence still fear that sharing salary information will result in employees clamoring for raises or leaving for a better-paying job.

Semco Group, Truss, Whole Foods, and SumAll—companies as diverse in size as they are in the products and services they offer— have turned pay secrecy into a transparent process.[2] Let's see what we can learn from a couple of these companies.

TRANSPARENCY IN ACTION

Visionary business leader Ricardo Semler grew Semco Group from $4 million in annual revenue to over $200 million in about 20 years. Based in Brazil, Semco Group was a centrifuge manufacturer founded in 1953 by Antonio Curt Semler, Ricardo's father. When Ricardo took over the firm, he modernized management practices and expanded the company by moving into the service sector, including environmental consultancy, facilities management, real estate brokerage, and inventory support.

During this expansion, the company worked with a variety of technology partners and developed a sophisticated joint venture model that combined Semco management practices with the partners' expertise and product lines. This fusion of skill sets created the business model that has been so successful in the Brazilian market.

In 2012, Semco Group became Semco Partners, transitioning into a structure featuring six directors who have worked together for many years. More about that later.

Early in Semler's tenure as CEO, several Semco employees felt dissatisfied with their salary levels. Known for his employee-friendly and somewhat radical ideas, Semler wanted to address the issue. He and his then HR leader came up with what some today, 40 years later, still consider a revolutionary idea: why not let employees define their own salaries?[3] To do that, what would employees need to know? It turns out there are only three pieces of information: how much people make inside the company, how much people make somewhere else in a similar business, and how much people make in the general marketplace. Semco provided that information.

We know what you're thinking: *you've got to be kidding!* Yes, in the beginning there was disbelief. When Semler and the HR manager proposed this idea in a meeting with all Semco managers, people thought that the idea was crazy and that it would cause too much disruption and discontent. The plan faced a lot of skepticism and resistance from management. However, with sustained effort over time, managers warmed to the idea and were ready to implement it.

Operationalizing pay transparency is in the details, and at Semco it looked like this: A computer was set up in the company's cafeteria where an employee could view how much he or she currently earns, what the additional compensation in benefits was, how much revenue the company was taking in, what the profit margins from that revenue were, how much other employees inside the company made, and how much employees in similar positions made in the marketplace. Armed with that information, the employee was then allowed to set their own salary. Semco also turned this information sharing into a teachable moment. Employees often feel like they're underpaid. In today's world, they have access to external, marketplace data. What they often don't have access to is internal data for pay comparison with their peers. Semco shared that internal data. And also detailed for employees the various considerations that went into defining pay ranges.

A company's effort such as this, to collate data and provide salary ranges or the average market rate for every position, fosters an atmosphere of trust and safety. Employees now have all the information needed to ensure they are being fairly compensated.

Next for Semco came a "self-set" pay approach, where nearly 25 percent of the employees opted to set their own salaries.[4] The process for self-set pay began with employees completing an evaluation form, helping them to focus on their roles and their value. Before suggesting what they believe they should be paid, employees were asked to consider four criteria: what they think they could make elsewhere, what others with similar responsibilities and skills make at Semco, what friends with similar backgrounds make, and how much money they need to live. To support this process, in addition to Semco sharing current salaries, it also shared with the entire company the results of the "self-set" pay surveys employees completed.

Did people pay themselves ridiculous salaries? No. It turned out that credible, well-researched information and peer pressure kept pay at industry norms. From that point forward, Semco employees set their own salaries, based on salary ranges culled from market research that was conducted by a trustworthy external partner.

Semco's participative approach was evident also in how it distributed profits through the company's profit-sharing program, with employees playing an active role. These approaches, and many others relating to Semco's programs and policies, continue to be radical decades after they were implemented. With intention, the company turned the old corporate hierarchy on its head by delegating as much decision power to the workforce as possible. Was the company successful? In 20 years' time, Semco grew its profitability and its workforce, from 90 to 5,000 through a period of acquisitions and joint ventures (national and international). The employee turnover rate? Two percent.

In 2001, Semler decided to change focus: "We proved that this democratic way of working worked. In fact, we proved that it worked really well. Now it was time to move on."[5] Semler wanted to see if similar approaches could be applied in other environments. That's why he started Lumiar (schools), Hotel Botanique (a luxury hotel), and Semco Style Institute (consultancy and training).

Semler operationalized this intentional transition by selling his Semco shares in 2001. And Semco Group evolved into Semco Partners, which employs approximately 200 people who work in the schools, hotel, and consulting company. Semler's passion is now "changing the system at the roots. We need to change the way we educate our children. If we start there, the impact of what we do can be so much bigger."

Businesses and business leaders can have significant influence on the societies in which they operate. This is one of the six reasons we described in Chapter 1 why the workplace is the perfect place to talk about race and racism.

A CONSCIOUS DECISION AND THE ART OF EXPERIMENTATION

Participative management has inspired a dedicated following, and many managers find it appealing and compelling in principle. However, it is often dismissed as utopian and naïve in the real world of conventional workplaces. If you've already dismissed this case study because you're thinking, "That's Brazil. It'll never work in my country," let's see how a US company removed secrecy from its compensation system.

"The reason why we conducted salary transparency was a diversity issue," says CEO Everett Harper,[6] whose story of Truss's origins opened up Chapter 8. "We knew women and people of color in the tech industry were being paid less for the same job. People like Erica Baker at Google and a couple of others had privately gathered data and exposed the pay disparities. So we said, "How can we solve this problem?"

How big was it? Pretty big. And not only in the tech industry. More than half a century ago, the Equal Pay Act and Title VII of the

Civil Rights Act was supposed to protect employees from pay discrimination based on race, gender, age, religion, national origin, or disability. "Equal pay for equal work" has made some progress since then, but the racial wage gap still exists. Black men and women, in particular, still earn substantially less than their White coworkers in similar positions.

In 2019, US-based compensation software and data company PayScale reported the findings from its two-year online survey of 1.8 million employees. Among the findings: Black men earned 87 percent of what non-Hispanic White men earned, and Hispanic workers had the next largest gap, earning 91 percent.[7] According to the US Census, on average all women, not parsed by race, earn 82 percent of what non-Hispanic White men earn in similar positions. When you look at the data by racial groups, Black women fare worse, earning only 63 percent of what non-Hispanic White men were paid in 2019.[8]

Most companies allow for a little wiggle room in salary negotiation. Say you negotiate a salary 5 percent higher than that of a peer who is performing the same job. Over time, that 5 percent compounds. It won't take long for the gap to grow larger and larger, especially if you have stellar negotiation skills and land a higher salary. However, addressing the wage gap one individual at a time is not going to solve the problem. Closing the wage gap requires institutional change.

Everybody can see everybody's salary. Harper is adamant in articulating this clarity. "Doing it halfway," he says, "doesn't make sense if you're trying to be transparent."

Truss consciously decided that its compensation strategy be both transparent and simple. "A big part of the work was testing our assumptions and asking folks if they would have a problem if we made salaries public," says Harper. "Would they leave if we did? Luckily we got overwhelming support."

But not before doing "the work before the work" (as we delved into in Part II). The next part of the experiment was figuring out the details of pay transparency. Harper and his cofounders knew their experiment would fail if it felt like something they were doing *to* people versus *for* people. So they assembled employee committees throughout the company to conduct research, collect salary data, perform leveling, and surface contrary opinions. Truss kept employees informed throughout the process. "Wash, rinse, repeat," says Harper, referring to the communication plan and frequent updates. By the time the company launched pay transparency, it was no big deal.

Did Truss get it completely right the first time? Of course not. As you might recall from Chapter 8, Harper is a big believer in experimentation. At the heart of experimentation is making mistakes. And Truss did. Assessing what was and wasn't working was all part of the learning for tweaking the process as they went. Truss's approach to experimentation has prompted other business leaders to invite Harper to participate in panels to share his company's experience. One of the most common questions posed to him is this: "Pay transparency only applies to employees, right? Not the founders or executive leadership?" No. Everybody can see everybody's salary. Harper is adamant in articulating this clarity. "Doing it halfway," he says, "doesn't make sense if you're trying to be transparent."

Harper recognizes that implementing pay transparency in a small company such as Truss is likely easier than instituting it within a large company that has been around for decades. And also because Truss holds transparency as a core value. Harper has spoken to companies with 1,000 to 10,000 employees. His advice for implementing pay transparency is always the same: "Set it up as an experiment. Be explicit that you want to learn. If you have a hypothesis that turns out to be wrong, great. Ask, 'What did we learn?' If the data validates your hypothesis, keep going and make sure that more people are on board."

PROMOTIONS AND YOUR LEADERSHIP PIPELINE

Promotions are another business practice that requires the same level of transparency as does pay to create a racially diverse and equitable workplace. The "glass ceiling" is the term commonly used to describe the invisible barrier women experience in the workplace. The term "concrete ceiling" describes the greater barriers women of color face in the workplace. Given the data below, we need to crack open the concrete ceiling for all people of color, and it begins by examining our current policies and practices, especially how promotions are handled. Despite decades of diversity programs and equal treatment laws, one of our colleagues, Javier Sanchez, a senior sales executive who self-identifies as Hispanic/Latino, shared his most burning race question with us: "Why is it that senior leadership appears to remain monochromatic?"[9]

Good question. As of October 2020, only 1 percent of the Fortune 500 CEOs are African Americans, 2.4 percent are East Asians or South Asians, and 3.4 percent are Latino.[10] To get more granular, as of May 2021, there were only three Black men[11] and two Black women[12] in the top job. They are Thasunda Brown Duckett, CEO of TIAA, the $1.3 trillion financial services giant; Marvin Ellison, CEO of Lowe's; Rosalind Brewer, CEO of Walgreens Boots Alliance, Merck CEO Kenneth Frazier who will retire in June 2021, and Rene Jones of M&T Bank. Currently, the senior leadership team of 97 percent of US companies does not reflect the country's ethnic workforce.[13]

"From where I sit, there doesn't seem to be a shortage of diverse talent within organizations," said a Black female professional who preferred to remain anonymous. "There is, however, a shortage of diverse leaders at the top of organizations."[14] She goes on to explain the disparity. For most of her career in corporate America there has been one constant: "I have never permanently worked under or reported to a leader of color." She also shared she has yet to be on a team where there were more than a handful of people of color.

In most large organizations, promotions are the outcome of a talent review process. A list of high-potential talent is compiled, and then each candidate is discussed by the executive team. To keep your biases in check, and to be sure everyone gets a fair shot, try this best practice we learned about while conducting research for this book. It demonstrates how a seemingly small action can have a big impact:

Start your next talent review, or "calibration" meeting as they are often called, by asking the leaders to write down their biases. Then remind people that we all have biases. We tend to favor people that are like us. The bias has a name: the "like-me bias." Also encourage people to focus on the strengths of the candidates and be consciously inclusive. Now here's the nuance. Who is responsible for kicking off the group discussion with this simple yet powerful exercise? The facilitator? No. The HR business partner? No. We recommend the most senior executive in the group be responsible for priming the discussion and setting the tenor of the meeting.

> Creating a racially diverse and inclusive workplace is not an HR exercise. It is core to your business strategy and requires intentionality about the racial diversity of your leadership pipeline.

By practicing conscious inclusion you increase the chances of retaining top racially diverse talent who might otherwise choose to go elsewhere because they've been passed over for promotion several times. Creating a racially diverse and inclusive workplace is not an HR exercise. It is core to your business strategy and requires intentionality about the racial diversity of your leadership pipeline. Says Heather Thomas-McClellan, CFRA Research's global head of talent (and mentioned several times earlier in the book), "When we're budgeting, we're now looking at the employees who are getting promoted. Even the CFO is asking the question, 'How do you feel about these decisions from a diversity perspective?' What was once thought of as an HR compliance exercise is now being seen as common sense and part of our decision-making process. We want to be sure as a business we are practicing what we are preaching."[15]

SPONSORS ARE DIFFERENT FROM MENTORS

In career advancement, mentorship, both formal and informal, has been a mainstay in most organizations. Typically an older, senior-level person guides, and serves as a sounding board for a younger junior-level employee. The mentee shares career challenges, and the mentor shares career advice. Reverse mentoring is also common, whereby a younger employee pairs with an older employee to share insights into contemporary culture or the latest technology.

Sponsorship is different and not quite as common. Yes, guidance is involved, but there's more. The sponsor actively advocates for the employee and seeks out growth and advancement opportunities for them. Rather than pair by age (younger and older) or gender as mentorships are often structured, sponsorships pair senior executives, who are still most often White, with BIPOC employees whom they want to develop into more senior leadership roles.

Sponsorship advocates for an individual employee when new or stretch opportunities arise. That talent review meeting we described earlier? If you are a leader in those meetings, this is your chance to "be loud," as Ray Martinez said in Chapter 10. What does sponsorship look like when institutionalized to advance a company's racial diversity goals? We asked Marianne Monte at Shawmut Design and Construction. She described it this way: "We took our typical talent review process and asked, 'Who are the women and people of color that can grow with our company? We identified 30 people to sponsor."[16]

In January 2020, Monte reported to Shawmut's board on the progress of the company's sponsorship initiative. "Thirty percent had been promoted into senior leadership positions, and the other seventy percent are continuing to work their way up the ladder with the idea that they could jump at least two levels." Monte herself sponsored one employee, Richard Hinton, who self-identifies as Black, Indian, and gay, and works in HR at Shawmut's New York office. Over the last 18 months not only has he excelled, also, he's been promoted to director of that region. After the

> When we can reframe potential threats as opportunities, we are better able to engage in productive conversations that result in constructive action.

murder of George Floyd, Shawmut doubled down on its sponsorship efforts.

We were curious if Shawmut's sponsorship initiative resulted in any backlash from its White employees, so we asked. While sponsorships for underrepresented groups didn't result in backlash, it did result in this question from the executive team: "'How do we explain to John, who is a talented employee and is White, that he's not getting sponsored?' The way we look at it is John has sponsorship mechanisms that already exist within our company," says Monte. "Of course he was hired because he had all the right skills, however, John may have been referred to us from one of our employees. Or maybe we found John because he went to the same college as someone else on the team. In both cases, a relationship already exists."

Monte continues: "There's plenty of opportunity for John to grow with the company as well, but there isn't as much opportunity for Jane or a person of color to grow because the mechanism isn't in place. So, we're putting the mechanism in place for other people who have not had access that already exists for John. That's been really eye-opening. No one is being hurt by this."

Notice what Monte didn't say. She didn't use the "P" word: "privilege." To be precise, White privilege. Instead she used the "O" word: "opportunity," which we defined in Chapter 8 when we explored the SOAR model of strategy development. When we can reframe potential threats as opportunities, we are better able to engage in productive conversations that result in constructive action. White privilege can be a lightning rod. The phrase can shut down conversations when you need them to open up. That's why SOAR is a useful tool, because it shifts the focus of any conversation, including race, from a deficit view to an asset lens.

WHAT ABOUT ME?

So far, we've focused on what the leaders of your company can do to be sure unconscious bias isn't preventing them from building a racially diverse pipeline. But what about me? you may ask. Perhaps you have been passed over for promotion one too many times. If so, as coaches we offer this advice: Be proactive. Don't keep your head down and think someone else will advocate for you. Not everyone has a sponsor. What most medium- to large-size companies do have is a process for promotions. However, just as for pay, the process is often not widely known. Make it your business to find out what it is. Ask your manager. If he or she doesn't know, ask your HR business partner. It will require work on your part.

Document your business case. Identify your accomplishments and how you have exceeded expectations. Once you present your business case to your manager and she agrees you've earned a promotion, you will probably have to wait for the next promotion cycle when these decisions are made. In many companies your manager will be required to fill out a promotion form with all the pertinent information. If he or she is not known for attention to detail, offer to complete the form. Be patient. But not too patient.

THE FINE POINTS

How much we pay and whom we promote traditionally have been closely held by HR. Not anymore. Innovative companies are turning these two processes on their head by making them transparent. No more secrets.

- Wage gaps in race and gender still persist in many companies across the United States.

- One way to close the wage gap is pay transparency.

- Reimagining compensation and promotions requires collaboration, research, experimentation, and ongoing communication. Treat this work like you would any other business project.

- Develop or reimagine your mentoring, sponsorship, and coaching practices to accelerate the development of your racially diverse leadership pipeline.

- If you believe you deserve a promotion, develop your business case; be proactive and persistent.

REFLECTION

- What are you or your company already doing effectively in compensation and promotion?
- What intrigued you about Semco, Truss, CFRA, or Shawmut's experience?
- How racially diverse are the senior levels at your company?
- What's one actionable step you can take to bring more transparency to pay and promotions at your company?

- Do you currently mentor, sponsor, or coach a BIPOC employee? Do you have a mentor, sponsor, or coach?

- The next time you hear someone from your country's dominant group ask, "Why am I not being formally mentored or sponsored?," how can you use this as a teachable moment?

CHAPTER 12

BUILDING STRATEGIC PARTNERSHIPS

Multiple Stakeholders, Multiple Pathways

It's an acknowledgment that we're always thinking about who is at our table and asking ourselves, "Who is missing from the table?" and "What are we missing by not having them at the table?" When you think about what assets we are missing, that's a very different question.

KATHY TAYLOR
Black American Professor of Legal Studies
and DEI Consultant[1]

No matter the size of your business, you have multiple stakeholders—people or groups that play an important role or have a keen interest in the success of the company. Of course, if you are a public company, you have shareholders. Whether you are private or public, you have other stakeholders: users, providers, influencers, and governance. In Part IV we explored the characteristics of leaders and the roles they play, at all levels in the organization, to create and sustain an antiracist workplace. In this chapter we examine five key stakeholders—boards, community, suppliers, customers, and employees—and show you how to build or strengthen your strategic partnerships with them to advance race work.

STAKEHOLDER #1—BOARDS

In June 2020, Alexis Ohanian, cofounder of the popular social news platform Reddit, announced his resignation from the company's board. He was stepping down and urged the company to replace him with a Black leader. "I'm writing this as a father who needs to be able to answer his Black daughter when she asks: 'What did you do?'" Ohanian wrote in a blog post.

Ohanian, who is Armenian American and married to African American professional tennis player Serena Williams, also committed to using future gains from his Reddit stock to serve the Black community and focus on curbing racial hate. To start, Ohanian said he would donate $1 million to former NFL player and activist Colin Kaepernick's Know Your Rights Camp.

> Businesses run on this fundamental formula: define your strategy, set specific goals with clear accountabilities, and then tie rewards to successful outcomes. Creating a racially equitable culture is no different.

"I believe resignation can actually be an act of leadership from people in power right now. To everyone fighting to fix our broken nation: do not stop," Ohanian said.[2] A week after his resignation, Reddit filled Ohanian's board seat request by appointing

Michael Seibel, who is Black. Seibel is CEO of seed capital firm Y Combinator, which helped launch Reddit in 2005. Seibel has advised and funded almost 2,000 startups and is on a mission to bring more racial diversity, inclusion, and equity to the startup world.

Businesses run on this fundamental formula: define your strategy, set specific goals with clear accountabilities, and then tie rewards to successful outcomes. Creating a racially equitable culture is no different. However, where many companies come up short is in accountability, and it starts at the top. The very top. Not only with CEOs and their senior leadership teams but also at the board level. You might recall from Chapter 3 that diverse representation on its board was one of the mandates of Coca-Cola's $192.5 million racial discrimination settlement. Both senior leaders and board members need to do their own inner work, examine the board's racial composition, and commit to bringing more racially diverse voices to the table. Some are. Some are not.

Today, in the United States, only 3 percent of C-suite positions are held by African Americans, and there are only five Black CEOs on the Fortune 500 list today. Of those five Black CEOs, only two are women—Roz Brewer—who you learned about in Chapter 7, and Thasunda Brown Duckett, CEO of TIAA. In addition, as of 2019, about a third—187 to be exact—of the S&P 500 companies had zero Black board members, according to *Black Enterprise*. It's time that corporate boards step up.

To this end, former Xerox CEO Ursula Burns, who currently sits on the board of Uber, calls on leaders in corporate America to look at the racial imbalances within their own companies amid their statements of support for protesters fighting against racial injustice. Burns, who was the first Black woman to serve as a Fortune 500 CEO, says that a huge part of racial inequality within corporate America starts at the board level. She points out that "most of the boards still have zero or one African American" member on their team and that "pressure in that area can help to speed up progress and transitions for companies."[3]

Too often, people from the dominant group (White in the United States) erroneously believe that if their company is committed to racial diversity, then that means its entire board or executive leadership team will be made up of nondominant-group members, leaving them out, as we learned from law professor Kathy Taylor in Chapter 7. Simply, that's not the case. One US state developed a method to include more racial diversity on boards that doesn't leave anybody out.

Much like it did for gender diversity in 2019, in 2020 California took a stand by passing a bill requiring all public companies headquartered in the state to include at least one board member from an underrepresented community (Black, African American, LGBTQ+, Native American, Hispanic, Latino, Asian, Pacific Islander, Native Hawaiian, or Alaskan Native) by 2021.[4] The size of a company's *current* board is what determines the minimum number of board members who must be from an underrepresented community.

> If you are an employee, it will take a bit more digging to find out your board's stance. Look beyond the public statements. Examine the board's annual report. Ask senior leadership. While some boards now tie CEO compensation to meeting diversity and equity goals, this is not the norm.

Whatever position you hold at your company, the first step is to be aware of the makeup of your employer's board. Everett Harper, the cofounder and CEO of Truss, the software development company that you first learned about in Chapter 8, also sits on two boards, one global and one domestic. Harper offers this practical advice:

> Take a look at your board. If you don't have any women, if you don't have any people of color, if they're all from the global North, as opposed to the global South, you have a diversity issue. The job of a board is governance. That means the people on the board need to have a composition that's blended, that can add specific value, because no one wants to be the token. You have to engage people on what the purpose of a board actually is, and then be thoughtful about how to set the board up for success as a governing body.[5]

The next step is to find out if racial diversity, equity, and inclusion are strategic priorities for the board members and an expectation they have of the company they govern. If you are a board member, that's easy to ascertain. If you are an employee, it will take a bit more digging to find out your board's stance. Look beyond the public statements. Examine the board's annual report. Ask senior leadership. While some boards now tie CEO compensation to meeting diversity and equity goals, this is not the norm. "The traditional accountability mechanisms that boards hold their CEOs to are missing or insufficient when it comes to racial equity," says Living Cities CEO Ben Hecht.[6] "Many boards don't hold their CEOs accountable for diversity goals, let alone racial equity goals. It's more of a 'nice to have.' How can a board hold its CEO accountable for this tough stuff when they don't even understand it themselves?"

If a company's board members are not willing to do their inner work and educate themselves on structural racism and how it expresses itself in the workplace, then they're not going to "hold the CEO accountable." In turn, the CEO isn't going to hold his or her organization accountable. If you are a senior leader in your company, engage your board as a strategic partner by making racial diversity a topic of discussion at board meetings and retreats. Board members have their own race work to do and can use their positional power to institutionalize racial equity changes to a company's policies and practices. But first, they must understand it. If the members of your board are looking for a formula, then advise them to stop looking. There isn't one.

> "Many boards don't hold their CEOs accountable for diversity goals, let alone racial equity goals. It's more of a 'nice to have.' How can a board hold its CEO accountable for this tough stuff when they don't even understand it themselves?"

Beyond your employer's board, look to influence the makeup of boards that run the companies you support as a consumer. You have choices about where you spend your hard-earned money.

STAKEHOLDER #2—COMMUNITY

The broader community in which your company operates is the second stakeholder the organization can partner with to advance its race work. Small businesses often support local food banks, youth sports teams, fund-raising events, and the like. Large businesses have entire departments dedicated to managing the company's public giving strategy. Often operating under a "foundation," corporations work with public and private nonprofit organizations to invest in communities and initiatives that align with their mission, values, and goals. You might think this sector is well ahead of its corporate partners when it comes to racial diversity. Think again.

Recruiting and promoting more people of color for leadership positions, which you learned about in the last three chapters, applies to the public nonprofit sector, too. In 2015, one of the world's largest woman-owned executive search firms, Battalia-Winston, analyzed the leadership teams of the largest foundations and nonprofits in the United States. Here's what the firm found: though 42 percent of the organizations surveyed were led by female executive directors, 87 percent of all executive directors or presidents, whether male or female, were White.[7] In these leadership positions there was minimal representation of African Americans (6 percent), Asian Americans (3 percent), and Hispanics (4 percent). These findings were not a blip in the racial equity research. A 2015 study by Washington DC's Community Wealth Partners, for example, found that only 8 percent of nonprofit executive directors were people of color. Another study conducted by D5, a coalition of more than a dozen organizations working toward advancing diversity, equity, and inclusion in the philanthropy sector, found that 92 percent of foundation executive directors were White.

> "Philanthropic efforts that don't consider race run the risk of exacerbating existing racial disparities or even creating new ones."

These numbers highlight the enormous disparity between the leadership of philanthropic organizations and the clients and communities served. Executives reflected in the statistics above, are tasked with paving the way for change in these same communities. Yet, they may never have faced the challenges that go along with being a person of color in a community of great poverty. Cheryl Dorsey, Jeff Bradach, and Peter Kim of the nonprofit advisors Echoing Green (Dorsey) and The BridgeSpan Group (Bradach and Kim) note that nonprofits ignoring the implications of race on the work they fund has only served to disadvantage people of color. "Specifically, philanthropic efforts that don't consider race run the risk of exacerbating existing racial disparities or even creating new ones."[8]

One way to influence the leadership that governs nonprofit organizations is to be aware of it's racial diversity before making a financial contribution. Visit the organization's website to find out who sits on the leadership team and board. If the people leading the organization are not diverse, provide that feedback. Consider withholding your donation until the organization addresses its racial diversity.

Large businesses typically look to their foundation to carry out public giving in support of causes such as eliminating poverty, hunger, and housing insecurities. Yet, they often overlook ways they can support underrepresented communities within the walls of their workplace. We asked Professor Kathy Taylor, who teaches business law at Naugatuck Community College in Connecticut, what advice she has for business leaders who want to make a difference in their communities. She offered two tangible actions: provide paid internships (the operative word is "paid") and sponsor scholarships for college students. "My best and brightest students have to work," she says.[9] "With a paid internship they can apply what they are learning in class and gain valuable, real-world experience. I hate to lose them to a retail job, just so they can get more hours to pay the bills." You might recall paid internships was one method LLNL also used to recruit more diverse scientists.

Businesses needn't provide scholarships for all four years, Professor Taylor explains. For example, once students at Naugatuck Community College earn their two-year associate degree, a nearby private institution, the University of Hartford, offers two-year scholarships so students can complete their four-year degree. "Imagine if businesses started to sponsor some of those scholarships," Taylor says.

Marianne Monte, chief people officer at Shawmut Design and Construction, sits on the state of Rhode Island's Board of Education, and her company partners with local colleges and universities. She says Shawmut has traditionally recruited from two private universities that offer four-year construction management and engineering degrees. However, she recognizes the need to expand these strategic partnerships. Industry jobs, such as project management, estimator, and superintendent, require strong math skills, Monte says. The company partners with high schools and colleges to provide scholarships that encourage more students of color to enter STEM (science, technology, engineering, and math) and STEAM (science, technology, engineering, arts, and math) programs.[10]

Strategic partnerships between business and educational institutions offer myriad mutual benefits. For students from underrepresented groups, internships provide real-life experience in applying what they are learning in the classroom and also networking and employment opportunities that they may not otherwise be exposed to. For businesses, internships create a diverse talent pipeline, allow you to test-drive that talent, and build your brand on high school and college campuses. For the educational institution, internship benefits include the ability to attract more students of color and strengthen its position in the business community as the go-to institution for diverse talent. And let's not forget the benefits of internship programs to the community at large. For students of color, internships are a way "to encourage local college students to stay within their community or region after graduation; this decreases the chances of valuable talent leaving the area, which positively impacts the local economy."[11]

STAKEHOLDER #3—SUPPLIERS

Suppliers are the third key stakeholder to partner with to advance your company's race work. A diverse supplier is a business that is at least 51 percent owned and operated by an individual or group that is part of a traditionally underrepresented or underserved group. Common classifications are small business enterprises, those owned by people of color, and woman-owned enterprises. Over time, the definition of diversity has expanded to businesses helmed by other underrepresented groups such as LGBTQ+, veterans, and proprietors with disabilities.

The history of supplier diversity in the United States is firmly rooted in the civil rights movement of the 1950s and 1960s.[12] Following race riots in Detroit in 1968, General Motors set up what is regarded as one of the first supplier diversity programs, and much of the US auto industry followed. Early movers and shakers in the electronics industry, such as IBM, established supplier diversity programs around the same time. Later, federal law established a program requiring government contractors to include underrepresented businesses in their supply chains. Then, nearly 30 years ago, UPS started its diversity supplier program and currently spends $2.6 billion annually doing business with around 6,000 small and diverse suppliers. Of course, UPS's program has evolved. For example, UPS partners with and supports multiple councils and third parties such as the Women's Business Enterprise National Council, the National Minority Supplier Development Council, and the US Hispanic Chamber of Commerce to run mentoring and training programs that support the growth and success of diverse suppliers. This includes workshops, professional matchmaking at supplier diversity conferences, enhancing opportunities for capital investment, and management education.

This is only the beginning.

"So much can be done outside of philanthropy, and they come up every single day; and most companies strike out every single day," a board director of an investment firm, who wanted to remain anonymous, shared with us. "It always makes me wonder why more pressure isn't put on procurement. This is money the company is spending anyway. How hard is it to give the job to diverse people?"

Apparently, very hard.

Rather than managing all the firm's portfolio internally, the board had made a strategic decision to move its fixed-income portfolio to an external company that specializes in money management. When it came time to make the tactical decision on which money management company to use, a not-so-unconscious bias reared its head. The chief investment officer insisted on moving the entire multibillion-dollar portfolio to one of the world's most powerful and Whitest financial institutions.

Both the CFO and CEO got involved in the tactical discussion, with the CFO ultimately getting his way. Though the outcome was not what this board director was seeking, he didn't storm out of the room in frustration or resign from the board. Rather, he plans to engage with each board member, one at a time. For the next big decision that requires a board vote, he will have built support. We like to call this the "meetings before the meeting." He will also be persistent. As he later reported, "I will keep bringing it up until I see the change I'm looking for."

A few months later we followed up with the board director, curious what progress had been made in bringing more racial diversity to the organization. We learned that the chief investment officer had identified five new people to manage the portfolio. "This was clearly an opportunity to bring more diversity and racial equity to the portfolio manager role, which is typically held by White men, not just at our company but across the investment management industry," he explained. "We ended up identifying four White women and one person of color. It's not exactly what I had wanted, but it is a step in the right direction."

Some large companies, however, do encourage and, in some cases, require their suppliers to create their own diversity initiatives. This broadens the racial equity impact throughout the procurement chain. For instance, as of 2019, the retailer Target spent $1.4 billion on goods and services provided by first-tier diverse suppliers—companies that provide parts and materials directly to a manufacturer of goods. Also, Target influenced its first-tier suppliers to buy over $800,000 worth of offerings from second-tier diverse suppliers—companies that supply materials or parts to another company that then supplies them to a manufacturer.

> Why would we make visible to our customers our ongoing race work? Because, like you, they are struggling with how to advance racial equity in the workplace, too.

Would it be easier to maintain a company's procurement process as a siloed administrative function? Yes. And in doing so, that company misses the opportunity of competitive advantage.

Adding diverse suppliers to your organization's procurement process may be lengthy and involved. We remind you that throughout this book, we've underscored that organizational race work is not easy. Good news: with small steps, it's entirely doable for your company to partner with racially diverse suppliers in equitable ways.

STAKEHOLDER #4—CUSTOMERS

A fourth stakeholder to engage in your race work is your customers. Forming, building, and strengthening strategic partnerships with customers is nothing new. For race work, though, it may be. You might be wondering, why would we make visible to our customers our ongoing race work? Because, like you, they are struggling with how to advance racial equity in the workplace, too.

The spice company McCormick wanted to benchmark its diversity and inclusion results against other organizations. So Nerida Perez, its chief D&I officer, approached the company's sales team and asked if she could speak to some of the customers about their race challenges. One corporate customer was struggling with how to talk to employees about diversity and inclusion. The customer had just named an individual to head up the work—someone who had a background in HR but had not worked specifically in D&I. "I was able to build a relationship very quickly and then give them some resources and tools that they could use," says Perez.[13] "I also invited them to some of our sessions so that they could see how the conversations were unfolding, and provided them with some guidance on the diversity strategy as they were building it."

Once word got out that Perez worked with one customer group, other salespeople began reaching out to her to ask if she would help some of McCormick's other clients. Now she is working with other business leaders at McCormick to help them build collaborative race work partnerships with their clients. "We're on this journey together," Perez says. Like a snowball that gains speed and gets bigger and bigger as it rolls downhill, your diversity and inclusion work also can gain momentum and grow in size. Perez says her next step is to create a network of diversity heads at other corporations. Her ultimate hope is that employee groups will come together to share their stories and to build an advisory council that employees across multiple businesses can turn to for support.

STAKEHOLDER #5—EMPLOYEES

This stakeholder group is arguably your most important partner because it is the face of your company to all other stakeholders. Too many companies view people as one-dimensional: you're either an employee, or a customer, or a shareholder, and that's it. That dichotomous thinking, rather than spectrum thinking that you learned about in Chapter 6, may be costing your business. Companies would do well to recognize that their employees embody dual or even multiple roles in relationship to their employer—within, alongside and outside the organization.

Case in point is a lesson that the National Football League (NFL) learned the hard way.

Diverse Teams Win Business; Homogeneous Teams Lose Business

In 2015, Nzinga Shaw, today the chief inclusion and diversity officer at Marsh & McLennan Companies, Inc., participated on a conference panel called "TWIN Global: Beyond the Game."[14] During the panel discussion, she told a story of her diversity and inclusion role while working for the NFL. The league was pitching PepsiCo to sponsor a long-term partnership. The NFL ended up sending 10 people to make the sales pitch. All were straight White men. Indra Nooyi, PepsiCo CEO at the time, told the sales team that she would not secure the partnership. "Based on the people we sent," said Shaw, "we weren't able to demonstrate that we had a depth of knowledge of what was happening in the world." That huge "aha moment" sparked reflection, and the NFL's diversity council got to work. Shaw said that was her first experience understanding how diversity can impact reputation and the bottom line, "and why we need to be having this conversation on a continual basis in organizations."

Your employees (and your marketing, which we'll get to in Chapter 14) represent your company. They are the most visible signs of how well your company mirrors the customers you serve and the communities in which your business operates. The employees you choose to represent your company in the wider community externally, and to participate in leadership development programs internally, say more about your company's commitment to racial diversity and inclusion than any public statement could. As the NFL learned through a failed partnership pitch to PepsiCo, so did another company learn a similar lesson the hard way, too.

At a previous employer, marketer Liz Rowan, whom you first met in Chapter 4, was selected to participate in the second cohort of a future leaders program. The entire leadership team, along with both the first- and second-cohort participants, was invited to take a trip to the Equal Justice Initiative in Montgomery, Alabama. Rowan was one of only two employees of color in the group.

On the first day of the trip, the group took a guided tour of Montgomery and learned about its history during the civil rights movement. The guide, a Black woman, asked the group the nature of their company's business. One of the executives replied that the company produced digital curriculum, including DEI content. The guide stopped short and observed the racial makeup of the group. Seeing so few people of color, she asked them to remain silent while en route to the bus, and to quietly reflect on the group's lack of racial diversity, especially given the company's work in DEI. "As we were walking back to the bus," Rowan told us, "which would take us to the next stop on our tour, one of the executives said, 'I feel like she thinks that this group represents our whole company, but it doesn't.'"

The executive was right; back at headquarters Black and Brown staff members held down the fort. So, what did this group's lack of racial diversity say about the company? It said that the company's "future leaders," would continue to look primarily like they always had—White.

Consumer and shareholder—these are two additional roles employees may play depending on the company's structure, products, and services. Erneshia Pinder, whom we have given voice to throughout the book, plays several roles in relation to the organization that employs her. She says, "I work for CVS Health, I shop at CVS Health, and I'm a shareholder of CVS Health."[15] However, all employees, no matter their role or position in the hierarchy, also play the role of ambassador for your brand. Sending an all-White sales team or a mostly White group of "future leaders," as did the two companies we've just highlighted, sends the message that your company does not value racial diversity. Neither does it represent your customers and the community at large. Employees represent your company on a sales pitch, at a professional develop-ment experience, industry conferences, community events, or even at a gathering of friends or family. The people you send to these events can enhance your brand's reputation for valuing a racially diverse and inclusive workplace or detract from it. When we partner with employees as strategic partners, we are expanding the employer-employee contract. A competitive business edge in an increasingly multicultural society requires that companies hold a spectrum view of the multiple roles their employees play, and partner with them to mutual advantage.

Engagement, Not Buy-In

"We must get employee buy-in," say business leaders when imple-menting large initiatives or advancing cultural change. In concept, we agree. Yet we take issue with the term "buy-in," that we're trying to *sell* people something, be it our strategy, product, or service. Save that for your sales team. Here's a more effective approach to raising awareness, changing behavior, and re-creating your policies and practices: *engage* people in this work instead. Then there is no need to jump through hoops to get their buy-in. They have been a part of the solution all along the way.

Buy-in looks like this: an executive team mandates unconscious bias or conscious inclusion training for all employees. Engagement looks like this: a cross-functional team, made up of employees and managers, and sponsored by one or more senior executives, develops a strategy. Then follows through with actions to advance the organization's race work. As many apps as there are on your smartphone, there are also pathways to engage your employees as strategic partners. So where do you begin? Let's get specific. Build upon what you already do well when engaging employees. And then consider these five additional approaches (Figure 12.1): articulate your employee value proposition,

FIGURE 12.1 How to engage employees in your race work. (*Illustration by Lucy Engelman.*)

reinvent your onboarding process, create or re-create employee/ colleague resource groups (ERGs/CRGs), replace exit interviews with stay interviews, and create high-quality connections.

Engaging employees as strategic partners in your race work begins even before they join your company. As you learned in the last chapter, companies such as Truss expressly tell prospective candidates that salaries are not secret, nor can they be negotiated as part of the hiring process. Making salaries public is one way innovative companies are closing the racial diversity wage gap. Don't like that approach? Then don't apply. Other companies such as Living Cities and Fractured Atlas make explicit on their website, the company's diversity, inclusion, and antiracist values and policies.

As does MassMutual. The company's chief D&I officer Lorie Valle-Yañez explains: "The value proposition is very humble. We're not perfect, and we know we have a lot more work to do, but we've made the commitment, and it's nonnegotiable. If you want to help us get there, then this is the right company for you."[16]

Once hired, engaging employees as strategic partners continues with a robust onboarding process to help them feel welcome and included. MassMutual and other companies are now incorporating learning labs on diversity, equity, and inclusion for new hires. From day one, new employees know that these values are core to the company's operations.

ERGS at Work

So your employees have been hired and onboarded. Now what? Another way to strategically partner with them is to create or re-create ERGs or CRGs. These are voluntary, employee-led groups designed to engender a sense of belonging and to foster a diverse and inclusive workplace. Media giant AT&T has over 50 ERGs with more than 147,000 employees participating. On its website the company states, "Employee group members are the cultural lifeblood of our organization and when it comes to advancing diversity and inclusion, they are the vanguard, helping to shape our path forward."[17]

Once an ERG or CRG is an organizational staple for engaging employees, you may find yourself re-creating its purpose. "Shaping that path forward" is especially important when dealing with a crisis. In the midst of the pandemic, company-sponsored Asian ERGs in the United States became both a source of emotional support and a way of educating others in the workplace in response to the rising hate incidents against Asian Americans that we highlighted in Chapter 4.

WHAT ARE MICROAGGRESSIONS?

Everyday, subtle, intentional—and oftentimes unintentional—interactions or behaviors that communicate some sort of bias toward historically marginalized groups. The difference between microaggressions and overt discrimination or macroaggressions is that people who commit microaggressions might not even be aware of them. Someone commenting on how well an Asian American speaks English, which presumes the Asian American was not born here, is one example of a microaggression. Presuming that a Black person is dangerous or violent is another example. A common experience that Black men talk about is being followed around in stores, or getting on an elevator and having people move away and grab their purses or their wallets. Oftentimes, people don't even realize that they're doing those sorts of things. And in fact, if you were to stop them and say, "Why did you just move?" They would deny it because they don't recognize that their behaviors communicate their racial biases.

—*Kevin Nadal, professor of psychology at both
the John Jay College of Criminal Justice
and the Graduate Center at
the City University of New York*[18]

"We had some conversations around what was happening in the Asian community because there are some racial concerns," says Heather Bodington of CVS Health. Bodington, whom you first met in Chapter 6, is the Korean American planning manager, adopted at birth by White parents and raised in a mostly White neighborhood.

"I didn't personally experience any prejudice in the workplace, but I definitely observed it in my everyday life outside of work."[19]

Companies that have established ERGs for Black and African American employees have proved especially critical as the Black Lives Matter movement continues to gain momentum throughout the United States and around globe. These employee groups are able to provide a safe space for race talk and guidance to the organization's leadership on DEI strategy and subsequent actions.

The Stay Interview

In Chapter 10 you learned about the hidden costs of hiring mistakes. When an employee doesn't feel included and decides the only way to advance her or his career is to leave, how do organizations respond? Typically, HR conducts an *exit interview*, by which time it's too late.

> What if we used our asset lens and conducted *stay interviews* instead of exit interviews to strengthen our partnership with employees?

"The problem with exit interviews is not only is it too late, but that person who is exiting has probably talked to their friends for the last six months," offers DEI consultant and law professor Kathy Taylor.[20] Let's not forget that those friends may also be prospective employees and/or customers. As Taylor points out, "They've probably also spread this to some current employees who are now also looking for another employer where they will feel more welcomed."

When customers have a poor experience with a company, product, or service, most businesses have a service recovery process to retain them. Examples range from restaurants that remove the price of your overcooked burger from your bill to Nordstrom's that accepts all returns no matter how long they have lived in your closet. But few companies apply this same rigor to retaining employees. What if we used our asset lens and conducted *stay interviews* instead of exit interviews to strengthen our partnership with employees?

Think of a stay interview as a conversation that can be initiated with any employee by a manager, HR professional, internal mentor, or external coach. The purpose? A simple check in with the employee to see how he or she is adapting to the new work environment. And, if need be, interrupt or disrupt the status quo. Also, conduct stay interviews with long-tenured employees to learn why they've stayed with the company. Once these attributes are known, they can be institutionalized: positive work environments, professional development opportunities, meaningful projects, or the feeling of being valued by their manager. Table 12.1 is a sampling of stay interview questions to ask of newly hired and long-tenured employees.

TABLE 12.1 Stay Interview Questions

For New Employees	For Long-Tenured Employees
• How would you describe your experience thus far to a friend or family member?	• What makes you want to stay with the company?
• How welcome do you feel?	• No matter how our company may change in the future, what organizational attributes must we be mindful to retain because they are crucial to your well-being at work and how you view the company?
• How can I help you better navigate and contribute to our company?	
	• What else do you aspire to do?

High-Quality Connections

In this digital age we often forget the most powerful and least expensive employee engagement tool we have at our disposal: one-on-one personal connections. Humans are intrinsically social beings. We crave genuine connections with others and have a need to belong. Researchers at the University of Michigan's Ross School of Business have found that short, positive, two-person interactions, or what people call "high-quality connections" (HQCs), are the building blocks for strong relationships that are characterized by trust, honesty, and resiliency.[21]

HQCs between people in the workplace are important to team effectiveness. They become more salient when people are faced with challenging situations and may feel isolated, such as the collision of the pandemic and violence against Blacks and Asian Americans and Pacific Islanders. Let's see how one business leader turned this uncertain and volatile period into an opportunity to build HQCs with employees in multiple cities around the United States.

City Club Apartments operates luxury real estate communities in the Midwest. Nina Davis, the company's VP of people and culture who self-identifies as Black, supports City Club Apartments' multiple sites spread across a half dozen cities. One of those cities is Minneapolis, the city where George Floyd was murdered. Davis had only been in her new job three weeks when Floyd was murdered and protests erupted across the country. As the newest member of the executive team, she could have laid low and taken a wait-and-see approach before wading into the emotionally charged topic of racism. She didn't.

"Between the pandemic and the civil injustices, our associates were feeling isolated," says Davis, who was living in Miami at the time.[22] Though the pandemic presented travel challenges, that didn't stop Davis from meeting face-to-face with City Club Apartments employees in Minneapolis. "Their city was shut down. I flew in and just sat there with associates and let them vent. Just being able to listen and let them know they are not alone. I also connected associates between sites."

Being visible, reaching out, and listening. So simple yet so powerful in cultivating HQCs and a workplace that feels inclusive. How do you foster connections with employees when gathering in person is not possible? In addition to her on-site visits, Davis also virtually connected associates across the company in cities such as Detroit, Chicago, Minneapolis, and Kansas City, where two months earlier Black medical worker Breonna Taylor was shot and killed in her home by White police officers.

City Club Apartments' employees are considered essential workers. Davis was clear, though, that operating "business as usual," didn't mean these employees had to "be the rock all the time." It's OK to be angry and confused and experience a full spectrum of emotions. Davis set the stage for these virtual meetings:

"I started by saying, 'Let's not talk at all about work, unless you want to. We're not going to come in with an agenda. We're just going to create a safe space. Let's just talk as human beings.'" She continues, "The reason I think no one was talking about it is because they felt they were walking on eggshells. They weren't sure who they might offend. We might be of different races, or you might be in an interracial relationship. I think that is where a lot of the anger was coming from; that no one was talking about it."

In 2020, a plethora of companies made public statements in support of Black Lives Matter. City Club Apartments decided on a different tack. "We took a really hard stance saying, 'We're not going to broadcast some statement to whoever is on the outside looking in,' but let's talk about this and create conversations from within. We talked about interracial relationships and how they're dealing with it. We talked about friendships that have been hindered because of differences of opinions. It helped people grow from those conversations."

THE FINE POINTS

Every day, multiple times a day, we encounter moments when we can either speak up against structural racism or remain silent. We can choose to influence the institution called work, or the do-nothing strategy. Regardless of your positional power, we hope you will choose the former to build or strengthen partnerships with your multiple stakeholders:

- Observe the racial makeup of your company's board and take action to advance changes.

- Examine your company's procurement policies to be sure they are racially equitable. Change them if they are not. Public giving is all well and good; however, your purchasing practices and the suppliers you choose to do business with can also have a profound impact on the communities you work in.

- Form strategic partnerships with industry peers, and your customers, to learn from each other ways to institutionalize workplace changes.

- Ask for the racial composition of the leadership team and board of nonprofit institutions before making financial contributions.

- Get involved in a nonprofit board whose mission speaks to you.

- Form ERGs/CRGs, or engage existing ones to advise leadership on strategic race work.

- Review your company's onboarding approach to be sure it is welcoming to all new employees and also helps them navigate the company infrastructure.

- Conduct stay interviews, instead of exit interviews, to boost engagement and learn what's working and what's not before employees head out the door.

- Speak up when you notice an imbalance in who is being selected to participate in professional development, high-profile projects, public panels, and meetings.

- Introduce yourself to someone who is from a different background, ethnicity, race, or religion and get to know each other through a high-quality connection.

- Create safe gathering spaces for employees to talk about how microaggressions, micro-opportunities, and current events impact their lives.

- Be intentional about whom you choose to represent your company externally and the racial makeup of the employees you perceive as your future leaders.

REFLECTION

- What are you or your company doing well in public giving, community relationships, and/or philanthropy? What changes might you make to invest your dollars in ways that will advance your race work?

- The next time you are in a meeting where a purchasing decision is being made, how will you raise the need to consider more racially diverse suppliers?

- Have you had a customer experience, similar to the NFL's PepsiCo pitch, where you lost a key account because of the lack of racial diversity on your team? How did you handle it?

- Does your company have strategic partnerships with customers or industry professionals? How might you leverage these relationships to advance your race work?

- How might you implement the stay interview?

- If your company already has ERGs or CRGs, how can you get more involved? If your company doesn't have any ERGs or CRGs, what might be your next step to create them?

- If your company has a board, what is its composition? How many people of color? How many women? What can you do to influence the diversity on your board membership?

PART VI

PUTTING IT ALL TOGETHER

Activity doesn't necessarily equal productivity. Black American actor Denzel Washington said, "Just because you are doing a lot more doesn't mean you are getting a lot done. Don't confuse movement with progress!"[1]

In business we measure everything. It is the only way to tell if our efforts are yielding the results we seek. Why should race work be any different? In the next chapter, Chapter 13, we examine ways to measure progress by looking both inside and outside your industry. We've said the "E"—equity—is a measure of your "D" and your "I." You will need to discover your own "E."

Though you may track diversity metrics today, you may not be examining them with sufficient granularity. Companies such as CVS Health and MassMutual, which are far along in their race work journeys, are now breaking down with specificity broad categories such as "diversity" and "people of color" to measure progress. By now we hope you've embraced the absence of prescription for creating and sustaining an antiracist workplace. Instead, we each must embark on our own journey, learn from and engage with others, be willing to experiment and make mistakes. In the final chapter, Chapter 14, we explore the power of narrative in the antiracist workplace of the future.

CHAPTER 13

DISCOVERING YOUR "E" AND MEASURING ITS IMPACT

Insights from Companies Outside Your Industry

Every other thing we do gets measured. I like to say a line that I learned from a CEO: Math has no opinion. But in this area [diversity], we want credit for trying. You don't get credit for trying to meet earnings expectations. You don't get credit for trying to deliver the product on time to your client. You either do or you do not.

MELLODY HOBSON
Black American businesswoman, Chair of Starbucks Board,
and Co-CEO and President of Ariel Investments[1]

Nereida Perez's DEI career spanned two industries prior to joining the spice company McCormick. Previously, she held positions in engineering and logistics at UPS, Shell, and National Grid. She already knew that business leaders use metrics to determine if they are meeting customer requirements and achieving financial goals. To get funded she had to show that her initiatives would produce measurable results for the company. "At

> In a manufacturing environment like McCormick, if the company is going to provide funding for your initiatives, you must show how they are going to increase productivity, improve retention, or open up new markets.

UPS it was 'I can't give you funding unless you tell me how much more revenue you're going to generate, the number of packages you're going to be able to sell, deliver, or pick up,'" she explains. Perez coined this approach the "UPS perspective" while she was working at the Latin American division of the company. Ever since, she has been applying this measurement rigor to advance her diversity and inclusion work.[2]

When she first arrived at McCormick, of course, there was race work under way; however, the company's diversity and inclusion strategy was broad. McCormick measured the diversity of its workforce and promotions, but it was not measuring the impact of inclusion on the business performance, such as productivity and profitability.

"In a manufacturing environment like McCormick, if the company is going to provide funding for your initiatives, you must show how they are going to increase productivity, improve retention, or open up new markets," says Perez.

In the last chapter, you learned that Perez benchmarked the company's D&I work to measure progress over time. She then partnered with customers, which accelerated McCormick's race work in other divisions. How? Perez was speaking the language of business: metrics.

She offers one other piece of advice as you develop or refine your metrics: don't use the term "targets." Here's a case where a common business term when applied to race work can create more problems than it solves. Use the term "goals" instead. When Perez coaches McCormick's business leaders, she explains it this way:

> You can use targets when talking about financial goals, but when you're talking about diversity and inclusion, it can raise very personal, gut reactions. "Wow, I'm a target, so you need X number of me to meet your target" or "What about our group? Now we're being discounted." The term we use is goals. The one question I get a lot is, "Does this mean that you're lowering the standards of who we're bringing in?" My answer is "No. The expectations of the skills needed to perform the job requirements are still there. That's not changing."

Perez admits that the measurement piece, like everything else in business, is still evolving. The results of the next employee engagement survey will tell the company even more. In the fourth quarter of 2021 McCormick also plans to roll out its first employee survey focused exclusively on diversity and inclusion.

Your company may already track diversity metrics that show 55 percent of your workforce is non-White. Those numbers can look impressive. However, it is only when you dig deeper that you find, say, that number plummets to 2 percent at the leadership levels. Depending on where your company is in its race work journey, it may be time to reexamine metrics. You might also find that your company isn't as racially diverse as you thought. Many companies take a "lumping approach" to diversity metrics. Lumping together broad categories, such as "gender" and "people of color," can give a false sense of progress. While numerous companies have made inroads in gender diversity by increasing representation of women at all levels, what gets lost is how well women of color—specifically Black, Native American, Hispanic,

> If creating and sustaining a racially diverse and inclusive workplace is one of your company's objectives, you need KPIs.

and Pacific Islander—are progressing. Heather Bodington of CVS Health shares this example: "It's not a true representation of our hitting the mark, because we box everyone together as people of color. I'm a person of color as an Asian, and so are Hispanics or Latinos, as well as Black individuals. And then when you tally that all up, especially because the Asian population I would say is pretty significant at our company, it looks like we're doing well when I know we could do a lot better."[3]

One way to reevaluate your metrics is to take a fresh look at your key performance indicators (KPIs). KPIs are a staple in most large companies to measure revenue, profit margin, and other business objectives. If creating and sustaining a racially diverse and inclusive workplace is one of your company's objectives, you need KPIs. You also need a baseline. One company taking this approach is MassMutual, which has added a KPI called "diversity in the pipeline." To measure progress, the people at MassMutual look at diversity by levels in the organization. They further break down diversity by looking at race, gender, ethnicity, age, LGBTQ+, veterans, and individuals with a disability. "We start by creating awareness of the data with business leaders; what the organization looks like today and how diverse the various layers are," says chief diversity and inclusion officer Lorie Valle-Yañez. "While it is important to have diversity at the top of the organization, you need people in the pipeline."[4]

DISCOVERING YOUR OWN "E"

In Chapter 3 we posited that the "E," equity, in DEI is a measure of how you are progressing in your "D" and "I." Like Coca-Cola, CVS Health, EVERFI, Prudential, McCormick, and MassMutual, your organization will need to discover its own "E."

Your "E," what you measure and how, when, and why, will be a function of deep conversations within your organization. It will also be a function of experimentation performed not in a vacuum, but in collaboration. It may include taking the pulse of your organization's readiness, as we described in Chapter 8. It may also include using the tool you learned about in the same chapter—SOAR. Recall that SOAR helps you to discover and name what you are already doing well (strengths), what needs to change in your policies and practices (opportunities), how you envision your workplace in the future (aspirations), and what outcomes (results) you seek. These strategic conversations will help you uncover the "E," unique to your workplace. Following are two measurements that can serve as jumping-off points for developing or reinventing your own metrics. Both measures come from an industry you may not work in but are familiar with as a consumer: media.

The first tool is the Bechdel-Wallace Test. It is a measure of the representation of women in fiction. It asks whether a work—films, books, plays, stories, video games, comics—features at least two women who talk to each other about something other than a man. The rules that make up the test first appeared in 1985 in Alison Bechdel's comic strip *Dykes to Watch Out For*. Bechdel, who self-identifies as White and lesbian, wrote a strip episode titled "The Rule." Two women are depicted discussing a film, and one woman explains that she only goes to a movie if it satisfies the requirements described above. "Bechdel, however, wasn't the originator of the test. She has long attributed the idea of what is commonly referred to as the 'Bechdel test' to her friend Liz Wallace [who is Black] who mentioned the standard to her as Bechdel was looking for ideas for *Dykes to Watch Out For*," writes Megan Garber.[5] "And now that the stuff of a 1985 comic strip has morphed into the stuff of broadly recognized cultural and literary criticism," continues Garber in *The Atlantic*, "Bechdel wants to return credit to Wallace.

Over the decades the Bechdel-Wallace Test has been adapted and has become a key film industry metric. In June 2018, the term "Bechdel test" was added to the *Oxford English Dictionary*. Simple in origin, the measure examines the rote, stereotypical plotlines of mainstream film. According to the user-edited database Bechdeltest.com, as well as media industry press, about half of all films meet these criteria. It is an indicator of the *active* presence of women in the entire field of film, versus the number of women seen on screen or in specific works.

Media industry studies indicate that films that pass the test perform better financially than those that do not.[6] Vocativ is an award-winning producer of long- and short-form video that uses proprietary technology to source unexpected stories from around the globe. Vocativ's authors found that the films from 2013 that passed the test earned a total of $4.22 billion in the United States, while those that failed earned $2.66 billion in total. FiveThirtyEight, an online statistical aggregator, found that the films that passed the Bechdel-Wallace Test had about a 37 percent higher return on investment (ROI) in the United States, and an equal ROI internationally, compared with films that did not pass the test. You might recall the McKinsey & Company findings from Chapter 2 that showed "companies in the bottom quartile for both gender and ethnic/cultural diversity were 29 percent less likely to achieve above-average profitability than were all other companies in our data set." How? As you will see below, the Cultural Insights Impact Measure™ (CIIM) shows how a genuine reflection of culture in marketing content favorably drives consumers to engage with a company's products and services.

Why write about the Bechdel-Wallace Test in a business book about race? Three reasons. First, it's a well-known measure in the storytelling business. And all businesses are in the business of storytelling—all day long in myriad ways to multiple stakeholders. You don't manufacture products and services to keep them secret, do you? You let your target audiences know what you are up to with your core business. Also, your public relations and community-giving functions tell stories about other aspects of your company's existence such as outreach, events, awards, sponsorships, and investments. Of the many ways businesses tell their stories, visual tends to top the list. Print marketing, sales collateral, website advertising, videos, and social media all tell stories. Not solely about your core business. Also, about how your business perceives itself, navigates the larger society, and engages with all people.

Second, the Bechdel-Wallace Test is easy to grasp. It's simple in origin and yet quantifies a human dynamic some might not consider easily measurable, given the complexity of gender as it continues to evolve today. That means the idea of the test is easily adapted to race. In your company's marketing and advertising materials, for example, is the White person the one always standing up at the front of the room leading the group or in some other way representing authority? Such a visual could easily be counted without Herculean number crunching. Useful, say, for small companies or solopreneurs, as well as large organizations.

Third, even if you do no such counting, our hope is that by sharing the Bechdel-Wallace Test, it will raise awareness that this type of measure exists. Maybe now you know something you didn't know (conscious competence from Chapter 5). It's like driving a make and model of a car new to you. You didn't notice it too much before you bought the car, but now that it's surfaced to consciousness, you see that same car everywhere. Now that you are aware of the Bechdel-Wallace Test, what ideas does it spark for measuring racial diversity and inclusion in your company's policies and practices?

CIIM, as we briefly described above, is the second tool that might help you uncover your own metrics. CIIM was developed by the Association of National Advertisers (ANA) and the Alliance for Inclusive and Multicultural Marketing (AIMM) in partnership with NBCUniversal. AIMM's mission is to elevate multicultural and inclusive marketing to promote business growth in an increasingly diverse marketplace. Founded in 2016, the AIMM represents multiple stakeholders including 135 member corporations, advertising agencies, media and research companies, and trade associations representing over 1,000 brands.[7]

CIIM changes the way businesses drive growth in a multicultural marketplace by reviewing the content of ads that depict people of color. It also examines the extent to which the people depicted reflect the *full spectrum* of their communities, and to what degree culturally relevant ads are a key driver of brand affinity and purchase intent.

Highlighted in the list below are the results of a September 2019 CIIM study of 10,000 individuals across demographics including Hispanics, African Americans, Asians, LGBTQ+, the disabled community, and non-Hispanic Whites. It shows how genuinely reflecting culture in marketing content favorably drives consumers to engage with a brand in the following five ways: learning about the brand, recommending it to others, personal relevance, likelihood of purchase, and likelihood of repurchase.

HOW *CULTURALLY RELEVANT* ADS* DRIVE CONSUMER BEHAVIOR, COMPARED WITH ADS THAT ARE *NOT* CULTURALLY RELEVANT

- Five times more likely to *learn* more about the brand when ads are culturally relevant versus not

- Eight times more likely to *recommend* the brand to others when ads are culturally relevant versus not

- Six times more likely to find the brand *relevant* to them when ads are culturally relevant versus not

- Seven times more likely to *purchase* a brand for the first time when ads are culturally relevant versus not

- Fifty percent more likely to repurchase a brand they have bought in the past when ads are culturally relevant versus not

CIIM and the Bechdel-Wallace Test are two measurement examples we hope will spark ideas to develop or refine your organization's "E"—how and to what extent your racial diversity and inclusion practices are equitable. Our intention in sharing these two tools is to expose you to how industries, perhaps outside your own, measure gender and racial diversity in their marketplace storytelling.

CIIM may not apply to you *directly*. If you are a local employer, say, in a small town such as Sarasota, Florida (population 57,000), chances are you are not advertising on national television because that's not your market. That means your ads are not being monitored by CIIM. However, your awareness of what it counts and how, might prompt you to examine the racial diversity in your ads, website, and other collateral.

If metrics are not your thing but you recognize the favorable business impact of measuring (and continually recalibrating) beyond diversity to substantive inclusion, then partner with the number lovers in your organization. They needn't be department heads or managers. Involve employees at all levels in helping to make a difference in measuring your company's race work. Maybe you'll create your own cross-industry alliance with other companies, like the ANA did to develop the CIIM.

HOW ELSE DO YOU KNOW IF YOU'RE MAKING PROGRESS?

A half-dozen years ago, MassMutual's chief diversity and inclusion officer Lorie Valle-Yañez, whom we mentioned above and in earlier chapters, did what we all do nearly every day in our professional and personal lives—she googled. Her research yielded a tool called the Intercultural Development Inventory® (IDI), developed by Drs. Mitch Hammer and Milton Bennett. MassMutual has been using the IDI as a measure of D&I progress, among other metrics such as the KPIs we described earlier in this chapter.[8]

The IDI measures intercultural competence—the ability to shift perspective and appropriately adapt behavior to cultural differences and commonalities. It measures where you think you are and where you actually are on a cultural competence continuum. "There's always a gap, especially for executives," says Valle-Yañez, "and with that awareness, you can have a constructive dialogue."

The IDI identifies a continuum of orientations. Figure 13.1 shows these range from the monocultural orientations of denial and polarization (defense/reversal), through the transitional orientation of minimization, to the intercultural/global orientations of acceptance and adaptation.

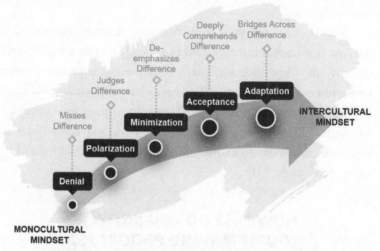

FIGURE 13.1 Intercultural Development Continuum (IDC™).
Licensed and copyright 2019 Mitchell R. Hammer, PhD
[*Intercultural Development Continuum® (2020), IDI, LLC. Used with permission.*]

Most people who take the 50-question, online assessment sit somewhere in the middle of the continuum at what's called "minimization." This worldview holds that people are basically alike. It downplays any differences among us and views them as inconsequential. The goal of the IDI is to move leaders from *minimization* to *acceptance,* which involves the ability to discern cultural patterns in one's own and other cultures.

Referring to minimization, Valle-Yañez says, "Everybody was kind of raised that way. We were raised to treat everybody the way you want to be treated, where everybody is the same. But you cannot create an inclusive culture if you stay in that place. We made a commitment to measure that movement."

Early in 2021 MassMutual received its third round of IDI results since it began using the assessment in 2015 to measure organizational progress along this continuum. "The first time we measured, 20 percent of our leaders were at the *acceptance* and *adaptation* stages," says Valle-Yañez. Those two stages represent leaders who have a deep understanding of cultural differences and are able to create bridges across them. The second time MassMutual measured intercultural competence using the IDI, 40 percent of the senior leaders were at *acceptance* and *adaptation*. The latest results, as of January 2021, show that 50 percent are at *acceptance* and *adaptation*. The trained professional who administers and interprets the IDI for the company is Mary-Frances Winters, also the author of several books including *We Can't Talk About That at Work!*, *Inclusive Conversations*, and *Black Fatigue*. Winters shared with Valle-Yañez that those numbers, reflecting behavior change in a five-year period, are "amazing." Winters should know; she's administered the IDI with dozens of organizations.[9]

In the fall of 2020, Starbucks announced that it would mandate antibias training for executives and tie their compensation to increasing racially diverse representation in its workforce. Starbucks also set a challenging and specific goal: it would aim for at least 30 percent of its US corporate employees—and 40 percent of its US retail and manufacturing employees—to be people of color by 2025.

We don't know what specific measures you should institute to gauge the progress your company is making on creating and sustaining an antiracist workplace. However, we learned from one of the business leaders we interviewed (and whom you first met in Chapter 6), Rajesh Ramachandran, executive director at CVS Health, that when exploring metrics, be thoughtful and be sure to involve a diverse group to help you create them.

Rajesh is no stranger to metrics, commonplace in the technology world of dashboards, objectives, key results, and KPIs. He advises that "We take some of the business analytics work that is available today and apply it to diversity." However, he adds "a bit of a cautionary tale." Diversity metrics are a "combination of science and art. We also must look at how we treat each other as human beings and show empathy. Find out what we have in common. You're not going to measure that in a dashboard or a box you can check to feel good that you've solved the issue."[10]

> To believe you will have zero defects on your race journey is magical thinking.

So how else can we measure systemic progress in forces so complex? There's no formula. We offer, instead, two more approaches that may run counter to what businesses call "quality assurance" (QA).

Quality assurance is built into nearly every business process. It's how companies minimize or prevent mistakes and defects in their products and services before they get into the hands of internal or external customers. Preventing mistakes and defects is crucial when manufacturing jet engines, monitoring food and drug production, performing surgery, and addressing other life-and-death situations. However, race work, as you now well know, embraces mistakes as part of the process. To believe you will have zero defects on our race journey is magical thinking. We don't need a QA test as much as we need a way to thoughtfully examine and then recalibrate two aspects of strategy: one, how we develop it; and, two, how deep does it go.

The components of a company's core business strategy will differ from one company to the next; so will the components of your racial diversity and inclusion strategy. In Part V, we examined a number of processes for you to consider. The salient takeaway from the companies and leaders featured in this book is *how* they developed their strategy, not what's in it.

Without exception, these businesses engaged their employees. And in some cases, such as McCormick, they engaged their customers, too. If you are developing strategy in isolation, with only those in senior leadership, HR, or DEI positions, then your progress will likely be slow. Anticipate greater progress if your company's ERGs or CRGs, advisory groups, and other committees that you learned about in the last chapter are funded and are working as strategic partners with the company's leadership. CFRA Research, a company of 120 employees globally that you learned about earlier in this book, implemented a social justice ERG to help develop its strategy. We asked its global head of talent, Heather Thomas-McClellan, how she perceives the progress her midsize company has made in its race work. "We are somewhere in the middle," she said. "When we did the unconscious bias training, I shared that this one-hour training didn't mean we could check off the box and say we're done. Instead, I reminded people that this was just the first step on our journey to make sure we have an inclusive workplace and that we're making progress toward CFRA being an even better place to work."[11]

Depth of strategy is the second place to look when measuring progress. To build a more inclusive culture, Living Cities CEO Ben Hecht writes, "We first needed to see the norms, values, and practices in our institutions that advantage White people and ways of working, to the exclusion and oppression of all others."[12] To do this, Living Cities committed both time and resources to develop staff members' understanding of history and personal biases, along with building skills such as empathy and vulnerability.

Law professor and DEI consultant Kathy Taylor, who opened up the last chapter, said that oftentimes organizations start their race work journey from a deficit stance. That's code for the company has been sued. Taylor comments: "People need to learn why it matters outside of being legally compliant. Legal is the floor; it's your lowest bar. If an organization is checking a box—'Well if anything happens, we can say we've done this training or that'—then they're really just honoring the letter of the law."[13]

MEASURING THE CHOICES WE MAKE

As much as we'd like to believe that race work starts at the top with a strategy that is developed collaboratively, that's not always the case. We agree with Ben Hecht who told us, "We can't wait. We shouldn't wait until our boards or our parents or whoever tells us that it's time to address race."[14]

The time to act now. And we all have a role to play, regardless of our position in a company's hierarchy. We noted earlier in the Part IV opener, neither of us—the coauthors of this book—has ever held a role at the VP level or above. While our roles have never given us positional power, we both have been able to influence up, down, and across the companies we've worked for. How? Not by *telling* people what to do. Rather, by asking thought-provoking questions, applying project management skills, and collaborating with others. Individual behaviors matter. Today's smartphones are packed with a dozen or more sensors that can pinpoint precisely where we are in the world, how many steps we've taken in a given day, our heartbeats per minute, and even ambient noise level. Sensors bring us intelligence and awareness, and that's exactly what we need to measure the effectiveness of our race work. We can build dashboards to measure *quantitative* progress to ensure effective policies and practices. We also need a way to measure *qualitative* progress at the individual level. We call these "micro-opportunities"—those seemingly small, everyday actions, most often carried out by individuals, that move us closer to creating a racially equitable and inclusive workplace.

> While we don't need to get stuck in history, we absolutely need to be committed to learning how we got here—through a skewed historic narrative that was designed to keep all of us from asking too many questions.

Let's look at a few micro-opportunities you might come across in your workday. How you choose to respond can demonstrate a *functioning* antiracist style that you learned about in Chapter 5. How you respond also can improve your company's performance through greater inclusion.

Micro-Opportunity #1

You introduce the topic of racial diversity with a coworker. She tries to shift the conversation to a broader definition of diversity. This may include: "What about [gender; LBGTQ+; people with disabilities—mental, physical, emotional, or cognitive; veterans; thinking preference]?"

You don't waver: "No, we're talking about racial diversity. Period. Using the all-encompassing term 'diversity' dilutes the conversation on race."

Micro-Opportunity #2

A conversation turns to race or racism and someone says, "What happened 400 years ago is not relevant. Let's move forward." Again, you don't acquiesce. Instead, you educate with courage and competence having embarked on your own inner work. And you help your coworkers connect the dots between today's racial inequities and the centuries-long reinforcement of systemic oppression.

Please remember: we can't solve what we don't talk about.

As Rochelle Newman-Carrasco shared with us recently, "While we don't need to get stuck in history, we absolutely need to be committed to learning how we got here—through a skewed historic narrative that was designed to keep all of us from asking too many questions."[15]

Micro-Opportunity #3

You are the only member of a nondominant group on your team. Or you are a member of the dominant group. You've taken the ASI (Chapter 5). You have a functioning antiracist style. In Chapter 1 we said businesses do not operate in a vacuum. Current events impact the workplace. A current event is affecting you, and you know it is negatively impacting other people in the organization. You realize that other members of your team do not see the racial disparities you see because those disparities don't affect them directly. You recall *unconscious incompetence* (Chapter 5) and recognize that they don't know what they don't know. You decide to turn this current event into a teachable moment. You bring voice to the struggles that people in your organization are experiencing.

A White woman with 13 years of business experience said it "grinds her gears"[16] when her company is not *consciously competent* about including people of color on external panels, in customer meetings, and in professional development opportunities. Every time she notices that no women or people of color have been invited, she speaks up and her company changes the composition of the group. Why is that important? In the last chapter you learned how the NFL lost a lucrative PepsiCo sponsorship because its sales team was completely homogeneous—all White males. PepsiCo's CEO at the time, Indra Nooyri, said the NFL's sales team did not reflect the customer base of a global organization. In the "gear-grinding" example above, right now we would say the company is *consciously incompetent*—it now knows what it didn't previously know. With this woman's continued advocacy, perhaps in the future, the company will no longer need her prodding. It will see how including gender and racial diversity at the table fosters progressive ideas, better decision-making, and enhanced marketplace reputation. Every day we have opportunities that can positively or negatively affect our lives and the lives of those around us. Starting today, notice the racial makeup of the people you interact with at work: in your live or virtual meetings, in client-facing meetings, at lunch, or when you take a break. Notice the racial makeup of your "go-to" people—the ones you most often rely on for highly visible projects, to serve as your thought partners or confidants. Notice the racial makeup of the authors of the business books your company uses in its leadership development programs. Better yet, notice who is teaching these programs or invited as a guest speaker. To whom are the quotes you use in your slide decks attributed? Who is on your marketing materials and company website? If you want greater market share, accelerated innovation, and access to a broader talent pool, notice and name what you see. When we give voice to our observations, we can begin to reimagine the system we call work.

> When we give voice to our observations, we can begin to reimagine the system we call work.

THE FINE POINTS

To be sure your race work is producing results, you must measure it. We offer the following actions for you and your organization so your race work is genuine, not window dressing:

- "E" is a measure of your "D" and "I." Experiment with what it looks like for your organization by drawing upon metrics from other industries and companies.

- Develop your strategy collaboratively, not in a vacuum, and go deep.

- Define specific goals and develop metrics to measure progress, just like you do for any other strategic priority. See what you can learn by studying how other industries measure racial diversity and inclusion.

- Speak directly about *racial* diversity rather than cloaking it in more general diversity terms.

- Look for and recognize micro-opportunities, those small, everyday actions that demonstrate progress in creating and sustaining an antiracist workplace.

- Educate your coworkers on the history of race and racism and how this social construct continues to shape our policies and practices today, both consciously and unconsciously.

REFLECTION

- Think about the actions your company has taken to create and sustain a racially diverse, equitable, and inclusive workplace. How would you describe the progress your company has made?

- How does your company measure diversity and inclusion today? If you don't know, how might you find out?

- How can you reimagine your company's metrics to capture the nuances of racial equity?

- Think about your own past behaviors and actions. Did you speak up when you saw racial inequities or heard racial slurs? Will you now?

CHAPTER 14

REIMAGINING THE FUTURE

The Power of Narrative

There have been great societies that did not use the wheel,
but there have been no societies that did not tell stories.

URSULA K. LE GUIN
White American science fiction author[1]

The stories we tell shape the world we live in. The stories we tell to ourselves, to our children, to one another, to consumers, in our history books, and to the world. Stories can entertain. But always, they've been humanity's tools of instruction for adhering to societal norms. To reshape our society, to reimagine the future, we must expand old narratives and introduce new ones. We must evolve into a collective where multicultural voices—historically underrepresented groups along with the dominant group—collaboratively create and occupy the center of those stories. For in them lies the foundation of our systems.

In Chapter 1 we quoted a red pill leader, Erneshia Pinder: "What we don't talk about, or can't acknowledge, we can't solve for." Color blindness, for example, is one story about race and racism that shuts down other stories. This narrative relieves those who tell it of the responsibility of examining, and by extension, fundamentally changing our society's imbalanced norms. The story goes like this: "We're all the same. Color doesn't matter. The United States elected a Black president, so we now live in a post-racial society." George Floyd's murder, #BLM[2] and #StopAAPIHate[3] protests surfaced the very stories this denial narrative attempts to suppress: the depth to which race and racism operate in and shape our global society. "Black people and people of color live in ghettos because of the individual choices they've made" is a story for which Citigroup's economists (Chapter 4) and other researchers provide evidence to the contrary. As does explicit language spelled out in housing covenants such as the 1921 deed of the Los Angeles home purchased in 1990 by Rochelle Newman-Carrasco and her husband (Chapter 1): "No portion of said premises shall ever be leased, rented, sold or conveyed to any negro, or any person of African descent, or of the Mongolian race, or of any race other than the white or Caucasian race."

> For all the reasons we outlined in Chapter 1, the workplace has a key role to play in evolving the race-based narratives that shape our global society: to introduce, advance and sustain stories that support all lives free of economic oppression.

"Race is biological" is a story deliberately crafted to hierarchically categorize human beings to advantage one group over all others. Evolutionary biologists and genetic researchers have long proved this to be false. "Color blindness" and "post-racial society" are stories that absolve the dominant group of accountability for systemic change. For all the reasons we outlined in Chapter 1, the workplace has a key role to play in evolving the race-based narratives that shape our global society: to introduce, advance, and sustain stories that support all lives free of economic oppression.

EXPANDING THE NARRATIVE

The pandemic has transformed business—where and how people work—and prompted organizations large and small to reimagine their footprint in the world. This is fertile ground for expanding workplace transformation by reimagining diversity and inclusion. Marketer Rochelle Newman-Carrasco admits this is tricky. "[Transforming the workplace] doesn't happen overnight and it doesn't happen because you draw a new org chart or because you hire a few more people [of color]."[4] There is figuring out what to do among and between cultures that, in many cases, know practically nothing about each other. The identities and the lived experiences of people from historically nondominant groups are no more homogeneous than those of people from dominant groups.

"Inclusion," by definition, implies an unspoken mandate to assimilate into a system of work created by dominant-group decision makers. In other words, these are the house rules: The dominant group says to the nondominant groups, welcome to "our" house. Help yourself to "our" food, served up in "our" traditions. We don't have enough dining room chairs to go around, so grab yourself a folding chair and sit at the kids' table. And listen carefully now, because around "our" table we'll be telling "our" stories. That form of inclusion, where one group dominates the center, is the status quo we are now living. It is a limiting and unsustainable business strategy, given an increasingly multicultural society. A solely dominant-centric view ignores the larger society in which businesses operate. It leaves untapped the resourcefulness, ingenuity, and imagination of wide-ranging lived experiences.

Expand the narrative. You now have tools to help you think about how you think. You have tools to help you understand the stages you go through when learning something new. Our hope: you now recognize that sitting with your initial discomfort of not knowing what you don't know is OK. It can even spark play. "The deliberateness and respect that produce fun result from deep dives into subjects rather than superficial explorations of them," writes Dr. Ian Bogost, Georgia Institute of Technology professor and award-winning game designer.[5]

PLAYING WITH THE "D," "E," AND "I"

Recall from Chapter 3 that we've defined the "E" as a measure of how and to what extent "D" and "I" are embedded into an organization's business strategy, and every policy and practice. In the last chapter, we played with the "E" by sharing examples of measurement tools that may exist outside your industry. And also, how other organizations are measuring "E." Let's now play with the "D" and the "I."

In discussing D&I, Newman-Carrasco asks, "As for inclusion—what could possibly be wrong with something that sounds so, well, inclusive? It rules out exclusion and promotes acceptance, right?"[6] Then answering her own question, she says:

> Yes, but it's inclusion into pre-existing structures with pre-existing rules written by . . . dominant culture decision makers. Without disruption there can be no real inclusion. Change, by definition, requires creating a new system. To quote French-Cuban journalist Paul Lefargue, "inclusion with strings attached is exclusion by another name."
>
> . . . Looking for new words to replace diversity and inclusion is pointless if we are not actively imagineering new ways of looking at our workplace and our world.

"Diversity and inclusion" get reduced to a quantity and quality conversation when what it's really about is disruption and innovation. We must get comfortable with cultural conflict and collisions as we navigate our intersected lives. Diversity isn't our [ad] industry's greatest problem. It's our most visible symptom.

At the outset of this book, we asserted that a shared lexicon is necessary in constructive race work, at both the individual and organizational levels. We are not imposing that on you. Rather, we are recommending that you explore that for yourself and with others in your organization. Use the tools we've suggested that "speak" to you. We explored the language of race and racism for ourselves, too, through the act of writing this book. Our lexicon surfaced through researching, learning, and generating ideas. Documenting that journey brought clarity to our conversations with each other, with interviewees, and now with you, the reader. One example of how race work surfaced our lexicon was the decision to write about *racial* diversity. Period. Because talking about all that is contained within the term "diversity" dilutes conversations on race and racism. The lexicon doesn't define the work. Rather, the work must allow the lexicon to surface, through experimentation, discovery, and more experimentation.

> The lexicon doesn't define the work. Rather, the work must allow the lexicon to surface, through experimentation, discovery, and more experimentation.

We invite you to notice how your lexicon surfaces organically. As your race work evolves, so will the words you use. And that is the beginning of *your* story. From that story emerges the reimagining of your workplace. We *can* reimagine a future that isn't zero-sum, where if some people win, others must lose. We *can* reimagine a future where members of all groups are *part* of the equation, and no single group occupies the *center*.

Let's play with the potential evolution of DEI, beginning with how the "I" in "inclusion" might change over time. Maybe the "I" comes to stand for "identity," which is multilayered, faceted, and filled with opportunities for discovery. "I" could represent "imagineering," which is experimentation, a shorthand for "try stuff." Learning in stages from your experiments surfaces yet another "I" for "iteration." Add to what you learn. Tweak. Remain open to the possibilities. When you hear, "That's never been done before," your response is, "Exactly." Remind your race work partners that with each iteration you are inventing something new. And that "inventiveness," another "I" to explore, can challenge you to use everyday resources in unusual ways. Do that and you find your way to "innovation," a whole new way of doing something familiar. Maybe what is new in your race work is the level of depth. What "insights" might you cultivate to deepen understanding of your organization's race work journey?

Through the work of redefining the "I," perhaps we also uncover a new "D." "Disruption" suggests "depth of transformation," to release attachment to what's come before. Let's play some more with what "D" might become. Bye-bye to the conference room brainstorming exercises, complete with markers and whiteboard! Instead, get deep down into it. We mean hands-on, roll-up-your-sleeves, muck-around-in-the-sandbox exploration. What would happen if your workplace brought a "D" for "a design engineering mindset" to what is currently called "diversity and inclusion"? Former PepsiCo CEO and now board director Indra Nooyi, who is Indian American, did just that when she became CEO in 2006. When Nooyi first assumed the helm of the company, it wasn't clear if she would survive as CEO of the second-largest food and beverage business in the world, behind Nestlé.[7] Pepsi's top brands were losing market share. And investors were critical of Nooyi's shift toward a more health-oriented product line. By 2015, the company enjoyed steady revenue growth during her nine years in the top job. Pepsi's stock price rose again after several flat years. All of this freed Nooyi to focus on what she said was driving innovation in the company under her tenure—design thinking. In 2012 she brought in renowned designer Mauro Porcini as PepsiCo's first-ever chief design officer. Nooyi proclaimed that, "design" has a voice in nearly every important decision that the company makes.

Design thinking is "the connection between empathy, strategy and prototyping," said Porcini in a *Service Design Show* podcast.[8] He explains: "Empathy is about understanding people's needs and wants; strategy looks for what is relevant for the business model. The role of the designer is to connect the two worlds." You might be thinking, nothing new. You know your customers through consumer insights, and as businesspeople you regularly develop strategy. So what do we need designers for? The design engineering mindset brings prototyping to race work expressed as business strategy. Once you understand what in your race work is relevant to key stakeholders—employees, customers, suppliers, board, and community—start to create. The ability to prototype allows a company to try on ideas. It is also an enabler of cross-functional innovation, a coalition builder among procurement, talent, finance, technology, sales, marketing, community relations, and others within the company. Prototyping grounds you. It concretizes ideas to share with others. A tangible creation is easier to react to than amorphous concepts. Everyone is looking at the *same* design, no matter how imperfect. This is preferable to each member of a work group reacting to a vision in their mind's eye that only they can see. Finally, prototyping advances productivity: each iteration allows for quick feedback about whether you are headed in the desired direction.

The authors of the book, *Think Wrong: How to Conquer the Status Quo and Do Work That Matters*[9] (who also run the design firm, Solve Next[10]), break it down this way:

"Green.

"Picture that color. What do you see?

"Maybe it's an azure-tinted green of the Caribbean ocean, or the saturated hue of a mountaintop tree line. Your green could be the oxidized tarnish of copper or the brightness of a lime. The point is we've got one simple word and myriad individual visualizations." What you see when someone says, "green," may be vastly different from what Jamal or Lisette sees. Or Joel. "This is why paint chips exist, and why hairdressers show clients synthetic samples of dyed hair first. This is also why it's imperative in the development of a new concept to move from thinking to making." You can dispute ideas forever. Why it will work, why it will fail, who will support it, who is going to pay for it. "Wait, what do you mean by GREEN?" Without anything to test your ideas against, you're simply speculating. You're mired in debate and supposition, so no progress. This is when it's time to start making stuff. "Making stuff puts physical form to the ideas in your head so you can understand them, share them, and quickly evaluate them."[11] You move from high-level abstract thinking to something more explicit. You ground the electricity of your creative energy in the tangible.

> Dismantling combined with imagineering asks, how can we take ideas and processes that have worked before and combine them with new ideas resulting from our experiments to advance our organizational race work?

Yes, you can prototype race work. Don't wait until you feel you have all your proverbial ducks in a row. Start with something and try it on. Do what Everett Harper from Truss advises: experiment. And discover what works and what doesn't through doing.

So what do a Danish designer and race work have in common? Christian Bason of the Danish Design Centre succinctly defines service design this way: "It is the creative process of gathering insights about people's experiences and behavior, generating new ideas about possible solutions and then testing, experimenting with those solutions to create new value for people and organizations."[12]

We think this crisp definition of service design thinking, or what we also call "iterative learning," very well suits the journey of organizational race work. But it requires a different look at the "D" and "I," which we began with the mini exploration above. One more experiment with the "D" is "dismantling" what we currently have in place. No, we don't toss everything out the window. Let's say you want to reexamine your recruiting and hiring practices. Collaboratively experiment with how the different components might be newly rearranged, not wholly discounted. Play. What might we add? What might we do away with to re-create something that advances us into a new future, driven by new narratives? Dismantling combined with imagineering asks, how can we take ideas and processes that have worked before and combine them with new ideas resulting from our experiments to advance our organizational race work?

NEW NARRATIVES: STEPPING INTO THE FOURTH BOX

While we were writing this book, we stumbled upon this meme—Figure 14.1—on Instagram. When we drilled down, we learned that its origins date back to 2012 when business school professor Craig Froehle cobbled together a graphic for his blog and posted it on the social networking site Google+. Froehle's meme—which showed the first two boxes, Equality and Equity—went viral. Since then, there have been "literally hundreds (perhaps thousands) of adaptations, most with wording changes."[13] Study the image. What does it mean to you? How do you define equality? Equity?

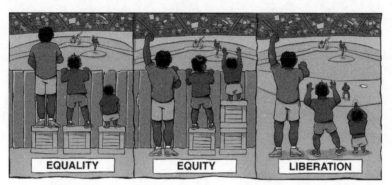

FIGURE 14.1 Equality, equity, and liberation. (*Interaction Institute for Social Change | Artist: Angus Maguire | madewithangus.com.*)

The team at the Center for Story-based Strategy (CSS), an organization that is reinventing how organizations develop strategy, uses this image in its work. The team discovered that the image prompts discussion and can create "aha moments" for some—and it can also "contain rather than unleash" deeper conversations.

COMMON REACTIONS TO THE EQUALITY/EQUITY MEME

- Participants with privilege or resources raise concerns about "their boxes" being taken away.

- Given a small contained world, arguments over identity and representations in the figures move to the foreground. (Why aren't there any girls in the story, and what proof do we have that they aren't there?)

- The either/or logic of two boxes erases the idea that we each might experience different boxes at different times/places in our lives.

- A focus on debating equality versus equity avoids deeper conversations about how did we get here and what else is possible?

Courtesy of the Center for Story-based Storytelling

We recommend that you expand your conversations beyond the two-box meme that can be seen all over the internet, because there's more to the story. This is why in Chapter 6 we introduced spectrum thinking using the Six Thinking Hats technique as a core muscle to develop and continue to strengthen for race work. Versions of the image depicting the third box, Liberation, as shown in Figure 14.1, reveal assumptions that hide in plain sight and get us further into the story. The CSS invites you to name the assumptions behind these three images.

One assumption after viewing the images is that "the conflict in the story isn't the same if the obstacle is removed." But CSS notes: "Still, this view is too simple and linear. Does the third box really come after the second? Wasn't the third box really *first, before* the fence was built?"[14]

In Chapter 9 we showed how Billy Beane explored assumptions about how to create a winning baseball team by recruiting where others didn't. Before he could challenge them, he had to name them. Just as we identify assumptions when developing any business strategy, we must explore our assumptions as we do race work. The assumption in Major League Baseball was that a single individual needed to possess multiple talents—that All Star Player. Once Beane removed that assumption, he crafted a different story for how to recruit talent and win games. Another assumption was that the best people to recruit talent grew up with the game—they played it; they managed it. Beane

> What assumptions about race and racism are keeping us from reimagining the workplace of the future?

removed those assumptions, and "one of his best hires, ever" (as noted earlier in the book) wasn't a baseball player. He didn't play sports, but he did follow baseball statistics. He was statistician Paul DePodesta, and together he and Beane told a new story and changed the game of baseball.

When we reveal assumptions, the whole conversation changes. New stories emerge. We encourage you to unpack and explore what's in the fourth box. Contemplate Figure 14.2. What assumptions about race and racism are keeping us from reimagining the workplace of the future?

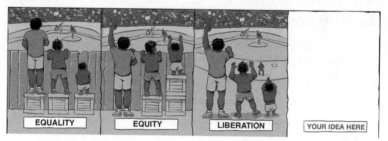

FIGURE 14.2 What's in the fourth box? (*A collaboration between Center for Story-based Strategy & Interactive Institute for Social Change | interactioninstitute.org.*)

NARRATIVES FROM THE MARKETING FUNCTION

A company's marketing function plays a critical role in the stories that a business tells about its products and services. Who shows up and how they appear in your marketing materials is your company telling a story—about its products and services *and* how it operates in the larger society. Founded in 1869, by John James Sainsbury with a shop in Drury Lane, London, Sainsbury's is the second-largest supermarket chain in the United Kingdom. During the 2020 holiday season, Sainsbury's proudly posted a Twitter clip sharing the first of its three festive ads. The full seasonal campaign would show three families enjoying the festivities along with one essential product that was purchased at Sainsbury's—gravy. One family was multiracial, another family was White, and the first family launching the campaign was Black.

The Black family was depicted doing what many families do that time of year—laughing, telling stories, singing, eating, toasting good cheer. Most of the footage used in the Sainsbury's commercial was the family's actual videos from past holidays. One of the home videos shows an adult daughter on the phone with her father. They reminisce about past Christmases and debate gravy-making skills. The tag line for the commercial: "Food is Home. Home is Christmas." The commercial clip quickly tallied over 1 million views.

Then came the backlash.

Critics of the Sainsbury's commercial accused the supermarket of virtue signaling and said that showing an all-Black family was not "inclusive." One critic said, "The UK is 87% White. The West is hell-bent on denigrating its White population while exalting ethnic minorities."[15]

Another viewer offered a different perspective, responding to the backlash: "This is an ad for gravy, mate. They didn't hire White people, that's the only difference. If it were only White people, would you be thinking that POC [people of color] couldn't buy Sainsbury's gravy? No. Shows how alienated you feel when you don't see yourself. Imagine it was like that all the time."

Thanking the supermarket for representation, another viewer added: "With all the other Christmas ads mostly featuring interracial couples/families, it's nice that you have done a Black family, a dark skinned one at that! Who you rarely see on TV. Thank you."

Emma Bisley, head of broadcast marketing at Sainsbury's, posted the company's response to the critics and fans. Referring to the challenges the pandemic presented, she wrote: "We wanted to take a different approach with our Christmas campaign by simply reminding people that Christmas dishes are gestures of love and care, served up by those who matter most. It's our memories of these dishes, prepared by the people we love, that have the power to transport us home—whether we're there or not." Sainsbury's choices in its gravy advertising represent a conscious decision to tell a story that advances a larger narrative about an increasingly multicultural society.

Aunt Jemima, a Quaker Oats brand, was one of several food brands—including Uncle Ben's, Cream of Wheat, and Mrs. Butterworth's—that decided to announce redesigns of its packaging as protests against structural racism erupted across the United States in 2020. After *132 years*, the Aunt Jemima brand, launched November 1889, was renamed the Pearl Milling Company in June 2020. "We recognize Aunt Jemima's origins are based on a racial stereotype," said Kristin Kroepfl, vice president and chief marketing officer of Quaker Foods North America, in a news release.[16] That stereotype dates back to slavery. And those images perpetuate a story told in minstrel shows where White actors wore blackface. The company added that the change is an effort "toward progress on racial equality." To advance that progress, Quaker Foods, owned by PepsiCo, is telling a new story. Kroepfl said that the company has worked to "update" the brand to be "appropriate and respectful" but that it realized the changes were "insufficient." Retiring Aunt Jemima matters. Why? Because the logo perpetuates an outdated narrative (slavery was abolished in the United States in 1865), premised on the idea of Black inferiority and otherness.

"Our perceptions are formed based on a combination of our real, lived experiences, and the images and stories we've been exposed to that fill in the rest," says Isis Dallis, managing director of Matter Unlimited, a New York City–based marketing firm.[17] "If you have no personal experiences with Black people to draw upon, (at home, in your social circles, or at work) then you're left with the images depicted in the media, in film, television, and literature that you choose to consume. Conversely, if you have real, lived personal experiences with a diverse range of Black people, then it will effectively balance or check any media images that contradict those experiences."

For example, say your company is a provider of health insurance. How do your marketing materials—brochure, website, or television ad—portray Black women? As college-educated, working professionals who make healthcare decisions on behalf of their family is one story. Depicting Black women as Medicaid recipients is another. And there are many others. People's experiences with a diverse spectrum of Black women will determine the stories they tell about them. To their friends. Family. Coworkers. Clients.

> Don't agree with what you hear but don't know the facts to seize a micro-opportunity to advance a new narrative? Then educate yourself. And add your voice to the chorus of new and emerging storytellers.

The dearth of people of color tells yet another story. Marketing manager Liz Rowan, whom you first met in Chapter 4, is always considering whether the photos in her corporate collateral represent the diverse customers her company serves. "There's this website I use. If I type in 'cloud technology,' it's all White people's hands on the mouse. That's not the message we want to send. Our customers are not only White."[18]

What Rowan is talking about is storytelling. Working on a more diverse team now, Rowan doesn't feel the burden she once felt at a previous employer, where she was one of the few people of color. And also one of the few who she felt cared about diversity, equity, and inclusion. "It was frustrating because I was the only person speaking up about the need to ensure our marketing materials represented the diverse customers we serve. At times I felt like a nuisance. At Amazon Web Services I feel like I have broader support. It feels more energizing and that our DEI efforts are going in the right direction."

The people you choose to represent your company at a meeting with a potential sponsor tell another race story. When a coworker whispers that the new guy is a "diversity hire" and you believe that isn't true and you say nothing, your silence perpetuates an old story. When you speak up and recommend a coworker of color who has the skills to represent the company on an event panel, you are advancing an antiracist narrative. When you hear "Why don't Black and Brown people just pick themselves up by their bootstraps" and then share what you now know about structural racism, you are telling a new, greater informed story. And if you do know the facts and don't share them, then your behavior is telling yet another story. Don't agree with what you hear but don't know the facts to seize a micro-opportunity to advance a new narrative? Then educate yourself. And add your voice to the chorus of new and emerging storytellers.

AROUND THE WORLD . . .
IN A MATTER OF MINUTES

Cell phones with built-in cameras are ubiquitous; so are social media, instant messaging, and a by-the-minute news cycle. The world is shrinking. An isolated incident half a world away, in a small, isolated town, cosmopolitan city, or developing nation, can travel around the globe in minutes. A digitally connected global population makes us more aware of what's happening in other countries. We saw this with the Black Lives Matter movement in the United States that has now spread throughout the world. Marketers pay particular attention to what's happening in the world because they know current events shape brand loyalty and affect sales.

When we interviewed Zakira Bhura, whom you first met in Chapter 5, she told us how the impact of the racial protests in the United States during the summer of 2020 made its way to her country of origin, India.[19] The Black Lives Matter movement prompted the manufacturer of a popular skin moisturizing cream called "Fair & Lovely" to rename the product, changing it to "Glow & Lovely." A name change, according to Bhura, in response to an awakening that Fair & Lovely implied that fair-skinned is coveted and dark skin is less desirable.

After our interview with Bhura, we explored this business case. We learned that Hindustan Unilever Ltd., the parent company of the product, announced on June 25, 2020, that "it will remove the terms 'fair,' 'whitening' and 'lightening' from Fair & Lovely's packaging and marketing material and feature women of all skin tones in future advertising campaigns."[20]

> Every action your business takes to advance race work is another chapter of a more expansive narrative. And with that story, you are wielding the power to influence the perceptions of the larger society. What stories will you tell?

Like Sainsbury, Hindustan Unilever took some backlash for this decision from a business peer, Emami, which had just launched an expensive marketing campaign for male consumers of its "Fair and Handsome" product line. According to Bloomberg, the global media and financial data and analytics conglomerate: "Triggered by incidents of police brutality against Blacks, the Black Lives Matter movement has gained traction around the world and spurred companies to reassess their businesses and marketing for signs of discrimination. J&J said a couple of weeks ago that it would retreat from its skin-whitening business, which includes the Clean & Clear Fairness brand in India and its Neutrogena Fine Fairness line in Asia and the Middle East."

Every action your business takes to advance race work is another chapter of a more expansive narrative. And with that story, you are wielding the power to influence the perceptions of the larger society. What stories will you tell? In the Introduction to this book, recall that we said this journey will be exciting and daunting. A journey that is both fraught with missteps and filled with surprising giant steps. A journey that at times is both self-reflective and other-focused. We hope you agree. We also asked you to reflect on why you picked up this book. And then asked you to write down your "why." Take a look at it now. How have the history you learned, the tools introduced, and the voices you heard informed your "why"? That you picked up this book tells us that you believe you can do something. And you can.

> No matter where you sit in your organization, you have the power.

You can be a Joanna Barsh, Heather Bodington, Zakira Bhura, Nina Davis, Everett Harper, Ben Hecht, Susan Somersille Johnson, Ray Martinez, Manuel Meza, Marianne Monte, Rochelle Newman-Carrasco, Nereida Perez, Erneshia Pinder, Rajesh Ramachandran, Christine Robinson, Liz Rowan, Karen Senteio, Kathy Taylor, Heather Thomas-McClellan, Lorie Valle-Yañez, or any of the other voices we shared on these pages. No matter where you sit in your organization, you have the power. It's our hope that *The Business of Race* has inspired you to use it.

We leave you with one last story. We hope it energizes you to start or continue your race work journey. To be curious about the people you work with. To reimagine a workplace where everyone can realize their dreams and fullest potential.

––––––––––

Her name is Liz.[21] When she was younger, she lived a few blocks from her dad's dad near the Van Ness Metro stop in Washington, DC. She called him Carl. Not Grandpa. Carl. It wasn't until she was in her twenties that she began to read his books and reflect upon his achievements and the sacrifices he made.

His full name was Carl Thomas Rowan. The American civil rights leader. The only Black reporter in the South in the 1960s. A friend of Dr. Martin Luther King Jr., whom he later helped to save the Montgomery Bus boycott. He also had collected many firsts:

> That's when I realized that every small, intentional act makes a difference, and it adds up.

the first Black nationally syndicated newspaper columnist; the first Black deputy secretary of state; the first Black director of the US Information Agency—the highest government position held by a Black man in 1964.

Liz Rowan (yes, the same Liz Rowan mentioned earlier in the chapter) is his granddaughter, a millennial who self-identifies as biracial: her father is Carl's son; her mother is White. Carl died when Liz Rowan was still a teenager, but he had a profound impact on her life and worldview. Rowan recalls:

> He used to get death threats. He would also get postcards delivered to his house with a photo of his face, usually cut from his newspaper column, with only the word "n****r" and "Washington DC" written on it. No name. No address. And it was still delivered through the US Postal Service.
>
> One time he opened a letter some woman wrote that read: "Dear Mister Rowan, life for you must be such a terrible burden being black and stupid at the same time."
>
> I asked him if he wrote back, and he said, "Well, I responded like I would all of my regular mail, and I wrote, 'Dear Madam, life for you can't possibly be so hard since you obviously only have half my burden.' He had lots of critics or haters, to say the least. People that threatened his life and wanted him to shut up. And he didn't do it because he knew that what he was doing was right and he believed in it.
>
> I used to feel like I could never make as big of an impact as my grandfather did. Where do I even start? But then I started thinking about all of the small things in his life that came together to make him able to have an

impact. That's when I realized that every small, intentional act makes a difference, and it adds up."

In June 2020, Rowan shared a few stories of her grandfather's work with her team at Amazon Web Services. She ended with a call to action for her team, for all of us:

When it comes to fighting for a society where Black lives are free from systematic dehumanization, I certainly can't claim to have the answers. But I know I am energized by the support of Black Lives Matter, the increase in donations to civil rights organizations, the push to change discriminatory policies and laws, the increase in strong and visible Black voices, and the pledges from so many of my friends, many of whom are already allies, that they will never again be complicit, and instead be proactively antiracist. And when I get overwhelmed by what I can do as one individual person, I revisit stories like Carl's and remember that every single intentional act against injustice and against racism made a difference in his life and will make a difference in this imperative fight for equality. With that, I challenge you all to think about what you can do to make a difference in the next Carl Rowan's life.

ADDITIONAL RESOURCES

Chapter 1

Book: *Blueprint for a Revolution: How to Use Rice Pudding, Lego Men, and Other Nonviolent Techniques to Galvanize Communities, Overthrow Dictators or Simply Change the World,* by Srdja Popovic.

Book/Play: *Twilight: Los Angeles, 1992,* by actor and playwright Anna Deavere Smith.

Chapter 4

Book: *The Big Sort: Why the Clustering of Like-Minded America Is Tearing Us Apart,* by Bill Bishop.

Website: National Museum of African American History and Culture at the Smithsonian, https://nmaahc.si.edu/.

Website: *Historical Foundations of Race,* National Museum of African American History and Culture at the Smithsonian, https://nmaahc.si.edu/learn/talking-about-race/topics/historical -foundations-race.

Book: *The Construction of Whiteness: An Interdisciplinary Analysis of Race Formation and the Meaning of a White Identity,* by David R. Roediger.

Website: The Equal Justice Initiative https://eji.org/.

Video: *How Can We Win,* by Kimberly Jones, https://digg.com/ video/how-can-we-win-kimberly-jones.

Book: *The Warmth of Other Suns: The Epic Story of America's Great Migration,* by Isabel Wilkerson.

Website: The Jim Crow Museum of Racist Memorabilia, https://www.ferris.edu/HTMLS/news/jimcrow/#.

Video: PBS's *Race: The Power of an Illusion*, https://www.racepower ofanillusion.org/.

Video: "A Class Divided," *Frontline*, https://www.pbs.org/wgbh/frontline/film/class-divided/.

Online course: Race and Cultural Diversity in American Life and History, University of Illinois at Urbana-Champaign, now offered for free by the giant online curator Coursera, https://www.coursera.org/learn/race-cultural-diversity-american-life.

Online course: Global Diversity and Inclusion: Beyond Microsoft, https://www.microsoft.com/en-us/diversity/beyond-microsoft/default.aspx.

Chapter 5

Book: *We Can't Talk About That at Work! How to Talk About Race, Religion, Politics, and Other Polarizing Topics*, by Mary-Frances Winters.

Website: The Race Card Project, https://theracecardproject.com/.

Antiracist Style Indicator (ASI): https://asi.dlplummer.com/.

Website: US Census Questions About Race on Form, https://2020census.gov/en/about-questions/2020-census-questions-race.html.

Website: VIA Character Strengths, http://businessofrace.pro.viasurvey.org.

Book: *How the Irish Became White*, by Noel Ignatiev.

Chapter 6

Book: *Awakening Compassion at Work: The Quiet Power That Elevates People and Organizations*, by Monica Worline and Jane E. Dutton.

Book: *The Empathy Effect: Seven Neuroscience-Based Keys for Transforming the Way We Live, Love, Work, and Connect Across Differences*, by Helen Riess and Liz Neporent

Book: *Mindset: Changing the Way You Think to Fulfill Your Potential*, updated edition, by Carol Dweck.

Book: *The Agile Learner: Where Growth Mindset, Habits of Mind and Practice Unite*, by James Anderson

Article: "Fixed vs Growth: Two Ends of a Mindset Continuum," by James Anderson, https://mindfulbydesign.com/fixed-vs-growth-two -ends-mindset-continuum/.

James Anderson Website: www.jamesanderson.com.au.

Mindset Continuum chart, James Anderson: https://mindfulby design.com/wp-content/uploads/2017/04/mindset_continuum.pdf.

Book: *The Net and the Butterfly: The Art and Practice of Breakthrough Thinking*, by Olivia Fox Cabane and Judah Pollack.

Book: *Six Thinking Hats*, by Edward de Bono.

Chapter 7

Film: Wachowski, Lana, and Lilly Wachowski. 1999. *The Matrix*. United States: Warner Bros.

Book: *The Fearless Organization: Creating Psychological Safety in the Workplace for Learning, Innovation, and Growth*, by Amy Edmonson.

Chapter 8

Book: *Thin Book of SOAR: Creating Strategy That Inspires Innovation and Engagement*, by Jacqueline M. Stavros and Gina Hinrichs.

Book: *Conversations Worth Having: Using Appreciative Inquiry to Fuel Productive and Meaningful Engagement*, by Jacqueline M. Stavros and Cheri Torres.

Report: Annie E. Casey Foundation's "Race Matters: Organizational Self-Assessment," https://www.aecf.org/resources/race-matters -organizational-self-assessment/.

Chapter 9

Book: *Moneyball: The Art of Winning an Unfair Game*, by Michael Lewis.

Professional Groups:
- Society of Hispanic Professional Engineers (SHPE), https://www.shpe.org/
- National Asian Pacific American Bar Association (NAPABA), https://www.napaba.org/
- National Association of Black Accountants (NABA), https://www.nabainc.org/.
- National Society for Black Engineers (NSBE), https://www.nsbe.org/.
- Society of Black Architects (SOBA) (UK), https://www.facebook.com/groups/5840238732/.
- National Association of Black Journalists (NABJ), https://nabjonline.org/.
- Wall Street Friends (Network of Black Finance Professionals), https://www.wallstreetfriends.org/our-team.
- Valence. Online centralized network of 10,000 Black professionals concentrated in the tech industry, https://valence.community/.
- OneTen. A coalition of leading executives who are coming together to upskill, hire, and advance one million Black individuals in the United States over the next 10 years. https://www.oneten.org/.
- Bridge Partners LLC. BIPOC-owned retained executive search firm that engages an inclusive search process from start to finish that purposefully brings diverse leaders to the table. https://www.bridgepartnersllc.com/.
- The Divine Nine and the National Pan-Hellenic Council (NPHC), http://www.blackgreek.com/divinenine/.
- Historically Black Colleges and Universities. There are 107 colleges in the United States that are identified by the US Department of Education as Historically Black Colleges and

Universities (HBCUs). Website includes alphabetical listing by state: http://www.thehundred-seven.org/hbculist.html.
* Hispanic-Serving Institutions (HSIs). Visit the Hispanic Association of Colleges and Universities (HACU): https://www.hacu.net/assnfe/CompanyDirectory.asp?STYLE=2&COMPANY_TYPE=1%2C5.
* Tribal Colleges and Universities (TCUs). Explore the tribal colleges and universities. More information about each college can also be found by clicking their name in the list below the map. See online, Tribal College, Journal of American Indian Higher Education: https://tribalcollegejournal.org/map-of-tribal-colleges/.
* American Indian Higher Education Consortium (AIHEC) is founded by six tribal colleges. In 1973, the first six American Indian tribally controlled colleges established the American Indian Higher Education Consortium (AIHEC) to provide a support network as they worked to influence federal policies on American Indian higher education. Today, AIHEC has grown to 37 Tribal Colleges and Universities (TCUs) in the United States. Each of these institutions was created and chartered by its own tribal government or the federal government for a specific purpose: to provide higher education opportunities to American Indians through programs that are locally and culturally based, holistic, and supportive. Visit online: http://aihec.org/index.html.
* The Asian American and Native American Pacific Islander-Serving Institutions (AANAPISIs). The AANAPISI program, one of eight federally designated Minority Serving Institution (MSI) programs, was established by Congress in 2007 as part of the College Cost Reduction and Access Act. It was expanded in 2008 under the Higher Education Opportunity Act. Visit online: https://www.aanapisi.net/.

Book: *I'm Still Here: Black Dignity in a World Made for Whiteness*, by Austin Channing Brown.

Chapter 13

Assessment: Intercultural Competence Using the Intercultural Development Inventory (IDI), https://idiinventory.com/.

Chapter 14

Tools: Center for Story-based Strategy (Creators of #the4thBox), https://www.storybasedstrategy.org/.

Website: Solve Next, https://solvenext.com/think-wrong-book

Book: *Think Wrong: How to Conquer the Status Quo and Do Work that Matters*, by John Bielenberg, Mike Burn, Greg Galle, Elizabeth Evitts Dickinson

NOTES

Chapter 1

1. Author interview with Erneshia Pinder, November 11, 2020.
2. Argyris, C., *Overcoming Organizational Defenses: Facilitating Organizational Learning*, Pearson, New York, 1990.
3. Personal conversation, Greenberg and Greenlee, June 2020.
4. Rich, M., "Restrictive Covenants Stubbornly Stay on the Books," *New York Times*, April 21, 2005.
5. Holtje, M., "It's Not Over: A Historical and Contemporary Look at Racial Restrictive Covenants," Homelight.com, September 14, 2020.
6. Newman-Carrasco, R., shared with authors, interview January 2021.
7. Watt, N., and Hannah, J., "Racist Language Is Still Woven into Home Deeds Across America. Erasing It Isn't Easy, and Some Don't Want To," *CNN*, February 15, 2020, https://www.cnn.com/2020/02/15/us/racist-deeds -covenants/index.html.
8. Popovic, S., *Blueprint for a Revolution: How to Use Rice Pudding, Lego Men, and Other Nonviolent Techniques to Galvanize Communities, Overthrow Dictators or Simply Change the World*, Random House, New York, 2015.
9. Latson, J., "How Poisoned Tylenol Became a Crisis-Management Teaching Model," *Time* magazine, September 2014.
10. Markel, H., "How the Tylenol Murders of 1982 Changed the Way We Consume Medication," *PBS Newshour*, September 29, 2014.
11. Ibid.
12. Kiger, P. J., "Minimum Wage in America: A Timeline," *History News*, October 28, 2019, https://www.history.com/news/minimum-wage -america-timeline.
13. Taylor, K., "Jeff Bezos Called for Amazon's Competitors to Raise Their Minimum Wage. Here's How Retail Rivals like Walmart, Target, and Costco Stack Up on Worker Pay," *Business Insider*, April 2019.
14. Smith, A. D., *Twilight: Los Angeles, 1992*, Anchor Books, New York, 1994.
15. Eswaran, V., "The Business Case for Diversity in the Workplace Is Now Overwhelming," World Economic Forum, April 29. 2019, https:// www.weforum.org/agenda/2019/04/business-case-for-diversity-in-the -workplace/.
16. Author interview with Nereida Perez, January 12, 2021.
17. Author interview with Erneshia Pinder, November 11, 2020.

18. Greenberg, M. and Greenlee, G, Race in the Workplace Online Survey, August–September, 2020.

Chapter 2

1. Eswaran, V., "The Business Case for Diversity in the Workplace Is Now Overwhelming," World Economic Forum, April 29, 2019, https://www.weforum.org/agenda/2019/04/business-case-for-diversity-in-the-workplace/.
2. Hunt, V., Prince, S., Dixon-Fyle, S., and Yee, L., "Delivering Through Diversity," McKinsey and Company, January 2019 , https://www.mckinsey.com/~/media/mckinsey/business%20functions/organization/our%20insights/delivering%20through%20diversity/delivering-through-diversity_full-report.ashx.
3. "2018 Deloitte Millennial Survey: Millennials Disappointed in Business, Unprepared for Industry 4.0," https://www2.deloitte.com/content/dam/Deloitte/global/Documents/About-Deloitte/gx-2018-millennial-survey-report.pdf.
4. Lorenzo, R., Voigt, N., Tsusaka, M., Krentz, M., and Abouzahr, K., "How Diverse Leadership Teams Boost Innovation," BCG Henderson Institute, January 23, 2018, https://www.bcg.com/publications/2018/how-diverse-leadership-teams-boost-innovation.
5. Creary, S., Rothbard, N., Mariscal, E., Moore, O., Scruggs, J., and Villarmán, N., "Evidence-Based Solutions for Inclusion in the Workplace: Actions for Middle Managers," Wharton People Analytics, Diversity Inc., May 2020, p. 2.
6. "70% of Job Seekers Value a Company's Commitment to Diversity When Evaluating Potential Employers," *PRNewswire*, June 18, 2020, https://www.prnewswire.com/news-releases/70-of-job-seekers-value-a-companys-commitment-to-diversity-when-evaluating-potential-employers-301079330.html.
7. Greenberg, M., and Greenlee, G., Race in the Workplace Survey, August–September 2020.
8. Hunt, Prince, Dixon-Fyle, and Yee, "Delivering Through Diversity."
9. Author interview with Kathy Taylor, December 14, 2020.
10. Peterson, Dana M., and Mann, Catherine L., "Closing the Racial Inequality Gaps: The Economic Cost of Black Inequality in the U.S.," *Citi GPS*, September 2020, https://www.citivelocity.com/citigps/closing-the-racial-inequality-gaps/.
11. Author interview with Ben Hecht, December 8. 2020.
12. Rojas, R., and Atkinson, K., "50 Years After the Uprising: Five Days of Unrest That Shaped, and Haunted, Newark," *New York Times*, July 11, 2017, https://www.nytimes.com/2017/07/11/nyregion/newark-riots-50-years.html.
13. Author interview with Susan Somersille Johnson, January 28, 2021.
14. Author interview with Ray Martinez, December 3, 2020.

Part II

1. American Psychiatric Association, "APA's Apology to Black, Indigenous, and People of Color for Its Support of Structural Racism in Psychiatry." January 18, 2021, https://www.psychiatry.org/newsroom/apa-apology-for -its-support-of-structural-racism-in-psychiatry.

Chapter 3

1. Macdonald , M., "'I Am Not Your Negro' review: A Poetic Journey Into The Heart Of The Civil-Rights Movement," *Seattle Times*, February 1, 2017, https://www.seattletimes.com/entertainment/movies/i-am-not-your-negro -review-a-poetic-journey-into-the-heart-of-the-civil-rights-movement/
2. Author interview with Lorie Valle-Yañez, December 17, 2020.
3. MultiCultural Institute, "Diversity & Inclusion: An Overview," *Diversity Primer*, Chap. 1, https://www.diversitybestpractices.com/sites/ diversitybestpractices.com/files/import/embedded/anchors/files/diversity_ primer_chapter_01.pdf.
4. Newkirk, P., *Diversity, Inc.: The Fight for Racial Equality in the Workplace*, Bold Type Books, New York, 2020.
5. Roberts, B., Women and Leadership Archives, Loyola University Chicago, https://www.luc.edu/media/lucedu/wla/pdfs/Roberts,%20Bari-Ellen.pdf.
6. Mulligan, Thomas S. and Kraul, Chris, "Texaco Settles Race Bias Suit for $176 Million," *Los Angeles Times*, November 16, 1996; https://www .latimes.com/archives/la-xpm-1996-11-16-mn-65290-story.html.
7. Anand, R., and Winters, M., "A Retrospective View of Corporate Diversity Training from 1964 to the Present," *Academy of Management Learning & Education*, vol. 7, no. 3, pp. 356–372, 2008.
8. https://www.hudson.org/about/history and https://www.amazon.com/ Workforce-2000-Workers-Century-Executive/dp/0160038871.
9. McCormick, Kate, "The Evolution of Workplace Diversity," State Bar of Texas 15th Annual Advanced Employment Law Course, Chap.16.1, February 1–2, 2007, http://www.texasbarcle.com/Materials/Events/6369/ 4079_01.pdf.
10. Author interview with Nereida Perez, January 12, 2021.
11. Ibid.
12. Anand and Winters, "A Retrospective View of Corporate Diversity Training from 1964 to the Present."
13. Newkirk, *Diversity, Inc.*
14. Newkirk, *Diversity, Inc.*
15. Newkirk, *Diversity, Inc.*
16. Newkirk, *Diversity, Inc.*
17. Holmes, Steven A. "Blacks, Citing Bias at Work, Sue Coca-Cola, "*New York Times*, April 23, 1999, https://www.nytimes.com/1999/04/23/business/ blacks-citing-bias-at-work-sue-coca-cola.html.
18. Email exchange between the authors and the anonymous person in May 2021.

19. Author breakout group discussion "How Can Companies Move Beyond Race Talk to Racial Equity," University of Pennsylvania Masters of Applied Positive Psychology (MAPP) Summit, October 24, 2020.
20. Newman-Carrasco, R., "Why the Ad Industry's Diversity Strategy Needs a New Brief: The Phrase 'Diversity and Inclusion' Is Doing Our Industry More Harm Than Good," *AdAge*, August 2016 , https://adage.com/article/agency-viewpoint/ad-industry-s-diversity-strategy-a/305638.

Chapter 4

1. Oliver, J., "America's Failures on Black America," *Broken News* (video transcript), June 2020, https://www.youtube.com/watch?v=aE8OqAtbn0s.
2. Author discussion with anonymous consultant, December 2020.
3. Author interview with Liz Rowan, December 21, 2020.
4. "George Floyd: Timeline of Black Deaths and Protests," *BBC News*, April 22, 2021, https://www.bbc.com/news/world-us-canada-52905408.
5. Ibid.
6. Ibid.
7. "Tamir Rice Killing: US Closes Investigation into 2014 Shooting," *BBC News*, December 30, 2020, https://www.bbc.com/news/world-us-canada-55481339.
8. "George Floyd: Timeline of Black Deaths and Protests."
9. Ibid.
10. Ibid.
11. Ibid.
12. "Federal Officials Decline Prosecution in the Death of Freddie Gray," *Justice News*, US Department of Justice, Office of Public Affairs, September 12, 2017, https://www.justice.gov/opa/pr/federal-officials-decline-prosecution-death-freddie-gray.
13. Serrano, Richard A. "All 4 Acquitted in King Beating: Verdict Stirs Outrage; Bradley Calls It Senseless: Trial: Ventura County jury rejects charges of excessive force in episode captured on videotape. A mistrial is declared on one count against Officer Powell," *Los Angeles Times*, April 30, 1992, https://www.latimes.com/archives/la-xpm-1992-04-30-mn-1942-story.html.
14. Hassett-Walker, Connie, "How You Start Is How You Finish? The Slave Patrol and Jim Crow Origins of Policing," *Human Rights* magazine, Vol. 46, No. 2, January 12, 2021, https://www.americanbar.org/groups/crsj/publications/human_rights_magazine_home/civil-rights-reimagining-policing/how-you-start-is-how-you-finish/.
15. Hassett-Walker, Connie, "The Racist Roots of American Policing: From Slave Patrols to Traffic Stops," June 4, 2019 (updated June 2, 2020), https://theconversation.com/the-racist-roots-of-american-policing-from-slave-patrols-to-traffic-stops-112816.
16. Robinson, Michael, "From the Slave Codes to Mike Brown: The Brutal History of African Americans and Law Enforcement," *Justice and Domestic Affairs* (blog), October 5, 2017, https://blogs.lse.ac.uk/

usappblog/2017/10/05/from-the-slave-codes-to-mike-brown-the-bruta
l-history-of-african-americans-and-law-enforcement/.

17. Potter, Gary, "The History of Policing in the United States," Gary Potter @ EKUonline, https://plsonline.eku.edu/sites/plsonline.eku.edu/files/the -history-of-policing-in-us.pdf.

18. Hassett-Walker, "How You Start Is How You Finish?"

19. Green, Jeff, "Floyd Killing Forces U.S. Business to Examine Its Record on Race," *Bloomberg News*, April 21, 2021, https://www.bloomberg.com/ news/articles/2021-04-21/floyd-killing-forces-u-s-business-to-examine -its-record-on-race. For information on the OneTen Coalition, go to https://www.oneten.org/.

20. "The Participation of Black Workers in the US Private-Sector Economy," February 2021 report by McKinsey & Co., https://www .mckinsey.com/featured-insights/diversity-and-inclusion/race-in-the -workplace-the-black-experience-in-the-us-private-sector#.

21. "A Class Divided," *Frontline*, March 26, 1985, https://www.pbs.org/wgbh/ frontline/film/class-divided/.

22. *Race: The Power of an Illusion*, California Newsreel, Larry Adelman, executive producer, 2003, https://www.racepowerofanillusion.org/.

23. University of Illinois at Urbana-Champaign: Race and Cultural Diversity in American Life and History, https://www.coursera.org/learn/ race-cultural-diversity-american-life.

24. Yoshino, K., "Inclusion and Covering," Beyond Microsoft, June 30, 2020, https://www.microsoft.com/en-us/diversity/beyond-microsoft/default .aspx.

25. The Human Genome Project: National Human Genome Research Institute, https://www.genome.gov/human-genome-project.

26. *Race: The Power of an Illusion*, Episode 1 (program transcript), California Newsreel, Larry Adelman, executive producer, 2003, https://www.pbs.org/ race/000_About/002_04-about-01-01.htm.

27. *Race: The Power of an Illusion*, California Newsreel.

28. The Human Genome Project, https://www.genome.gov/human-genome -project.

29. Definition of Race: National Human Genome Research Institute, https:// www.genome.gov/genetics-glossary/Race.

30. Night, S., "Are Humans Naturally Tribal?," Be Human Project, March 5, 2014, https://behumanproject.org/why-are-we-tribal/.

31. Bishop, B., *The Big Sort: Why the Clustering of Like-Minded America Is Tearing Us Apart*, Mariner Books, Boston, 2008.

32. "Historical Foundations of Race," National Museum of African American History and Culture at the Smithsonian, https://nmaahc.si.edu/learn/ talking-about-race/topics/historical-foundations-race.

33. Ibid.

34. *Race: The Power of an Illusion*, California Newsreel.

35. Jefferson, Thomas, *Notes on Virginia*, 1781, Thomas Jefferson Foundation, https://docsouth.unc.edu/southlit/jefferson/jefferson.html.

36. The White House: James Madison, https://www.whitehouse.gov/about-the-white-house/presidents/james-madison/.
37. *Race: The Power of an Illusion*, California Newsreel.
38. Ambrose, Stephen E., "Founding Fathers and Slaveholders," *Smithsonian* magazine, November 2002, https://www.smithsonianmag.com/history/founding-fathers-and-slaveholders-72262393/.
39. Kindy, D., "New Research Suggests Alexander Hamilton Was a Slave Owner," *Smithsonian* magazine, November 2020, https://www.smithsonianmag.com/history/new-research-alexander-hamilton-slave-owner-180976260/.
40. Iaccarino, A., "The Founding Fathers and Slavery," *Britannica*, January 2007, https://www.britannica.com/topic/The-Founding-Fathers-and-Slavery-1269536.
41. History.com Editors, "Trail of Tears," November 2009, updated July 2020, https://www.history.com/topics/native-american-history/trail-of-tears.
42. *Race: The Power of an Illusion*, California Newsreel.
43. Blakemore, Erin, "The Brutal History of Anti-Latino Discrimination in America," *History Stories*, updated August 29, 2018, https://www.history.com/news/the-brutal-history-of-anti-latino-discrimination-in-america.
44. *Race: The Power of an Illusion*, California Newsreel.
45. Jones, K., *How Can We Win*, June 2020, https://digg.com/video/how-can-we-win-kimberly-jones/.
46. Wilkerson, I., *The Warmth of Other Suns: The Epic Story of American's Great Migration*, Penguin Random House, New York, 2011.
47. "The Origins of Jim Crow," home page, Jim Crow Museum of Racist Memorabilia, Ferris State University, https://www.ferris.edu/HTMLS/news/jimcrow/origins.htm.
48. "What Was Jim Crow?," Jim Crow Museum of Racist Memorabilia, Ferris State University, https://www.ferris.edu/HTMLS/news/jimcrow/what.htm.
49. Ijeoma Oluo on Talking About Race and Racism, New York State Writers Institute, October, 2019, https://www.youtube.com/watch?v=2b_twxTjaoE&t=379s.
50. Equal Justice Initiative, "On this day Apr 24, 1877: Federal Troops Leave South, Ending Reconstruction," https://calendar.eji.org/racial-injustice/apr/24.
51. Traub, A., Sullivan, L., Meschede, T., and Shapiro, T., "The Asset Value of Whiteness: Understanding the Racial Wealth Gap—How Past Racial Injustices Are Carried Forward as Wealth Handed Down Across Generations and Reinforced by 'Color-Blind' Practices and Policies," Demos, February 2017, https://www.demos.org/sites/default/files/publications/Asset%20Value%20of%20Whiteness_0.pdf,
52. Peterson, Dana M., and Mann, Catherine L., "Closing the Racial Inequality Gaps: The Economic Cost of Black Inequality in the U.S.," *Citi GPS*, September 2020, https://www.citivelocity.com/citigps/closing-the-racial-inequality-gaps/.
53. Osbourne, H., "Financial Inequality: The Ethnicity Gap in Pay, Wealth and Property," *The Guardian*, June 2020, https://www.theguardian

.com/money/2020/jun/20/financial-inequality-the-ethnicity-gap-in-pay-wealth-and-property.

54. Jeung, R., Horse, A. Y., Popovic, T., and Lim, R., "Stop AAPI Hate National Report," March 2020, https://secureservercdn.net/104.238.69.231/a1w.90d.myftpupload.com/wp-content/uploads/2021/03/210312-Stop-AAPI-Hate-National-Report-.pdf.

55. "Authorities Name All Eight Victims in Atlanta Spa Shootings," *The Guardian*, March 19, 2021, https://www.theguardian.com/us-news/2021/mar/19/atlanta-spa-shootings-victims-named.

56. Lang, Cady, "The Atlanta Shootings Fit into a Long Legacy of Anti-Asian Violence in America," *Time* magazine, updated March 19, 2021, https://time.com/5947723/atlanta-shootings-anti-asian-violence-america/?utm_medium=email&utm_source=sfmc&utm_campaign=newsletter+brief+default+ac&utm_content=+++20210318+++body&et_rid=150152715.

57. Suyin Haynes, "As Coronavirus Spreads, So Does Xenophobia and Anti-Asian Racism," *Time* magazine, March 6, 2020, https://time.com/5797836/coronavirus-racism-stereotypes-attacks/.

58. Chow, K., "'Model Minority' Myth Again Used as a Racial Wedge Between Asians and Blacks," *Code Switch*, NPR, April 19, 2017, https://www.npr.org/sections/codeswitch/2017/04/19/524571669/model-minority-myth-again-used-as-a-racial-wedge-between-asians-and-blacks.

59. Lang, "The Atlanta Shootings Fit into a Long Legacy of Anti-Asian Violence in America," To learn more about Vincent Chin, see Little, Becky, "How the 1982 Murder of Vincent Chin Ignited a Push for Asian American Rights," *History Stories*, May 5, 2020, https://www.history.com/news/vincent-chin-murder-asian-american-rights.

60. Lang, "The Atlanta Shootings Fit into a Long Legacy of Anti-Asian Violence in America."

61. Ibid.

62. Author interview with Ray Martinez, December 3, 2020.

Chapter 5

1. Author interview with Joanna Barsh, January 5, 2021.

2. Plummer, D., Antiracist Style Indicator, https://asi.dlplummer.com/.

3. Vincenty, S., "Being 'Color Blind' Doesn't Make You Not Racist—in Fact, It Can Mean the Opposite," *Oprah Daily*, June 12, 2020.

4. Eberhardt, J., "Science: The 'Colorblind' Approach to Racism Doesn't Work: You Can't Make Your Kids Nonracist by Pretending Race Doesn't Exist," Literary Hub, April 2019, https://lithub.com/science-the-colorblind-approach-to-racism-doesnt-work/.

5. Wilkerson, I., *Caste: The Origins of Our Discontents*, Random House, New York, 2020.

6. Hirsch, Afua, "The 'Playing the Race Card' Accusation Is Just a Way to Silence Us," January 16, 2020, https://www.theguardian.com/commentisfree/2020/jan/16/playing-the-race-card-racism-black-experience.

7. NALEO Educational Fund, https://naleo.org.
8. "2020 Census Questionnaire Guidance for Latino Respondents," Hagase Contar, https://hagasecontar.org/wp-content/uploads/2020/03/Census-form-instructions-NEF-03092020-Final-1.pdf.
9. Travae, M., "Racial Classification and Terminology in Brazil," *Black Brazil Today*, November 2011, https://blackbraziltoday.com/racial-classification-and-terminology-in-brazil/.
10. Jean-Philippe, M., "So, What's the Difference Between Race and Ethnicity?," *Oprah* magazine, August 2019.
11. Author interview with Susan Somersille Johnson, January 28, 2021.
12. Author interview with Zakira Bhura, January 13, 2021.
13. Author interview with Manuel Meza, January 12, 2021.
14. Parvini S., and Simani, E., "Are Arabs and Iranians White? Census Says Yes, but Many Disagree," *Los Angeles Times*, March 2019.
15. Jean-Philippe, M., "So, What's the Difference Between Race and Ethnicity?" Oprah Daily, August 26, 2019. https://www.oprahdaily.com/life/a28787295/race-vs-ethnicity-difference/
16. Ignatiev, N., *How the Irish Became White*, Routledge, London, 1995.
17. Author interview with Lorie Valle-Yañez, December 17, 2020.
18. Author interview with Ruth Pearce, December 2, 2020.

Chapter 6

1. "Apple CEO Tim Cook Speaks on Diversity and Inclusion at Auburn University," *Silicon Review*, April 10, 2017, https://thesiliconreview.net/ceo-review/apple-ceo-tim-cook-speaks-on-diversity-and-inclusion-at-auburn-university.
2. Author interview with Erneshia Pinder, November 11, 2020.
3. Author interview with Heather Bodington, December 21, 2020.
4. Hughes, B., Camp, N., Gomez, J., Natu, V., Grill-Spector, K., and Eberhardt, J., "Neural Adaptation to Faces Reveals Racial Outgroup Homogeneity Effects in Early Perception," *Proceedings of the National Academy of Sciences*, vol. 116, no. 29, pp. 14532–14537, July 2019, https://doi.org/10.1073/pnas.1822084116.
5. Author interview with Susan Somersille Johnson, January 28, 2021.
6. Author interview with Joanna Barsh, January 5, 2021.
7. Author interview with Rajesh Ramachandran, January 21, 2021.
8. Worline, M., and Dutton, J., *Awakening Compassion at Work: The Quiet Power That Elevates People and Organizations,* Berrett-Koehler Publishers, Oakland, CA, 2017, p. 5.
9. Riess, H., *The Empathy Effect: 7 Neuroscience-Based Keys for Transforming the Way We Live, Work, and Connect Across Differences*, Sounds True Publishing, Boulder, CO, 2018, pp. 45–62.
10. Dweck, C., *Mindset: Changing the Way You Think to Fulfill Your Potential*, Random House, New York, 2017.

11. Anderson, James, "Fixed vs Growth: Two Ends of a Mindset Continuum," https://mindfulbydesign.com/fixed-vs-growth-two-ends-mindset-continuum/.
12. Ibid.
13. Gross-Loh, Christine, "How Praise Became a Consolation Prize," *The Atlantic*, December 16, 2016, https://www.theatlantic.com/education/archive/2016/12/how-praise-became-a-consolation-prize/510845/.
14. https://mindfulbydesign.com/fixed-vs-growth-two-ends-mindset-continuum/.
15. Anderson, J., *The Agile Learner: Where Growth Mindset, Habits of Mind and Practice Unite*, Melbourne, Hawkerbrownlow, 2017.
16. Rush, B., Rush Studios, https://rushstudios.briannarush.com/contact-2/.
17. Cabane, O. F., and Pollack, J., *The Net and the Butterfly: The Art and Practice of Breakthrough Thinking*, Portfolio, New York, 2017.
18. Author interview with Nina Davis, December 16, 2020.
19. de Bono, E., *Six Thinking Hats*, rev. and updated, Back Bay Books, Boston, 1999, https://www.amazon.com/Six-Thinking-Hats-Edward-Bono/dp/0316178314.
20. de Bono, E., Lateral Thinking, https://www.edwddebono.com/lateral-thinking.
21. Six Thinking Hats® content republished under license from the copyright holder deBono.com.

Chapter 7

1. Noah, T., *Born a Crime: Stories from a South African Childhood*, Spiegel & Grau, New York, 2016.
2. Greenberg, M., and Greenlee, G., Race in the Workplace Online Survey, August–September 2020.
3. Author interview with Kathy Taylor, December 14, 2020.
4. Starbucks Race Together Campaign, https://stories.starbucks.com/stories/2015/what-race-together-means-for-starbucks-partners-and-customers/.
5. Carr, A., "The Inside Story of Starbucks's Race Together Campaign, No Foam," *Fast Company*, June 2015.
6. Brooks, K., "Why So Many Black Business Professionals Are Missing from the C-suite," *CBS News*, December 2019, https://www.cbsnews.com/news/black-professionals-hold-only-3-percent-of-executive-jobs-1-percent-of-ceo-jobs-at-fortune-500-firms-new-report-says/.
7. Alcom, C., "Rosalind Brewer Officially Takes the Helm at Walgreens, Becoming the only Black Woman *Fortune* 500 CEO," CNN Business, March 15, 2021.
8. Author interview with Ben Hecht, December 8, 2020.
9. Author interview with Susan Somersille Johnson, January 28, 2021.
10. Author interview with Ray Martinez, December 3, 2020.
11. Author interview with Kathy Taylor, December 14, 2020.
12. Author conversation with Mhayse Samalya, June 2020.

13. Email conversation between Meghan Donahue and the authors, January 19, 2021.
14. https://quotecatalog.com/quote/iyanla-vanzant-if-you-trust-yo-adbA2R7.
15. Author interview with Karen Senteio, January 7, 2021.
16. Edmondson, A., *The Fearless Organization: Creating Psychological Safety in the Workplace for Learning, Innovation, and Growth*, Wiley, Hoboken, NJ, 2019.
17. Duhigg, C., "What Google Learned from Its Quest to Build the Perfect Team," *New York Times*, February 25, 2016.
18. *Creating Psychological Safety at Work in a Knowledge Economy | Amy Edmondson, Harvard* (video), July 2018, https://www.youtube.com/watch?v=KUo1QwVcCv0&t=7s.
19. Author interview with Christine Robinson, December 21, 2020.
20. Bennett, J., "What if Instead of Calling People Out, We Called Them In?," *New York Times*, November 19, 2020, https://www.nytimes.com/2020/11/19/style/loretta-ross-smith-college-cancel-culture.html.
21. Author interview with Ben Hecht, December 8, 2020.
22. McGlinchy, A., "After 'Damaging' Diversity Training, City Won't Use Company Again for Similar Workshops," Austin Monitor, September 11, 2020.
23. Author interview with Ben Hecht, December 8, 2020.
24. Author interview with Heather Thomas-McClellan, November 17, 2020.
25. Hecht, B., "Moving Beyond Diversity Toward Racial Equity," *Harvard Business Review*, June 2020.

Chapter 8

1. https://obamawhitehouse.archives.gov/blog/2016/03/08/international-womens-day-3-women-who-inspire-us.
2. Author interview with Everett Harper, November 19, 2020.
3. Author interview with Marianne Monte, December 11, 2020.
4. Slowey, K., "By the Numbers: Women in Construction," Construction Dive, March 6, 2019, https://www.constructiondive.com/news/by-the-numbers-women-in-construction/549359/.
5. Mishel, L., "The Increased Diversity of New York City Union Construction Employment," *Working Economics Blog*, January 19, 2017, https://www.epi.org/blog/the-increased-diversity-of-new-york-city-union-construction-employment/.
6. US Bureau of Labor Statistics, Industries at a Glance: Construction, https://www.bls.gov/iag/tgs/iag23.htm#workforce.
7. Prudential newsroom, "Prudential Deepens Commitment to Advance Racial Equity," August 5, 2020, https://news.prudential.com/prudential-deepens-commitment-to-advance-racial-equity.htm.
8. Author interview with Nereida Perez, January 12, 2021.
9. Author interview with Jackie Stavros, January 7, 2021.
10. Author interview with Heather Thomas-McClellan, November 17, 2020.

11. The Annie E. Casey Foundation, "Race Matters: Organizational Self-Assessment," January 12, 2006, https://www.aecf.org/resources/race-matters -organizational-self-assessment/.
12. Author interview with Lorie Valle-Yañez, December 17, 2020.
13. Smith, R., "How to Make Your Small Wins Work for You," Ideas.TED.com, January 29, 2019, https://ideas.ted.com/how-to-make-your-small-wins -work-for-you/.
14. Author interview with Christine Robinson, December 21, 2020.

Part V

1. Author interview with Susan Somersille Johnson, January 28, 2021.
2. Author interview with Joanna Barsh, January 5, 2021.
3. Author discussion with Leslie Ashford, January 5, 2021.
4. Author interview with Ray Martinez, December 3, 2020.

Chapter 9

1. Nigamboyz, "12 Motivational Quotes by Indra Nooyi, One of the Greatest Female CEO [*sic*] in the Present World," Bumppy, November 2, 2017, https://www.bumppy.com/12-motivational-quotes-by-indra-nooyi-one -of-the-greatest-female-ceo-in-the-present-world/.
2. Lewis, M., *Moneyball: The Art of Winning an Unfair Game*, W. W. Norton & Company, New York, 2004.
3. Haun, L., "Billy Beane and the Science of Talent Management, the Moneyball Way," ERE Media, February 28, 2012, https://www.tlnt.com/ billy-beane-and-the-science-of-talent-management-the-moneyball-way/.
4. Gardner, Hayes, "The Iowa State Dropout Who Started Baseball-Reference," *Ames Tribune*, October 4, 2019, https://www.amestrib.com/ sports/20191004/iowa-state-dropout-who-started-baseball-reference. Sean Foreman is the "Iowa State dropout." His LinkedIn page says that he is president of Sports Reference, LLC, and that he sets "direction and strategy for the largest group of sports statistics websites in the world."
5. Goldstein, P., "Splunk .Conf2017: Oakland A's Billy Beane Says Data Analytics Has Transformed Baseball," BizTech.com, September 28, 2017.
6. Zettelmeyer, F. and Bolling, M., "Billy Beane Shows Why Leaders Can't Leave Data Science to the Data Scientists," *Forbes*, September 23, 2014, https://www.forbes.com/sites/forbesleadershipforum/2014/09/23/billy -beane-shows-why-leaders-cant-leave-data-science-to-the-data-scientists/ ?sh=7abca1a74c7c.
7. Ibid.
8. "Wells Fargo CEO's Comments About Diverse Talent Anger Some Employees," *CNBC*, September 22, 2020, https://www.cnbc.com/ 2020/09/22/wells-fargo-ceo-ruffles-feathers-with-comments-about-diverse -talent.html.
9. Author interview with Ted Fleming, October 22, 2020.
10. "Wells Fargo CEO's Comments About Diverse Talent Anger Some Employees," *CNBC*, September 22, 2020, https://www.cnbc.com/

2020/09/22/wells-fargo-ceo-ruffles-feathers-with-comments-about-diverse-talent.html.

11. Anonymous, email exchange, October 20, 2020.

12. "About Us," National Association of Black Accountants, Inc., https://www.nabainc.org/about_us.

13. National Society of Black Engineers website, https://www.nsbe.org/home.aspx.

14. Wall Street Friends website, https://www.wallstreetfriends.org/our-team.

15. Stofer, A., and Quintard, B., "Diversity in U.S. Startups," RateMyInvestor in partnership with Diversity VC, https://ratemyinvestor.com/Diversity VCReport_Final.pdf.

16. Valence Community, https://valence.community/about.

17. Valence Community.

18. OneTen, https://www.oneten.org/.

19. Ibid.

20. Bridge Partners, https://www.bridgepartnersllc.com/.

21. Office of Civil Rights, Minority Serving Institutions Program, https://www.doi.gov/pmb/eeo/doi-minority-serving-institutions-program.

22. The Divine Nine website, http://www.blackgreek.com/divinenine/.

23. A History of Historically Black Colleges and Universities," https://hbcufirst.com/resources/hbcu-history-timeline.

24. White House Hispanic Prosperity Initiative, U.S. Department of Education, https://sites.ed.gov/hispanic-initiative/.

25. White House Initiative on American Indian and Alaska Native Education, https://sites.ed.gov/whiaiane/tribes-tcus/tribal-colleges-and-universities/.

26. The Asian American and Native American Pacific Islander-Serving Institutions (AANAPISIs), https://www.aanapisi.net/about_aanapisis.

27. Ibid.

28. MasterClass.com online course: Spike Lee Teaches Independent Filmmaking.

29. TDU website, "Teamsters Deserve Leadership That Looks Like the Membership and a Union That Fights For Social and Economic Justice for All Workers," reported the TDU, November 6, 2019, https://www.tdu.org/black_teamsters_are_building_power.

30. Teamsters website, https://teamster.org/about/leadership/.

31. Brown, A. C., *I'm Still Here: Black Dignity in a World Made for Whiteness*, Convergent Books, New York, 2018.

32. Kang, Sonia, DeCelles, K., Tilcsik, A., and Jun, S., "Whitened Résumés: Race and Self-Presentation in the Labor Market," *Administrative Science Quarterly*, Vol. 61, No. 3, pp. 469–502, September 2016.

33. Woodman, C., Greenberg and Greenlee Race in the Workplace Survey Results, September 28, 2020.

34. Wainwright, O., "Architects Elsie Owusu and Shawn Adams: 'Above the Glass Ceiling Is a Concrete Ceiling,'" *The Guardian*, June 25, 2020, https://www.theguardian.com/artanddesign/2020/jun/25/architects-elsie-owusu-and-shawn-adams-above-the-glass-ceiling-is-a-concrete-ceiling.

35. Author interview with Nereida Perez, January 12, 2021.

36. Author interview with Everett Harper, November 11, 2020.
37. Author email with Everett Harper, February 2021.
38. Author interview with Heather Bodington, December 21, 2020.

Chapter 10

1. Author interview with Karen Senteio, January 7, 2021.
2. The National Registry of Exonerations, a joint project of the University of California Irvine Newkirk Center for Science & Society, University of Michigan Law School, and Michigan State University College of Law, https://www.law.umich.edu/special/exoneration/Pages/casedetail.aspx?caseid=3191.
3. Author interview with Marianne Monte, December 22, 2020.
4. Author interview with Manuel Meza, January 12, 2021.
5. Liu, J., "The Simple, but Meaningful, Interview Question This Anti-Racist Company Asks Job Applicants," *Make It*, CNBC, June 23, 2020, https://www.cnbc.com/2020/06/23/the-job-interview-question-this-anti-racist-company-asks-applicants.html.
6. Fractured Atlas company website, https://www.fracturedatlas.org/.
7. Liu, "The Simple, but Meaningful, Interview Question This Anti-Racist Company Asks Job Applicants."
8. Author interview with Ben Hecht, December 8, 2020.
9. Author interview with Heather Thomas-McClellan, November 17, 2020.
10. Author interview with Ray Martinez, December 3, 2020.
11. Domise, A., "What Black People Have Always Known About Diversity Policies," *Fast Company*, April 17, 2018, https://www.fastcompany.com/40560291/what-black-people-have-always-known-about-diversity-policies.
12. Jim Crow Museum Timeline, Part 4 (1877–1964) from Ferris State University Jim Crow Museum of Racist Memorabilia, https://www.ferris.edu/htmls/news/jimcrow/timeline/jimcrow.htm.

Chapter 11

1. Harper, E., personal interview, November 11, 2020.
2. Cooney, S., "Should You Share Your Salary with Co-workers? Here's What Experts Say," *Time* magazine, August 2014, https://time.com/5353848/salary-pay-transparency-work/.
3. Kruse, K., "The Big Company That Has No Rules," *Forbes*, August 2016, https://www.forbes.com/sites/kevinkruse/2016/08/29/the-big-company-that-has-no-rules/?sh=42baa14356ad.
4. "Semco: A Participative Approach to Pay," *Build It: The Rebel Playbook for Employee Engagement*, https://www.rebelplaybook.com/bonus-plays/a-participative-approach-to-pay-semco.
5. de Morree, P., "Fixing Work That Sucks: Semco's Step-by-Step Transformation," Corporate Rebels, 2018, https://corporate-rebels.com/semco/.
6. Author interview with Everett Harper, November 19, 2020.

7. Miller, S., "Black Workers Still Earn Less Than Their White Counterparts," SHRM, June 11, 2020, https://www.shrm.org/resourcesandtools/hr-topics/compensation/pages/racial-wage-gaps-persistence-poses-challenge.aspx.
8. "The Simple Truth About the Gender Pay Gap," AAUW, https://www.aauw.org/resources/research/simple-truth/.
9. Sanchez, J., Greenberg and Greenlee Race in the Workplace Survey, August 28, 2020.
10. Zweigenhaft, R., "Fortune 500 CEOs, 2000–2020: Still Male, Still White," *The Society Pages*, October 28, 2020, https://thesocietypages.org/specials/fortune-500-ceos-2000-2020-still-male-still-white/.
11. Wahba, P., "Only 19: The Lack of Black CEOs in the History of the Fortune 500," *Fortune*, February 1, 2021, https://fortune.com/longform/fortune-500-black-ceos-business-history/.
12. Fairchild, C., "Seeing Only Two Black Female CEOs in the Fortune 500," *Working Together* (newsletter), LinkedIn News, March 3, 2021, https://www.linkedin.com/pulse/seeing-only-two-black-female-ceos-fortune-500-should-make-fairchild/.
13. Tulshyan, R., "Racially Diverse Companies Outperform Industry Norms by 35%," *Forbes*, January 30, 2015, https://www.forbes.com/sites/ruchikatulshyan/2015/01/30/racially-diverse-companies-outperform-industry-norms-by-30/?sh=5eed3a921132.
14. Anonymous, Greenberg and Greenlee Race in the Workplace Survey, August 19, 2020.
15. Author interview with Heather Thomas-McClellan, November 17, 2020.
16. Author interview with Marianne Monte, December 22, 2020.

Chapter 12

1. Author interview with Kathy Taylor, December 14, 2020.
2. Rodriguez, S., "Reddit Co-founder Ohanian Resigns from Board, Urges Company to Replace Him with a Black Candidate," *CNBC*. June 2020, https://www.cnbc.com/2020/06/05/reddits-ohanian-resigns-from-board-in-support-of-black-community.html.
3. Connley, C., "Ex-Xerox CEO Ursula Burns: Companies Should 'Improve Representation for Women and for Blacks' or Be Forced to Meet Targets," *CNBC make it*, June 17, 2020, https://www.cnbc.com/2020/06/17/ex-xerox-ceo-ursula-burns-calls-out-corporate-america-for-lack-of-diverse-leadership.html.
4. Sumagaysay, L., "California Will Require Public Companies to Have Diverse Boards," *MarketWatch*, September 2020, https://www.marketwatch.com/story/california-will-require-public-companies-to-have-diverse-boards-11601504807.
5. Author interview with Everett Harper, November 19, 2020.
6. Author interview with Ben Hecht, December 8, 2020.
7. "The State of Diversity in Nonprofit and Foundation Leadership," Battalia-Winston white paper, 2017, https://www.battaliawinston.com/wp-content/uploads/2017/05/nonprofit_white_paper.pdf.

8. Dorsey, C., Bradach, J., and Kim, P., "The Problem with 'Color-Blind' Philanthropy," *Harvard Business Review*, June 2020, https://hbr.org/2020/06/the-problem-with-color-blind-philanthropy.
9. Author interview with Kathy Taylor, December 14 , 2020.
10. Author interview with Marianne Monte, December 22, 2020.
11. "Giving Back to Your Community Through an Internship Program," *Intern Matters* (blog), March 31, 2010, https://internmatters.wordpress.com/2010/03/31/giving-back-to-your-community-through-an-internship-program/.
12. Bateman, A., Barrington, A., and Date, K., "Why You Need a Supplier-Diversity Program," *Harvard Business Review*, August 2020, https://hbr.org/2020/08/why-you-need-a-supplier-diversity-program.
13. Author interview with Nereida Perez, January 12, 2021.
14. *TWIN Global 2015 Beyond the Game* (video), https://www.youtube.com/watch?v=yc4CFocQnIo&t=472s.
15. Author interview with Erneshia Pinder, November 11, 2020.
16. Author interview with Lorie Valle-Yañez, December 17, 2020.
17. AT&T website, https://about.att.com/pages/diversity/employee_groups.
18. Limbong, Andrew, "Microaggressions Are a Big Deal: How to Talk Them Out and When to Walk Away," *NPR Life Kit* (interview), June 9, 2020, https://www.npr.org/2020/06/08/872371063/microaggressions-are-a-big-deal-how-to-talk-them-out-and-when-to-walk-away.
19. Author interview with Heather Bodington, December 21, 2020.
20. Author interview with Kathy Taylor, December 14, 2020.
21. Dutton, J. E., *Energize Your Workplace: How to Build and Sustain High-Quality Connections at Work*, Jossey-Bass, San Francisco, 2003.
22. Author interview with Nina Davis, December 16, 2020.

Part VI

1. Washington, D., Good Reads, https://www.goodreads.com/quotes/9450482-just-because-you-are-doing-a-lot-more-doesn-t-mean.

Chapter 13

1. "A Happy Warrior: Mellody Hobson on Mentoring, Diversity, and Feedback," McKinsey Global Institute (podcast), June 18, 2020, https://www.mckinsey.com/featured-insights/diversity-and-inclusion/a-happy-warrior-mellody-hobson-on-mentorship-diversity-and-feedback.
2. Author interview with Nereida Perez, January 12, 2021.
3. Personal interview with Heather Bodington, December 21, 2021.
4. Author interview with Lorie Valle-Yañez, February 3, 2021.
5. Garner, Megan, "Call It the 'Bechdel-Wallace Test," *The Atlantic*, August 25, 2015, https://www.theatlantic.com/entertainment/archive/2015/08/call-it-the-bechdel-wallace-test/402259.
6. "Bechdel Test," *Wikipedia*, https://en.wikipedia.org/wiki/Bechdel_test#:~:text=Media%20industry%20studies%20indicate%20that,For%20the%20test%20first%20appeared.

7. "The ANA's AIMM Introduces the Cultural Insights Impact Measure™ (CIIM™) Proving That Cultural Relevance Drives Real Brand Results," *PR Newswire*, September 2019, https://www.prnewswire.com/news-releases/the-anas-aimm-introduces-the-cultural-insights-impact-measure-ciim-proving-that-cultural-relevance-drives-real-brand-results-300920266.html.
8. Author interview with Lorie Valle-Yañez, December 17, 2020.
9. Ibid., February 3, 2021.
10. Author interview with Rajesh Ramachandran, January 21, 2021.
11. Author interview with Heather Thomas-McClellan, November 17, 2020.
12. Hecht, B., "Moving Beyond Diversity Toward Racial Equity," *Harvard Business Review,* June 16, 2020.
13. Personal interview with Kathy Taylor, December 14, 2020.
14. Author interview with Ben Hecht, December 8, 2020.
15. Author interview with Rochelle Newman-Carrasco, August 2020.
16. Anonymous, Greenberg and Greenlee Race in the Workplace Survey, October 19, 2020.

Chapter 14

1. Le Guinn, U. K., *The Language of the Night: Essays on Fantasy and Science Fiction*, Putnam, New York, 1979.
2. https://blacklivesmatter.com/.
3. https://stopaapihate.org/.
4. Newman-Carrasco, R., "Why the Ad Industry's Diversity Strategy Needs a New Brief: The Phrase 'Diversity and Inclusion' Is Doing Our Industry More Harm Than Good," *AdAge*, August 2016, https://adage.com/article/agency-viewpoint/ad-industry-s-diversity-strategy-a/305638.
5. Bogost, I., *Play Anything: The Pleasure of Limits, the Uses of Boredom, and the Secret of Games,* Basic Books, New York, 2016.
6. Newman-Carrasco, "Why the Ad Industry's Diversity Strategy Needs a New Brief."
7. Ignatius, A., "How Indra Nooyi Turned Design Thinking into Strategy: An Interview with PepsiCo's CEO," *Harvard Business Review*, September 2015, https://hbr.org/2015/09/how-indra-nooyi-turned-design-thinking-into-strategy.
8. Porcini, M., "Closing the Gap Between Business and Design," *Service Design Show* (podcast), Episode #44, January 25, 2018, https://www.youtube.com/watch?v=MlkOcBd1xpg.
9. John Bielenburg, Mike Burn, and Greg Galle, with Elizabeth Evitts Dickinson, *Think Wrong: How to Conquer the Status Quo and Do Work That Matters*, Instigator Press, 2016, https://www.thinkwrongbook.com/.
10. https://solvenext.com/about.
11. *Think Wrong.*
12. Fonteijn, M., "What Is Service Design," *Service Design Show* (podcast), Episode #75 June 9, 2019, https://www.youtube.com/watch?v=gLp-2QFRVXs.

13. Craig, "The Evolution of an Accidental Meme," *Medium*, April 14, 2016, https://medium.com/@CRA1G/the-evolution-of-an-accidental-meme-ddc4e139e0e4.

14. "Why We Need to Step into #the4thbox," Center for Story-based Strategy, https://www.storybasedstrategy.org/the4thbox.

15. Gayle, Latoya, "Customers Accuse Sainsbury's of 'Virtue Signalling' over Christmas Advert Showing an All-Black Family and Claim the Retailer Is 'Not Inclusive,'" *Daily Mail*, November 16, 2020, https://www.dailymail.co.uk/femail/article-8954151/Twitter-call-Sainsburys-boycott-release-Christmas-advert-showing-black-family.html.

16. Kesslen, Ben, "Aunt Jemima Brand to Change Name, Remove Image That Quaker Says Is 'Based on a Racial Stereotype,'" *NBC News,* June 17, 2020, https://www.nbcnews.com/news/us-news/aunt-jemima-brand-will-change-name-remove-image-quaker-says-n1231260.

17. Dallis, I., "We Need to Talk About How Media and Creatives Portray Black People: An African American Leader in the Media Industry Pens an Open Letter to the Industry on the Power of Images and Stories," *Fast Company*, June 4, 2020, https://www.fastcompany.com/90512750/we-need-to-talk-about-how-media-and-creatives-portray-black-people.

18. Author interview with Liz Rowan, December 21, 2020.

19. Bhura, Z., personal interview, January 13, 2021.

20. BQ Desk, "Fair & Lovely Gets a New Name—Glow & Lovely. Emami Fumes," BloombergQuint.com, July 2, 2020, https://www.bloombergquint.com/business/fair-and-lovely-gets-a-new-name-glow-and-lovely.

21. Rowan, L., personal interview, December 21, 2020.

IN GRATITUDE

The Business of Race would not have been written without the support, advice, and encouragement from our friends, colleagues, clients, interviewees, and family members who so graciously gave their time to this project. In particular, we will be forever grateful to the following collaborators:

To our agent, Jill Marsal, who believed in this book and us from the very start.

To our editors at McGraw Hill, Amy Li and Cheryl Segura, who are as passionate about this topic as we are. Also, the production team who brought this book to market: Daina Penikas, Peter McCurdy, and Maureen Harper; copy editor Judy Duguid for her keen observations and constructive questions, Patty Wallenburg, for interior design and layout, and the grace to work so closely with us to accommodate a unique editing schedule; in marketing, Amanda Muller and Scott Sewell; and our amazing cover designer Jeff Weeks and the team at Matchbook Creatives.

To our talented illustrator, Lucy Engelman, who translated our conceptual ideas into beautiful images. To our dear friend and designer extraordinaire Michelle Mazzarella and dear friend and colleague Senia Maymin, who helped us fine-tune the cover design.

To all of our survey participants who shared their struggles with us, which helped shape the direction of this book.

To the Masters of Applied Positive Psychology (MAPP) alumni who showed up at a virtual luncheon in October 2020 and shared their perspectives on "How companies can move beyond race talk to racial equity": Grace Ahao, Andrew Brady, Jordana Cole, Rephael

Houston, Sydney Kastner, Christine Robinson, Andrew Soren, Pam Teagarden.

To our thought partners and early readers of our book proposal, select chapters, and/or the entire manuscript: Dana Arakawa, Leslie Ashford, Laurie Bates-Weir, John Bermel, Valorie Burton, Tracy Chen, Mia Chernick, Sulynn Choong, Xaviera Diaz, Meghan Donahue, Ted Fleming, Sophia LaRusso, Bob Mauterstock, Senia Maymin, Betsy Nealon, Rochelle Newman-Carrasco, Ruth Pearce, Tom Rath, Christine Robinson, Mhayse Samalya, Javier Sanchez, Karen Senteio, Toni Serofin, Nuntiya Smith, Shirley Suhenda, Karen Towle, Doug Turner, and Babbie Van Dyk.

A special thanks to Rochelle Newman-Carrasco, our lifetime friend and social justice and diversity thought leader, for mentoring us while we stumbled toward knowing what we didn't know: helping us to surface our biases, deepen our explorations, stay in our lane, and keep it real.

We are deeply grateful to the following leaders who gave so generously of their time and experiences by granting us an interview. This book would not be what it is had it not been for their stories, rooted in action, specificity, and courage to share the raggedy parts. They will inspire readers to do the same. Thank you for coming along on this journey, helping us reimagine the workplace: Joanna Barsh, Heather Bodington, Zakira Bhura, Nina Davis, Everett Harper, Ben Hecht, Susan Somersille Johnson, Ray Martinez, Manuel Meza, Marianne Monte, Rochelle Newman-Carrasco, Ruth Pearce, Nereida Perez, Erneshia Pinder, Rajesh Ramachandran, Christine Robinson, Liz Rowan, Karen Senteio, Jackie Stavros, Kathy Taylor, Heather Thomas-McClellan, and Lorie Valle-Yañez.

In gratitude,

Gina and Margaret

To my family, whom I owe the greatest gratitude.

To my eldest daughter, Maegan, with whom I share office space (aka home office), for always being willing to pick up her head when I'd ask, "How might a millennial perceive or approach this?" or "What another word for . . . ?"

To my youngest daughter, Carolyn, for reminding me that her degree in English was a good investment. Thank you for being an early reader.

And finally, to my husband, Neal, for keeping me fed, watered, and cared for. Thank you for reading umpteen versions of our chapters and being patient when "5 more minutes" turned into 50.

MARGARET

To chosen family member Sophia for creating a space called "home" in so many ways.

To neighbor, friend, and beautiful spirit Babbie for letting me commandeer your condo, Internet, ear, and open heart during the early phases of this unexpected journey.

To Rochelle: cultural mentor, childhood friend, sister artist-on-the-journey.

To my Gulf Gate Library literary friends, research mavens, fun-makers and progressive thinkers who've created for me a safe and welcoming nest.

GINA

INDEX

ABOUT THE AUTHORS

Margaret H. Greenberg is president of The Greenberg Group, a consulting firm founded in 1997 to coach executives and their teams to lead large-scale organizational change. She is recognized by the International Coaching Federation as a Professional Certified Coach. She is also coauthor of *Profit from the Positive*, which has been translated into three languages, and developed into an online certificate program that has trained coaches, consultants, and business leaders in 17 countries. Greenberg, who has a keen interest in people and cultures, earned her undergraduate degree in sociology from the University of Hartford. She is also a graduate of the inaugural Master of Applied Positive Psychology from the University of Pennsylvania and is a sought-after speaker on the intersection of positive psychology and the workplace to boost employee engagement and results. Greenberg also teaches in the Master of Positive Leadership program at Universidad Tecmilenio in Monterrey, Mexico, and Mexico City. Her research and thought leadership have been published in *Entreprenuer* magazine, *Forbes*, *Gallup Management Journal*, LinkedIn, *Live Happy* magazine, *Positive Psychology News*, *The Economic Times*, and Wharton@Work among others.

Gina Greenlee is an organizational development, project management, communications, training, and educational professional with more than 25 years of experience. She holds a Bachelor of Arts in English from Hunter College and a Master of Science from Queens College in Education, with specialties in experiential learning models and stages of readiness for behavioral change. She is trained in

Advanced Facilitation by Johns Hopkins University and Johnson & Johnson to motivate demographically diverse populations in widely varied settings. The author of 19 books, Greenlee has been published in *The New York Times Magazine*, *Essence* magazine, and the *Tampa Bay Times*. She was an Opinion Columnist for the *Hartford Courant* for seven years.

LET'S CONTINUE THE CONVERSATION

The authors would love to hear from you:

What has been most helpful?

Which tools or stories most resonated with you or have sparked your own ideas?

What's missing?

How have you reimagined your workplace?

Use any of these avenues to connect with Gina and Margaret:

https://www.businessofrace.com

https://www.linkedin.com/company/the-business-of-race

https://www.linkedin.com/in/margaret-h-greenberg

https://www.linkedin.com/in/ginagreenlee/

Gina@businessofrace.com

Margaret@businessofrace.com

Instagram: businessofrace

Facebook: https://www.facebook.com/businessofrace/